# Umbrellas into Parasols

## Turn Life's Fizzle Into Sizzle

Bill Kimmett

Published by Answering Breeze Publications

ISBN: 978–0-9938081-0-4
ISBN: 0993808107

"Everything in time,
Umbrellas into parasols"

# Dedication

Lovingly offered to my wife Janette who continually sustains me, our daughters Fionna, Natalie and Lisa, and our grandchildren Maya, Liam, Rory, Logan, Sophia and Emily who are our ultimate teachers.

# Umbrellas into Parasols

## The Ultimate Guide to Your Complete Inner Makeover

## Foreword:

## The Bonfire Within: Voyage to the Centre of Your Being

Many of us spend our lives drifting aimlessly through a monotonous maze of predictable events and seemingly unconnected intrusions which annoy, entertain, or which we studiously ignore. Our days are full of the trivia of our existence, the jobs we struggle through to pay a torrent of bills; gossip of the world which washes over us; interminable television shows which invariably fail to add anything to the overall quality of our lives; and the occasional nagging question which leaps into our minds at whimsical moments: "Why am I here? Is this all there is to life?"

There is a mind-numbing certainty to it all, and we tend to leave the anticipated answer to time-tested escapist responses. "I have a reasonably well-paying occupation, a good family, and we manage to take a nice holiday every year or so; what more do I need?"

"Let's leave the answer to this form of soul-searching analysis to the experts," we mutter; or better still, we skulk off to meditate on the daily horoscope in the local newspaper. "Oprah or Dr. Phil can provide a logical incisive response to the ponderous questions of our age, but not I." Think again, for who better to know who we are, than ourselves; that is, if we take the time to interview the stranger lurking within and pass the test of "Who Am I and How Can I Live My Life?"

We must redefine our existence so that we are not merely filling our days, but instead are embarking on a voyage of exquisite discovery which resonates with the bliss of knowing that we are continually honing and discovering the uniqueness of who we are. For after all, how can we know and understand others, if we remain a stranger to ourselves.

**Falling Pine Cones and Day-dreams**

As a poet with an obsession for capturing the quiet flurry of life around me, I've spent a lifetime writing about what to most people are inconsequential events. I endeavour to describe poetically a storm-battered sail boat crawling back to harbour, the last leaf of Autumn struggling to cling to a wildly waving branch, and a million other events or feelings which deluge my senses. I paint them in either crystal clarity or with shades of subtleties; giving them a raison d'être; at least to me and hopefully to others. I strive to endow everything I witness with a purpose and use; always eliminating the negativity and embracing the positive, which I store away in my gunny sack of potpourri resources, to season and temper future vignettes when they occur unexpectedly.

We are sitting relaxing on our sunny deck, day-dreaming, when from high above us a pine cone falls from a tree and lands beside us. It then rolls into a corner and nestles against the railing. We observe this fleeting episode, and then ignore it; for after all there is no real relevance to what just happened, right? Later, in the kitchen, a cup we are drying slips and breaks; merely an accident? At the end of the day, we stroll out onto our deck and casually watch the dizzying panoply of an exquisite sunset searing the end of another day. Then we sleep and, if we are lucky, we dream.

Most of the time we sleep-walk through our allocated hours, barely noting the incredible variety of events, moments, sensations, scents, voices and abundant forces around us. We ascribe no meaning to trivial episodes – the pine cone simply fell; the cup breaking on the floor was a silly accident. There is no correlation to any of these events, you say. They have no meaning or consequence to my life, therefore why should I bother about them?

This book is my attempt to give some insight to the deluge of trivia which fills our memory banks often at a subconscious level. We may think that these individual events I have described have no specific, pivotal influence on our overall destiny, or the world, but I sincerely believe that we can attribute analogous reasons to everything, whether collectively or in isolation, and that we can use all that new-found knowledge to understand ourselves more deeply.

Through stories and analogies, on a practical level, we will explore in this book how this diversity of events is a series of lessons to be learned, and after some creative analysis, can be used in resolving some of our minor, and previously insurmountable issues and dilemmas.

The reason we squander this idiosyncratic bounty happening daily around us, is mainly because it doesn't fit into the logical, analytical pigeon-holes we have made; "these cannot be of any conceivable importance, or as possible answers for our problems," we state.

This attitude is fostered, and ably assisted by the whiplash of society's conventions, perceived convictions, and conventional thinking. We teeter on the tight-rope of conformity, staring straight ahead, and never daring to look around at the whimsical side of life; and certainly not at the barely decipherable challenges beckoning above and below us.

The tide of time lulls us into complacency and rolls us along, while constant reminders of discontent and lack of fulfilment casually drift beside us as a persistent reminder of what we have become.

We may equate happiness with a feeling of comforting, non-threatening sense of complacency. "If it ain't broke, don't fix it," we may say, when someone suggests that we make even a minute change to our routine.

"You cannot buck the tide," we mutter; and then perpetuate our discontent by steering the same course. All of this may sound as though I believe that everyone is living miserable unhappy lives. No! What I do believe is that we can make positive changes to energize our lives, and give a motivational boost to the exploration of the most important individual on the planet we can influence: ourselves. For when push comes to shove at the final accounting when we have to justify the purpose, value and contribution made by our existence; we stand alone, with no team of experts to guide and protect us. We alone have made the decisions that have charted our life's course.

## Drop an Anchor and Look Around

So hold it right there! Drop an anchor for a moment and let us rethink all of the components of our current life; our direction; our goals which may be hazy or seemingly well-formulated; our relationships with others; our values; how we perceive and are perceived by others; how we deal with issues and problems in our lives; how committed we are to making ourselves as perfect as we possibly can; and how we observe a sunset, and a falling pine cone.

I have written this book, influenced by how, at a macro level I see the world, and at a micro level, the minutiae of life surrounding me; for often, I have discovered that the Lilliputian viewpoint is more meaningful to understanding, and is a superior tool for positive change than the overpowering Goliath side of the world which can swamp us. Hopefully, after you have read these thoughts, you will be able to hoist up your anchor with new-found enthusiasm and forge ahead with a renewed sense of who you are, and with a clearer sense of what footprints you are ready to make.

## Don't wait to be awakened

The piercing moan of a freighter's horn booming across this deserted beach which has been my temporary refuge has awakened me from my lulling sense of sunny serenity. An hour before, I strolled along this tranquil beach; wading in tidal pools and clambering over silver, sculptured, basking piles of driftwood, seeking the perfect site to sit in the sun and write. Eventually, shirt off, back against the smooth end of a log; the sun in perfect broiling mode, and with a chilled drink beside me, I quickly drifted towards a state of euphoric sleepiness however, and not towards energized scribbling on a waiting blank page.

Then, "boom!" Across the bay lapping serenely in front of me, criss-crossed by a flotilla of bobbing sail boats and frenetic speedboats, a freighter sounded a dramatic warning signal – "Get out of my way or suffer the consequences!"

This is what the following pages are all about: being constantly aware of the dangers of being lulled into a hypnotic sense of acceptance of our position in life, and remaining blinkered towards the world around us, and our purpose in life. Simply, and most critically, not listening to the impending warning signals around us. In fact, not listening and paying attention with every antenna we possess, which should be tuned to the slightest vibrations and influences around us.

"Didn't you hear it coming?" exclaims someone in shock over a relationship shattering- "Didn't you feel the vibes"– "There must have been warning signals," and on and on. "I guess I must have been blind," we mutter. "I didn't feel the changes. It seemed to be the way it always was." We just weren't listening or paying attention; our sensing antenna was turned off, or not working through lack of use. Once again: that overwhelming, lulling sense of complacency had blinded us to the realities of changing situations; for life is a continually evolving process.

We must change, or risk the danger of being left behind. Taking things for granted in life and relationships, is like walking down a precipitous cliff path on a dark night with no flash-light; because after all, we have walked down here before. Don't practice the habit of wandering through life with your eyes wide shut.

Yet, just like those aimless pleasure boats drifting on the sun dappled waves, oblivious to the looming bulk of the freighter, many of us coast along through life or relationships a heartbeat from disaster. Not sensing warning signals until, "smash" we are broadsided by "unexpected' heartache."

In this book, as well as utilizing the abundant latent meaningful events around us, we will explore how to resurrect the dormant, vital soul lying slumbering within us and to revitalize the mystical stranger called "Me." It is my hope that you will experience a positive awakening in your existence, similar to my sudden epiphany on the beach, when the freighter, by firing its "I am coming" broadside, shattered my siesta, but gave me another tidbit of finding a reason behind every event, and its subsequent application as a tool to explain and assist in resolving life's dilemmas.

Since I started writing this introduction to Umbrellas into Parasols on this deserted beach, the tide has been steadily encroaching. I looked up from my pages a few minutes ago and saw that the path I had taken to this idyllic spot had now gone the way of Atlantis – submerged! Another beach lesson taught, and quickly learned.

Life is like this – we have a certain way of living; of going about our business. Sometimes we are awakened by encroaching tides of worries and concerns. What do we do? One way is to throw our arms in the air and scream, "I can't take this anymore." That will not resolve anything. My answer is to find a new path to that resolution! Just like how I will now have to take a new direction by scrambling over the rocks to get back to the safety of my car.

Always remain flexible, do not become entrenched in situational problem-solving by always using the same clichéd tried and true answers; because the tried and true have a nasty habit of having become obsolete and useless while we were drifting along in Lala Land. We simply did not notice that our world had changed while we slept.

We must explore new trails in the wilderness of our being; wander off that old predictable trail we are on, and peek around every corner. Adventures beckon to stimulate our slowly awakening being. "I never thought of that before," as we encounter ever-expanding philosophies and viewpoints.

With each new experience, our sensory, emotional and spiritual heartbeats will beat faster and faster, and we will learn to build incrementally on each lesson learned until our path traverses every corner of our previously unexplored interior. We will become like Lewis and Clark on an epic voyage of discovery overcoming obstacles and pitfalls; and if we reach a dead-end; an impasse, we can simply return to "Go" and start again, until we hit the jackpot and shout aloud: "I tried something different and I liked it."

*one*

# Galloping Towards Your Identity

**Introduce Yourself to the Stranger Within.  AKA You**

Recently I met an old friend, whom I had not seen in years, and after the usual catch-up conversation, he hesitantly confided, "I am retiring next year, and I am truly scared of this next phase of my life." It turns out that he was not so much terrified of this upcoming chapter of his life, but of losing his identity. He had been a teacher and university professor for thirty-five years; and now his persona, his individuality, his status was about to be left behind. "How can I suddenly assume a new identity?" he pondered. What he was struggling with was the eternal question: "who truly am I?"

He knew that the professorial role was his occupation, his job, but deep inside he also realized that he was unfamiliar with his true essence. He had been caught up in the frenzy of his scholastic endeavours, teaching eager students to become what he was: a teacher; and although intellectually, on the surface, he had a façade of sophistication, he had forgotten that poor neglected Stranger Within. Suddenly, he recognized that with the removal of his identity, categorized by his social and academic status, he had nothing to replace it.

After much meaningful discussion, he later phoned me to say that his mission now was to explore his neglected inner self, and present a new identity to the world. He still was nervous and apprehensive, but he had made a commitment to introduce himself to the Stranger Within, and gracefully adopt his long-awaited identity: after he discovered what it really was.

That is why we are reading this book. We all need to know and understand the intrinsic qualities that stamp us as individuals; that introduce us to the Stranger Within, and later in the book we will explore how, in a deeper way, to discover our neglected identity. A sad indictment of our culture is that when we hear the word "identity," the word "crisis" often springs to mind. It would appear that in our complex society, the two concepts are interconnected; bound together with a Velcro hook.

As we tackle our identity odyssey, towards our goal of achieving a profound sense of happiness, fulfilment, and purpose, I feel that we need to ask ourselves three questions. "Do I know myself? Do I love myself? And, how do I serve myself?"

Many people will automatically equate the word "seeing" with knowing, and therefore with understanding. To give you an example. We walk into a room filled with strangers and our eyes scan the room; we quickly have a visual image imprinted on our mind of a sea of faces. But to say we know these people would be stretching credibility. In order to know them, we would first have to observe them; notice their mannerisms; their body language; how they interact with others; how others interact with them; how they are regarded by others. Even then, only a superficial picture of the identity of these strangers would be obtained.

Time would have to be spent in close conversation with each stranger to find out their likes and dislikes; their idiosyncrasies; their values; moral code and so forth. Yet paradoxically, we often spend more time trying to "know others" before we know ourselves. Later we will discuss the relationship between positive self-discovery and its beneficial effect on those around us.

Similarly, we need to love ourselves first, before we can ever hope to love anyone else in a meaningful manner. If we display and offer a picture of self-loathing and a lack of self-worth to the world, we will attract like-minded people. Once we know the real "Me" and what makes us tick in our own unique way, a commitment must be made to accept the Stranger Within, who, by now, will no longer be such a stranger. We will have come to terms with our specific brand of humanity; with its perfections and flaws.

As long as we can truthfully say that we have embarked on an adventure of positive self-discovery, and have made a concerted promise to polish our inner core until our noticeable glow illuminates the way for others, ultimately we will fall in love with ourselves. Love yourself, and others will instinctively respond in a reciprocal manner.

Always remember that we are not talking about the Narcissistic syndrome of self-worship or ego projection, but about giving ourselves credit for the shining example we now are. My acronym for this form of love is Light and Life Giving, Optimism, Value to others, and Eternally committed to others.

The last of the three questions; How do I serve myself? Naturally follows. A doctor's service is offering health care; a writer's service is communication; a mother and father's service is providing love and sustenance to the family; and we will serve ourselves by serving others. Sharing our positive spark, encouraging self-improvement, lighting the way for others; and always emphasizing the positive aspects of life by discarding negativity in every form. Always remember, that to see is not to understand, but to understand is to see.

**Clothes Do Not Spell Identity**

We live in an age of uniformity where clone-like culture is the norm, and among the young and hip, clothes must be of the requisite brand to make them acceptable. But despite what many believe; clothes do not denote identity; individuality does. However, sometimes cultural trappings can inexorably affect identity, and mould people in negative ways; yes, I say, "you can make silk purses out of sows' ears." No insult intended to the reader. This is what this is all about.

If we believe in ourselves, and project an image of consistent optimism and positive thinking; others will take scant notice of our exterior façades and will concentrate instead on our inner glow which will be beneficial to all.

When I was growing up in Scotland, all school-age children wore uniforms. As money was scarce in most families, these clothes were worn at all times; before school, at school, after school and at play.

To place things in perspective, there were two distinct classes of children; those whose parents could afford to purchase school uniforms, and those unfortunates who relied on the municipal governments to provide them. This latter group consisted of families who were destitute; the father was typically unemployed and on welfare; so there was little money for the bare essentials of life; never mind school uniforms. The clothes between the two groups were essentially the same, with a few noticeable differences. Those who "had" wore leather shoes, and those who "had not," wore hob-nailed footwear which resembled paratrooper boots.

This was in the days before T-shirts, denims, sneakers, baseball caps and brand name clothing, so school uniforms were the normal dress for all children. The "had not" children were given nondescript versions of the uniforms, consisting of a white shapeless shirt, a tie resembling a discarded piece of colourful string, rough grey short pants and the ubiquitous "paratrooper boots." The "had" children wore a more sophisticated uniform. So no matter where you were, walking in the street, at school, going to church on Sunday, if religion was part of your life; playing in the summertime - you could always identify these two distinct castes.

The "had not" kids were easily identifiable and typically teased; therefore many of them had an identity crisis which lasted throughout their lives in some cases. They had been placed in a cast and moulded as a lesser mortal by the unthinking actions of others. Not of whom they were inside, but superficially by what they wore. However, thankfully casts can be broken, and new identities allowed to evolve by those determined enough to struggle to break the inherited negativity, and show their inner worth: their true identity.

Now, we tend to explore our identities, portray our identities and change our identities in different ways. One particular classmate was of the hobnailed boots variety and he chose a specific method to express his anger, his sadness, and his incredulity that he came from a family that could not afford to buy him anything. He would select the fanciest, most expensive extravagant car he could find, climb on top of it, and jump and dance his anger out on the rapidly damaged car. He was leaving his signature on top of the car; "this is me, this is my identity, I'm a hobnailed boots loser, I'm angry, I don't understand why others have and I haven't."

His only recourse to his overwhelming anger at his perceived lowly status was to express aggressive anger. Constructive, analytical soul-searching would come later, and a new persona formed. Anger resolves nothing, but simply exacerbates the feelings of inadequacy and perpetuates feelings of being fragmented and hurt. We must learn to discard negativity; learn to break unhealthy moulds and forge new optimistic positive versions of who we now wish to become.

*two*

# Things Are Not Always What They Appear To Be

## Throw Away Your Blinkers and Loosen the Reins

This story will illustrate how things are not always what they appear to be. Identities can be concealed or obscured, until that moment when a creative, perceptive soul spies a glimmering spark, when all everyone else sees is a blackened dead fire. Once the spark is discovered, by careful fanning of its fragility, a blaze can be created.

The late 1940's in Scotland was a time of transition, when traditional ways were slowly succumbing to changes brought about by the end of the Second World War. In this age before Elvis, home deliveries such as coal and milk were still carried out by horse and cart, although trucks were increasingly being used. The horses that were used to pull the large heavy loads were Clydesdales; enormous, ponderous, yet majestic blinkered beasts as they plodded head-down through our neighbourhoods.

I was about three or four years of age at the time of this story, but I still remember the circumstances very clearly. My family lived with my mother's aunt, who was like my grandmother, and every morning, the local milkman would make his deliveries. He would wander down our steeply inclining street, with his heavily laden cart pulled by a huge Clydesdale horse wearing its ubiquitous blinkers. The man would walk along the sidewalk picking up bottles of milk from the cart for delivery to the next house, while the horse plodded along on the road. The horse was like an automaton, as he was programmed to stop at only the milkman's clients. This beast knew from years of trekking through the streets where to stop, and it would stand patiently outside the customers' houses, while the man delivered the milk, before ambling on to the next house.

One day, the milkman came to my elderly Aunt Alice's house and said "I'm really puzzled, Lomond stops at every single house where the milk is to be delivered. He knows the right houses, and won't move on until I've delivered the milk. But when he gets to your house he just won't stand still, and starts to fidget. Every time I return to the cart he's stamping his feet, and I don't know why" With a puzzled look he asked, "Do you have a dog?" My aunt said "no."

One day the mystery was finally solved. In front of my Aunt Alice's house, there was an old hawthorn hedge, resembling a Disney forest, with gnarled branches and small secret tunnels where the foliage had died – just big enough for a little kid to get into and pretend he was wandering through the unexplored jungle in the Amazon.

That day, the milk man pretended he was going back to the house with some more milk, but instead just stood and watched as a clearly agitated Lomond started stamping his feet. Suddenly out of the tangled jungle of the hawthorn hedge I appeared – a little kid the size of one of the horse's feet; and taking a few small pebbles threw them at the horse's feet. Thinking back, I didn't do it with any intent to injure the horse but to see him dance and become animated.

Of course the outraged milkman was convinced that I was maliciously trying to injure his work horse and that ended my jungle adventure. But the reality was, even as a little child I viewed that horse with different eyes. I felt a sense of sadness at this beautiful, magnificent beast plodding down the street, stopping at homes, head down and plodding on again with no spark of life. What I was trying to do in my imagination, and in the reality of the childish stone-throwing, was to make that horse dance; to make it feel animated and feel life: to give it a feeling of freedom from its blinkers.

This is a story of perceptions: I perceived the horse as a noble steed majestically galloping like the wind over never-ending plains. The milkman saw me as a naughty child attempting to hurt, and at the least stampede his bread and butter; or milk as applied in this case.

We must learn to cut through perceptions which cloud the realities of many situations in our lives.

Again, remember the difference between seeing as opposed to understanding or knowing. Perceptions are how you "read" an occurrence; and as we all have unique viewpoints, there ultimately will be many variations of perceptions for every event. We will however learn to hone our search for truth as we voyage into our inner self, with clarity of perception.

Every time I thought of Lomond, I saw blinkers. Remember the expression; "oh! "Johnny or Jenny is wearing blinkers." On a horse, blinkers are leather eye guards which are fastened to the bridle beside the horse's eyes to limit his peripheral vision; so he can just look ahead. I guess we could also call that tunnel vision. This was to avoid distractions for the horse; to make him agreeable, amenable; a slave in essence, going only in one direction, the direction that was imposed by the owner. In some ways the horse would become content, some would say complacent. It would switch off its mind, soul and spirit and just plod along wearing his blinkers.

How many of us do that? How many of us in life wear blinkers? Society teaches us to keep those blinkers on to avoid distractions. We're also told, sometimes in our lives; from our employer, our partner, lover; could be anyone, "stick to the straight and narrow, don't digress, don't veer, stay on track and you'll get where you're going; be focused, don't meander down side trails, that's a waste of time. You're going from A to B and the fastest way to get there is to go straight." We are bombarded with "eyes down, focus, nose to the grindstone."

Doesn't that sound pathetic? Do we truly wish to lead a life like that? If we spend our precious life with our nose to the grindstone, our view-limiting blinkers on, concentrating on our tunnel vision, being always focused, we will be like a song bird in a dark cage. Our songs will wither and our life's journey will become purely routine, and the Stranger Within will always remain so. We will deprive ourselves of the spontaneous luxury of dipsy-doodling down inviting shady trails where sun-beams slant over havens which are hiding day-dreaming glades. We will never know if around that intriguing bend in the road, we would have met the Stranger Within and redefined our odyssey.

No, we are told, "stay on the main highway; it's a faster and straighter route." Of course, that's why the highways were built; for speed. When we sit in the carriage of a speeding train, the scenery outside the window is a blur. Yes, we are hurtling along at break-neck speed towards our destination, but just think of what is being missed. The sights and sounds of a vibrant world, intoxicating scents from an abundance of wild flowers, and the hands we have no time to shake. Yet that's what most of us do. Every morning we crawl out of our beds, put on our blinkers, and hit the highway.

As the old 60's pop song said, "slow down, you move too fast, gotta make the morning last." Take a deep breath, look around with open eyes, and walk instead of running. Hold hands with our inner friend; that stranger who is starting to resemble someone we faintly remember. We are starting to know, love and serve ourselves; and this pace is more our style.

As for blinkers, I threw those away a long-time ago, because I had decided as a child that I hated them. The things I enjoyed and found meaningful and purposeful were the things many others said were a waste of time. Sometimes peripheral views are more appealing than the straight-ahead variety. We will talk about this concept later. So, shake hands with yourself, and make a friend for life.

*three*

# The Joy Of Daydreaming Or The Art Of Creative Contemplation

**Yes! There is Another Way to Ponder Our Existence**

This may seem heretical to some, but I am a great advocate of the noble art of daydreaming, or to give it another name; the art of creative contemplation. Yes, I am talking about giving our imagination permission to take us to places we never knew existed; that is, until we empowered our creative, contemplative mind to roam unhindered. In a later chapter I talk about the therapeutic positive benefits of practising visualization. This is a method whereby we can achieve an easier outcome to problems or tasks by imagining the task completed in our mind, before we actually start the process of tackling it.

Daydreaming is more than merely passing a few escapist minutes or hours in order to run away from "reality." It is a pleasurable form of reverie, in which we indulge in a form of abstracted musing; which in its turn is really creative contemplation or thinking meditation. The end result is that we will encounter moments of epiphanies when we come to the understanding that things which we assumed were impossible to achieve were actually within the realm of possibility.

The process is similar to keying in a "search word" in a computer, and then watching as lists of related, and in some cases unrelated connections appear. Our daydreaming imagination accepts our drifting thought and wanders through the storage tunnels of our memory bank searching for connections. The thought or word is acting like a catalyst, and is throwing Velcro hooks to bring to our attention what our creativity is encountering. We have given this enthusiastic process full authority to create an encyclopedia of visions or images for us to choose from, and in some ways we become an interested bystander, shopping among the amazing discoveries we are witnessing.

We are not analyzing or filtering all of our creative encounters, but viewing their progression until we find one that "fits" the specific issue at hand. Our intuitive side has given us a present which our analytical side could not. Remember; in the art of daydreaming or creative contemplation expect the unexpected, because we are viewing the world, both internally and externally with fresh uncomplicated eyes.

I remember a story in elementary school which focused on "don't daydream; don't waste your time; stay focused." I believe the story was called "Johnny Head in the Air" and involved a boy who appeared to spend his life with his head in the air. He was a daydreamer.

As he travelled through life; instead of keeping his nose to the grindstone, and going from A to B with tunnel vision; blinkered to the specific chore he had to perform, he would walk along with his head in the air. He would gaze at the sky and marvel at the serenity of drifting clouds, and the way the leaves moved in the breeze. He would peer at butterflies in their seemingly aimless journeys, similar to the activities of the cartoon character in "Family Circus." He may have been taking the long way to his destination, but he would always arrive there.

Of course I discarded the moralistic viewpoint being made that daydreaming was lazy and wrong, and adopted my own rationale of using the power of positive daydreaming in a productive way. I would use this tool to view the world from a different perspective; that of the creative contemplator. Like Johnny Head in the Air, we can use productive daydreaming as a tool as we continue to voyage to the centre of our being.

Take time to look at the ever-changing shape of clouds; watch the lances thrown by the sun as they splash into the ocean; listen to the gossip of tiny bumblebees as they whisper their mantra of "always search for the nectar, the holy grail of who you are." Learn the lessons taught all around us, and allow our creative mind to meander through realms unknown where answers lie in the most unlikely places.

Forget long-entrenched admonishments: "for heaven's sake stop day-dreaming," or "little Johnny's in a world of his own," or "Annie's mind is somewhere else?" Sometimes it is therapeutic and beneficial for a mind to be somewhere else. Not just "attending to the business of daily toil," but exploring our essence. Don't become a tunnelled, blinkered version of that Clydesdale horse delivering milk, stopping where it's supposed to stop, moving when it's supposed to move without spontaneity.

*four*

# Wearing Armour Becomes A Habit

### Strip Down to Essentials and Get a Life

We all have heard the expression; "I have the weight of the world on my shoulders." When I hear that, I think back to Lomond, our old blinkered Clydesdale friend who is going to teach us another lesson on how we can crawl out from under our self-imposed suits of draining, exhausting armour, and lift the weight of the world from our shoulders.

Horses like the behemoth Lomond, were bred in medieval times as steeds for legendary knights in armour like Sir Lancelot and the other knights of King Arthur's round table; they were bred for their incredible strength, and I am sure for their intimidating presence. These elite knights were encased from head to foot in the finest, heaviest armour of the day; chain-mail; mammoth ornate helmets, and even steel boots. The weapons they wielded were also extraordinarily heavy: long lances; maces and chain, and huge slashing swords.

Because of the overpowering weight to be carried into battle, enormous horses like our Clydesdales were required. However the excessive weight of the knights' armour made them extremely vulnerable if they should be thrown from their horses. This is where their vulnerability spelled their doom, as they simply could not move or stand up due to their cocoon of metal. Consequently, they were easily killed by foot soldiers, as they lay on the battlefield. Just like these doomed knights, we too can become immobilized by the layers of protective armour we surround ourselves with. Sound familiar?

In our age people say we don't wear armour any more, but I'm talking now in terms of protective psychological armour that we wear; some self-imposed, some of it imposed by others and some of it we just accept without thinking about it, or the consequences. At an early age we can be a "Johnny Head in the Air," we can be a dreamer, a drifter through the wonders of our mind, and a wanderer of our soul. We can see the butterflies with rainbow wings taking us to unimaginable adventures; we can admire rays of sunlight drifting through the trees before dissolving in pools of gold. Optimism sits unchallenged on our shoulder, until admonishments force a layer of armour against our inherent innocence.

Therefore we construct an imaginary protective wall around ourselves, and call this refuge; "my space", and project an image of, "intrude at your own risk." As problems develop in our lives, we find it easier to construct another layer of amour around us, in an attempt to keep the issue at bay. After all, that is how we have trained ourselves.

In relationships we pile the armour on, until one day we have trouble moving. We feel that we are suffocating. We are struggling to stagger through a quagmire as thick as treacle. Our limbs are becoming heavier by the moment, and despite our best efforts, we are getting nowhere. Heaven help us when we actually trip and fall: like the poor doomed knights in their protective armour, we lie there wondering how life came to be like this.

We have perhaps been bombarded by the litany of; "stay focused, don't daydream, plod along your course, you'll get there, don't be flighty, don't kick up your heels," and so inevitably we have retreated inside ourselves and pulled up the draw-bridge. If we are lucky, we keep our secret dreams alive, but all too often, a feeling of despair and anger builds the armoured layers around us. "Keep out of my space," and on and on.

Maybe some of us, like my elementary school friend, who danced in hobnailed boots on top of expensive cars experience uncontrolled rage: the weight of armour can do that. They react and respond to their partners, their children, their accomplices, their workmates. They're angry in different ways, and mainly at themselves, and the "hole that they have dug for themselves." They're dancing their anger, maybe through their speech, and their actions, but we need to change this dance into a graceful waltz, where harmony is re-established.

If we consider however, that the present moment is all there really is, then the past with its tentacles of "I should have done that," "if only I had said yes to that chance," "I should have handled that situation better" only produces draining negativity. All of this nail-biting, self-flagellation achieves nothing, except making us unbearably unhappy and angry at ourselves.

Dwelling in the emotions of the past is like living in the basement of our house with all of the lights turned off: we will have submerged ourselves in darkness, and that is how we will stay, until we switch the light of optimism back on, and surge towards our future.

The first step to removing our armour is to simply accept that we are wearing it. The second stage is to remove it systematically; bit by bit. Now, if we try to lift multiple layers of piled wood at the same time, we will find it impossible to lift them. A layer at a time and the task is manageable. Start by tackling the minor skins of armour, such as minor irritations which irritate you and which you have built armour against. Is this really such a major problem? Probably not. Next time, when this annoying event occurs, smile instead of scowl; and watch that specific layer of armour drop away.

So far so good. Incrementally outline occurrences in our life which have caused us to manufacture our debilitating suits of armour. Let the sunshine of optimism thaw and melt them away. We will feel a growing lightness in our movements; we can actually move with a spring in our step. The more layers we remove, the easier our life will become.

There will be those who feel uncomfortable as they witness our progressive change in attitude about life; mainly because this will reflect upon their negative viewpoints. Accept this, and gradually our lightness will help them also explore their trail to a brighter existence.

Think back to how you used to react; like my school acquaintance who used to dance his "hobnailed boot rage" on top of those cars. His suit of armour required multiple doses of therapy to remove it; the longer one wears it the more difficult it is to remove; but resolution always starts with a simple step forward.

# *five*

## Try The Zigzag Course To Your Destination

**Get To Your Destination Any Way Other Than a Straight Line.**

Have you ever been on a sail boat? To get from A to B you have to tack back and forth in a zigzag course, until you reach your destination; if you try to keep on a straight heading, you will get nowhere. You have to savour the breeze, sniff the wind, watch the tides, and gracefully head away from your port of call; turn the other way and then head back on another course.

Some people may say this form of heading for a destination is aimless. "Hey, we're supposed to be going that-away, but you're heading east then you're heading west; I'm confused because we seem to be going all over the place; any direction but straight." But the reality is we are getting to our projected arrival point, because we are sensitive to the influences around us, and are using them all to our best advantage.

If we have tunnel vision; if we are blindly focused; if we are wearing blinkers on a sail boat we are dead in the water. We have to be a little bit of a "Johnny Head in the Air;" we have to smell the breezes and tack back and forth to get from A to B because after all we know how to manoeuvre our individual sails.

Some people would like to try this method of travelling. I can hear you saying, "But I don't have time to wander all over the place; I have a busy life." But this is what you will be doing, heading to your destination with the realization that tacking towards the destination can be its own reward; in the diverse, unexpected positive encounters experienced.

Take a chance and experience the joy of digressing from the main trail now and again and just like the sail boat, still arriving at the destination. Taking the "scenic route," is to be like Robert Frost wandering down the trails less travelled. But often we don't do that because we're dredged in armour; we're covered from head to toe in dos and don'ts. We have become like old Lomand, following the blinkered trail of, "do one thing, stop and go, stop and go." This is the red/green light syndrome, responding somewhat like laboratory rats. We have a house, so we need to earn a pay cheque to put food on the table.

But, surely, we don't have to give up the "Johnny daydream" side of our existence. We have to learn to keep spontaneity in our lives. Our armour is weighing us down – throw it off, toss it away, open up, expose our inner selves. Soon we will be sailing an armour-free course on a gentle sail boat, coursing imaginatively towards our future, and relishing the abundance we have found, in the realization of the perfection to be found in living in the present moment. Goodbye past, thank you present and hello future.

Yes, we may get sun in our faces on our imaginary sail boat; we may get a thorn in our finger when we reach up to caress a rose; we may trip sometimes when we are daydreaming through the forest, but we will always pick ourselves up. We will be living; we will be experiencing a reality instead of living a tunnelled, blinkered, focused existence. We can give it a try by opening up our hearts.

All of this sounds easy doesn't it? Just by opening our hearts and souls, we can become Johnny Head in the Air. Drifting along to our own horizons and relishing our own daydreams; but what about this armour; this cumbersome coat around us weighing us down? We're scared to go swimming in case we drown with this lead balloon around us. What do we do, how do we get rid of it? Well, in the next chapter, we are going to find the Achilles Heel in the armour and "make the largest monolith into a pile of gravel."

*six*

# Break The Largest Monolith Into A Pile Of Gravel

**Become a Mouse by Nibbling Problems into Small Pieces**

We've all heard the statement about finding the chink in the armour; the Achilles Heel of vulnerability The following story highlights how we can reduce an insurmountable problem to a pile of gravel; using my process of finding answers to issues in everyday situations.

Some years ago I decided to extend our driveway up to the side of our house. Our lot is very steep and challenging, and the existing driveway ended some distance from our home, which entailed a strenuous hike through the forest, carrying the inevitable loads of groceries.

Decision made to build the driveway! Now came the action plan. So in my normal poetic, simplistically-achievable manner, I strolled through the trees in front of the house, pinpointing where the driveway could go; and in my usual positive attitude, the task looked pretty easy. There were a few trees that would have to come out I decided, and though it breaks my heart to cut down part of the majestic forest, it would have to happen. I hammered in some stakes and figured "that's where the driveway is going to go." I had set my goal to put the driveway through the treed part of the forest mountainside; first remove the trees; next hire a local bulldozer operator to come and clear the trail; and lastly have the black top company pave the driveway. In my mind I pictured it; I saw it, hence it was done.

After the trees had been removed from the future driveway site, I wandered over the area removing some bushes and debris from the chainsaw massacre; and that is when I saw it. I don't know how I could have missed it before, but there was this huge rock right in the middle of where the driveway was going to go. In reality it was more like the tip of the iceberg. The tree removal had exposed this monolith of a rock, which sat grinning at me and asking, "How are you going to remove me?"

Now, this rock was armour plated; it sat there like Australia's Ayers Rock, [Uluru] just inviting me, daring me to move it. Some tentative exploration revealed that this was indeed the tip of the iceberg – what you see is not what you get! I looked at this rock sitting there and concluded that there were two ways to remove it; the easy way and the difficult way.

As I enjoy manual labour, I thought that what I would do was to clear around the rock and maybe I would be able to roll it to the side, and down the mountain, where it will lodge against another rock or a tree and. It will be then "out of sight and out of mind." Wishful thinking.

In my imagination I saw this rock moving, but as I dug around it, I saw some little cracks radiating across its face like veins. There were mosses and ferns growing in the cracks, and as I probed them, they became little fissures, and I thought "maybe this rock isn't as tough as it looks, maybe I can nuzzle a wedge in there; maybe I can break it into more manageable pieces." So that was the next part of my strategy.

No longer was this beast an immovable, intractable, armour plated rock. This was a problem I could break down into small manageable pieces and tackle them one at a time. Sound familiar? So, I went and purchased a sledge hammer and a cold steel chisel and set to work. Slowly, systematically I started nibbling. I was like a mouse with a piece of cheese, nibbling away trying to work the chisel into a crack, before coming to the realization that to try and exert too much brute strength would accomplish nothing.

A little finesse was needed as I pondered how to find the right pivotal crack to start the disintegration of the rock. Like a problem staring you in the face; if you tackle it in the wrong way or in an inappropriate place, it will remain an unresolved problem.

Like dominoes; I had to find the linchpin fissure into which I could drive the steel chisel, which would open and in turn, force another crack to open and, like the whole domino effect, the destruction of the rock would take place. Very patiently and tenaciously I started breaking down the armour and suddenly, from being an enormous, unbeatable foe, I saw it as a collection of gravel that was going to dissolve into easily removable pieces.

In a relatively short space of time this problem had been broken down into manageable pieces that I could tackle one piece at a time, and achieve my final goal of building my driveway. In problem solving always search for the linchpin to provide the key to a final resolution.

This exercise was the result of intellect and brawn, with a liberal dose of visualization tossed into the equation. When I said that I enjoy physical labour, the satisfaction of getting my hands in the dirt; this was the tenacious rock in me, indulging in this contest of brawn and intellect. I didn't tackle the rock because I hated it; I tackled it because, unfortunately, it just happened to be in the wrong place at the wrong time.

Satisfaction came quickly as I gradually started breaking up the rock, mainly because I had taken the initiative in this problem-solving exercise, and was moving along the path to its resolution. Now, I learned that tackling a problem as big as this rock wouldn't succeed unless I tenaciously kept the momentum going. In other words, if one chunk of this rock was going to splinter off – and I sat back and rested –the rock, and therefore the crack, would start to settle into place; so when I found the gap was wide enough, I had to fill it with smaller rocks, wedge it apart, wedge it deeper, until a piece would come off and the armour was ultimately broken down.

This monster rock had been removed, not by trying to muscle it down the hill, but by systematically breaking it down into bite-sized portions. We must always maintain momentum to all of our problem solving.

Many people, when they are presented by a new or different problem, instinctively say, "There is no way I can do that." The problem to them is like the "impossible dream," or "fighting the unbeatable foe." Think about that. If we progress through our lives with dreams that we say are impossible; constantly seeing, or seeking obstacles to justify why we cannot succeed; we will always be facing the unbeatable foe; if we surrender, we'll never get anywhere. The game's over, the fun of life and living is gone. Take that specific problem and like our rock, break it into a pile of gravel. Nibble it to death. Look at it from different angles, and use creative imagery to paint the picture of the problem resolved.

Problems are usually tackled with analytical aggression; however, some problems can be resolved through intuition, or the path of creative contemplation. Eureka, the light bulb just came on; "I don't know what triggered that, but this is the answer." Look at issues through different eyes and diverse perspectives. Let the search engine in your imagination take over some time, and you may be surprised when you wake up in the middle of the night with the surprising knowledge, that the problem's resolution came when you were asleep. Try handing over your problem to the Stranger Within and see what happens.

In all of our endeavours we should retain a sense of childlike optimism and dream-making ability, for dreams are the icing on the cake in our imagination, and we should never give up on them. Can you imagine if a general is going to fight a battle and is told, "by the way, the foe is unbeatable; he's the unbeatable foe." The general is going to think "what's the point, we'll just surrender." Where would the world be now? We must always fight, we must always battle. But remember, in the combat of problem-solving, we must break things down into incrementally achievable portions.

*seven*

# Leaving, Arriving And The Magical In-Between

**What Kind of navigator are you on the River of Life?**

I believe that there are four categories of travellers voyaging through this odyssey called life; each traversing the course in their own distinct manner.

If we imagine the start of life as a spring in a remote part of a mountain-range, we will then be able to witness a sparkling, life-giving river flowing ultimately to the ocean. This river possesses an energy and life of its own as it creates its own route to its destination. It gently flows through the tranquillity of mountain meadows, where it relaxes in shady pools before surging forward again, around bends, through torrents, and plunging over waterfalls.

It is always changing direction as it encounters impediments to its goal of reaching the ocean. It spreads itself thin on flood plains, and then has to cram its bulk into narrow canyons. It practices patience as it spends aeons carving its way through granite cliffs; but always it surges creatively forward to its ultimate wedding with the waiting waters of the sea.

Our four life travellers start their voyage high in the mountain where the river gently starts its journey. The first traveller is the Aimless Drifter with a vision of life as simply going where the river dictates. This traveller has a belief that there is no control over influencing destiny, so he or she fatalistically climbs into the fragile boat of destiny, and allows the river to dictate where they will ultimately wash up. "Along for the ride," is the mantra, and if the boat beaches itself in a remote back-eddy pool, or spins uncontrollably in a whirlpool; "well that is life; these are the cards I have been dealt." This level of consciousness is barren of any thought of "there must be a better way," regarding life almost as merely something to be tolerated.

The next traveller is the Conscious Drifter who on climbing into the life's boat to start this cruise on the river of life, looks around and says. "I feel that there must be more meaning to this trip than just blindly drifting where the river takes me." That said, shoulders are shrugged and complacency descends as the voyage starts, with an occasional twinge of regret as the river bank drifts by. "I don't know how to steer this boat, otherwise I would have liked to have visited some of those fleeting scenes." The river dictates the Conscious Drifter's life however, which coasts along with intermittent moments of despair, apathy, and glimpses of what might have been, at this lack of direction and uncontrollable momentum.

The next traveller is the Determined Dreamer, with a strong vision of how the trip is going to evolve. "I have decided that I am not going to permit the river to simply take me where it wishes. I want to steer my own course so that I can stop and visit and explore all that I see on this trip down the river. I want to learn and understand all that I can, and become the best navigator that I possibly can be."

The saying and the doing are two extremely different things, as the Determined Dreamer quickly learns. Naively, attempts are made in a hit-and-miss method to learn the idiosyncrasies of this river of life; how to navigate around jagged rocks in the channel; how to avoid the mazes of swamps; the boat-ripping teeth of waiting rapids, and unexpected surges of adrenaline-laced floods. This traveller attempts to learn by trial and error. In this form of a life lottery, success may be achieved by sheer willpower, luck, determination, and an ability to learn from mistakes.

The final traveller called the Dedicated Dreamer intuitively understands that in order to survive the vagaries of the river, the complex art of life, navigation will need to be learned. Not content with the trial and error approach, knowledge is sought through different sources to teach the neophyte all the tricks of the river. The art of navigating with confidence; how to steer a steady course through all of the challenges thrown by the river; and also when it was appropriate to take a "time-out" to portage around aggressive rapids.

A dedication to becoming the finest steersman on this river of life personifies this traveller who uses every available resource around. Commitment, perseverance, optimism in adversity, unafraid to turn around sometimes and try again, an openness to ask for assistance and directions when the horizons seem cloudy and unpredictable; and most important on this ever-changing river, adaptability.

Debates about whether the journey or the destination is more meaningful have their corresponding share of enthusiasts, and every-one has their own rationale, or in some cases a "no opinion".

I remember a television show I used to devour many years ago in Scotland. It was called "ON SAFARI," and the hosts, who lived in exotic Kenya in Africa took viewers initially on vicarious adventures into the Dark Continent, and later to other equally adventurous destinations. Now, this was in the '50s before people had access to mass transporta-tion, or to charter flights winging them away to the far corners of the world: to a time when distant lands like Africa, the mysterious Far East, mythical Egypt and similar achingly exotic landscapes were mysterious places visited by explorers, archaeologists, and soldiers, but certainly not you nor I.

In an interview once, the interviewer stated in some awe, "you've been everywhere," and they said "no, there's one place we've never been to; Venice, Italy, although it is the one place in the world we consider to be the ultimate destination." Now, this is a place that's very accessible; within easy reach from most parts of the world, and yet they'd never been there!

At this response, the interviewer exclaimed. "You've been to Indonesia, the Amazon, the darkest recesses of Africa, but you've never been to Venice although you want to go there; why not?" The response really was that they were scared to go there, because, to them, Venice epitomized the zenith of earthly perfection. It was almost like "see Venice and die." It seemed to me that what they were articulating was: that visiting the city would be the end of their expedition through life. This example shows that to some, the journey is more relevant and important than the destination; whether simply travelling from A to B or from this life to the next.

Robert Louis Stevenson also shared the philosophy that the journey was more meaningful than the destination, and in a later chapter we will unravel the two disparate beliefs in greater detail. The process of "just journeying" has a life and synergy of its own, similar to sailing. Ask sailors as they set out on their sail boats on a sunny day; "Where are you going now?" "We have no destination in mind, we're just sailing for the fun of it", they will probably reply. Later we will explore the; "darn we are there already" syndrome.

# *eight*

## Open Your Eyes And Surge Forward

**Learn the magic of reinterpreting the meaning of words as you start your journey**

One of the reasons that a lot of us don't even start the journey of self-discovery, is because we are caught up in the negative snares of, "not, don't, can't," and similarly debilitating words. Maybe at some time in our lives, we threw up our arms and lashed out at this entangling web of impediment to change. However, we soon became wrapped in this net like a trapped dolphin thrashing in a fishing net, and as our energy faded, so did our resolve to implement positive improvements in our life's journey. "What is the point?" we muttered, and allowed ourselves to be dragged through life, wrapped in a confining shroud which appeared to be unbreakable.

Words can be construed as nails in the coffin of resolve. However, if we melt negative words down and hammer them into having a different, positive meaning, we can then use their power in our creative portfolio of looking at life.

"How do we do this?" You may ask. Before we lift up the hammer to forcibly force the words into a different shape, and a positive meaning, we need to free our mind and give it wings to fly. Remember our creative contemplation practice.

Once we decide to explore our life's purpose, and to allow our way of thinking to digress from the conventional paths of thinking, the first thing we must do, is give every awakening thought that flies into our mind a chance: don't negate them by cutting them off prematurely.

Negative, draining visions have no place in our minds or lives, and these are the only thoughts that we refuse to entertain.

Don't always be influenced by what other people say and do, or follow the current trends. Always try to follow the intuitive flow of our heart and soul, and listen to the wisdom which is being whispered to us from deep inside. "I don't hear it, or it is too faint for me to understand," we will initially complain. Can you learn a new language in a few days? No, it takes time, effort and a sense of commitment.

Look at the world through new-born, wondering eyes without expecting or anticipating the images you are used to. "I didn't see that for looking." In other words, if we expect to see something in a certain way, then that is how we will end up seeing it. We have trained our eyes, and therefore our minds to format images in routine ways. Similarly, we have become programmed into hearing a word; reading a word and instantaneously making a decision as to what that word really means.

However, think about the magic of words in the following way by practising the art of word alchemy. For example let us examine the word, "not." When we hear that word, instinctively our mind states, "it means don't, it's a barrier, it's a wall, it's a fence, and it's a negative word." However a positive mind-set will hear the word "not" and in their imagination they're sailing over the ocean in a schooner, because they heard the word as "knot" which defines measuring distance on the ocean; a nautical mile, they see vast, rolling waves stretching from the shore into eternity, and their mind travels along for the ride. This exercise shows that we can use our ears to hear sounds in different ways. Creative thoughts lead to creative actions.

Someone else hears the word "not'" and thinks of a knot in a tree; pictures the aesthetic spiralling whorls, circular lines, intricate patterns and subtle colours that constitute a wooden knot. So, just by initially hearing a word, don't make an assumption that it's negative. It's not, as we have just proven. We've already decided you can run away to sea in a majestic schooner, or you can picture an artistic knot of wood with all its beauty. By adopting this concept of using diverse meanings for words, we will be permitted to tie the loose ends of our lives together.

We can become so entrenched in a way of thinking, seeing or hearing, and feeling that we may consider that is impossible to change.

However, we are quickly learning, and using our creative flow to break down that dam of complacency and allowing our river of life to flow with new and revitalized energy and direction.

Following on our discussion about a knot in a tree; when a tree is growing, there is no preordained plan where the branches will grow, it's idiosyncratic. A knot is where a limb or branch grows out of the trunk, and later we will use the analogy of a growing branch to show how some beliefs become entrenched and difficult to remove. Using the Velcro form of thoughts "leaping up to join the one before" we will now discuss the elements of the old expression "out on a limb."

You may be one of those committed visionaries who is willing to go "out on a limb" for your belief; and you may be considered to be as one of the fringe element; someone with a philosophy not in keeping with established thoughts or practices. However, this is what we are trying to do, to change our thought patterns to reveal a new energized you.

The fringe element groups stand up and say "Hey! We don't accept the rationale you're giving us for this scientific theory; we don't accept current forestry practices; we don't accept the direction that society is taking; we don't accept this military process; this religious belief; this type of painting; this type of music; this type of writing," et etcetera! They stand up for their usually unpopular views, and say ''why don't we try a different process, or why don't we look at this issue in this way?"

Now, the accepted norm is to do something, or perform a duty in a specific conventional way, and the mass of people say "this must be right because we've always done it that way; this is the way we do things. This is the established procedure." At one time, when some daring Renaissance innovative thinkers stated; " the world is round, not flat, and the earth is not the centre of the universe," the response from the conventionalist was; "if you don't believe in established thought, then you are an agnostic, an atheist; you cannot believe in God."

People in the fringe element groups; the people who are out on a limb, who sway in the breeze and sense issues, philosophical, spiritual, artistic patterns; who listen to brave new ways of looking at the world, are the ones who start off as a fringe group; the minority. Think small and grow large, as the following outlines.

Some years ago, there was a spindly cedar tree growing beside my deck, and as the top of the tree obscured the afternoon sunlight, I decided to top it. I hate to cut trees, but to benefit from some much-needed sunshine; I cut the trunk of the tree, just above a branch that was artistically swaying out to the West. It was fairly easy to do; you might say I "nipped it in the bud," because that tree hadn't become established, and the trunk had not yet become a solid mass.

Time passed, and the branch that was now growing from the top of the tree, started angling out from its position, parallel to the ground. Eventually, as more time passed, that branch started to turn up toward the sun, higher and higher. I ignored it, until suddenly that branch became the tree!

So what had started off as a fringe element; what started as a branch that was doing its own thing and growing away from the main body of the tree in a different direction, had gradually become the essence of the tree. Slowly, methodically, that branch had gradually turned and tilted toward the sun until it became the tree. I had ignored it and suddenly that branch was no longer out on a limb, it was no longer part of the fringe. It had become the tree.

Again, this demonstrates how we can learn lessons from events that happen around us, using analogies to help to explain issues in our lives. We have learned that something that starts off as a fringe, like the branch, can ultimately become the main body. Similarly, we can use the analogy of saying that if we ignore something long enough; it will become so entrenched that it will be difficult to remove. Finally, if we are not careful, as we will now discover, we can become the actual tree; despite our best judgement

In our lives some times, if we are not careful and attentive, this is what happens to us. We have individual ideas, feelings, emotions, desires; we have tendencies that are leading us in a certain direction; we want to do things in our own inimitable way; we want to experiment; we want to explore unknown terrain. Whether it's our mind, our body, or our soul; whether it's some artistic concept we want to tackle; we want our particular stamp or brand on it. This is when outside influences may prevent, or alter the outcome of our crucial creative experimentation.

We may be bombarded by statements that talk about the eccentricity of what we are contemplating. From the undiplomatic, "don't you realize that that is a stupid idea? The way you should do things is the way the rest of us do them, better people than you have tried to alter destiny, what makes you think that you are any better?" And on and on.

The temptation, the tendency, the sad reality is if we always listen to "not, don't, you shouldn't do that, you must do this," we will feel a noose of negativity like a lasso around us, which will pull us, tug us and drag us, sometimes screaming, towards the body of the tree, back towards the established order and procedures that will make everyone happy; except yours truly of course.

If we surrender, and allow ourselves to be manipulated back to the tree of status quo, we will become on the surface apparently solid as the tree, and one of the masses; but inside, our Stranger Within who was reaching out with welcoming hands to us, will turn away and wait to be discovered another day.

It is very difficult to be "one of a kind"; to be someone who stands up and says "Hey! I'm doing this my way." A person who is willing to expose their vulnerability is an incredibly strong individual. No one said that reaching for the stars, or reaching inside would be easy, but with a belief in ourselves, a strong sense of optimism, and persistence we will achieve.

To all the naysayers; when you hear that negative spike containing the word "not" being driven into your dream, think of this acronym for not. Negativity or Terminal. However, by using our creative Velcro-thought linking again, we can transform this into something positive, that we can use on our life's journey.

When we think of the word terminal, it's commonly associated with a terminal disease with its inevitable conclusion; that's a pretty sad ending; something has ended or is coming to an end; something we have no real control over. However, even with something as tragic as a fatal illness, there can be a brighter positive side to it.

I bumped into a friend recently, and in the conversation, he blurted out that he had just been diagnosed with inoperable terminal bone cancer. "It's strange," he continued, "but after the initial shock had faded, I had a feeling of gratitude; almost that I had been given a blessing. It has allowed me to no longer procrastinate in fulfilling all the dreams I have been harbouring for years. Trips, creative projects, and more important, a realization that love of family and friends is eternal."

This is why we are pondering this book; to find avenues to open ourselves to change and fulfilment. It should not take a wake-up call like my friend's, but simply a commitment to open ourselves up to the positive energy around us, and take the first step of saying; "I live in the present moment, and I am going to transform myself to accept all the blessings flowing around me."

But think of another definition of terminal; as a transportation terminal; a train terminal; a bus terminal; an air terminal. These terminals serve as departures for voyaging to distant realms, but are also destinations. This word contains dualities; two things in one. The reality is that in everything there is a duality. Learning to find many meanings, reasons and analogies in everything around us will enable us to steer the course we truly want on our river's journey and enable us if we are required, to swim against the current.

*nine*

# Melting Ruts While Swimming Against The Current

**It is OK to live in the Grey Zone where you make the rules**

Traditionally we have been trained to view things in neatly stacked columns of black and white; as much for conformity and uniformity as for any other reason. We have been taught to be oblivious to the grey area; or the middle ground, for after all we have been told that a thing is either one way or another; it's either right or wrong, or left or right," and so on. Therefore, an object cannot be two things at the same time; or can it?

Departure is different from arriving. But think about it... At the terminal you can be either arriving or departing. It is a corollary to the Eastern sense of Yin and Yang; plus and minus; negative and positive; black and white; dominant and subservient. Look at any battery and you will see at each end there's a terminal. One is a negative current and one is a positive current. They are both terminals, a negative and a positive, simply because you cannot have one without the other.

Or a simple cardboard box; there is a top and a bottom, opposites; black and white, night and day. There is a duality in everything. So start to think of things and events you encounter in life in different ways. Allow your mind to venture beyond "conventional wisdom", and make black white and white black. Don't revert to a life where every situation, every day, every moment is an unbroken routine; where everything must be done in a certain sequence. Discard the statement; "No deviations or creative thinking allowed."

We have learned the complicated art of living by observing, and learning to live by rote. Years ago at school in Scotland, we would sit mesmerized in front of the teacher who would chant incantations about multiplication tables; famous dates in history; the colours of the rainbow; everything was learned by rote; boom-boom-boom, it was drummed into us. There were no opportunities to explore creative thinking; thus the rote method of learning became our blue-print for laying out our life. This form of habitual repetition can easily become our daily routine.

I am advocating changing our repetitive life-style. We start our day by crawling out of bed at the same time each day; probably muttering the same tired litany. A mantra of discontent. We have our coffee break at the same time; eat at the same time and same place. Even our meal, probably is predictable. That is what we become: predictable and easy to read. We are swimming along with the current in a flood of accepted complacency. We have been superbly trained in the fine art of evading the Stranger Within, and we are perfect students who will certainly not rock the boat. So life hypnotically hums away with occasional hiccoughs and bumps, and we sleepwalk along with it.

If you've ever seen a ploughed field on a frigid winter day, you will notice the neat corded furrows frozen solid. If you accidentally steer your cart wheels into the ruts, there's no way you can move; you're stuck; you are committed to following those ruts where they lead, because to break out of them requires a great deal of effort. But it's not impossible! So, maybe, if we feel we are getting into a situation where we are riding the waggon of our imagination along ruts and we can't get out, just start to feel the sun slowly bathing that ice-bound field of ruts; just envision the sun of optimism softening and melting the icy grip. Now it will be easy to pull the cart out of them; to break through the sides, to leave the ruts behind; to branch off, to veer off and create a destiny on a track of your own making, into a place where no one has ventured before. Don't always follow the pack, or the entrenched rut: use the warmth of optimism and commitment to thaw them and plough ahead.

Years ago I read one of my favourite novels of all time Lorna Doon. This story which I still reflect on, is set in 17th century England and centres on a young protagonist, John Ridd, who lived in an isolated area of Devon during a time of turmoil after the English Civil War. The pivotal moment in the book, which speaks volumes to me about perseverance and commitment to explore something different, occurs when John Ridd finds a waterfall in the country-side, and decides he'll clamber up it to the top.

Now, he's going against the grain; he's going to climb against the flow; he's drawn to reach up for something and he's not sure why. He starts to climb laboriously up this icy waterfall, with torrents of water pouring over his freezing body. Despite the rigours of the climb as he slips and slithers higher and higher, he never once says, "to heck with this, I'll take another way. I don't know why I'm doing this anyway." But he was inexorably drawn to the summit of the waterfall, and ultimately he succeeded.

On arriving at the top of the waterfall John Ridd met the love of his life; Lorna Doon; a young black-haired girl, and the novel then developed into a moving, resilient love story. But if John had never gone against the flow, crawled and fought and clawed his way against the current, he never would have found the love of his life.

Just like salmon in their millions fighting their way against the currents; leaping up over cataracts; smashing themselves against rocks; being thrown back, but continuing to fight to get to the spawning beds. The life force within them is pushing them against the grain, against the current. It would be so easy for them to give up and drift through the water allowing the water to roll them back; it would take them somewhere, but not where they want to go. These tenacious fish battle against the current, until they get to their destination and their mission of renewing life. It's a continual battle, this overpowering sense of mission, but that's what they must do.

This is what this book is all about: the renewal of our spirit; the revitalization of our inner core against all obstacles and currents.

We hopefully are starting to think differently about our life, and the creative ways we can explore change, and its ultimate outcome of shaking hands with the Stranger Within. Finding a special place in which to contemplate the unravelling of our old lives, and the construction of our new improved version of ourselves is beneficial, but certainly not essential.

We may say that we have a little haven where we can go for reflection; maybe a little alcove at home with a study lined with treasured favourite books; or a special hideaway in the woods where we can sit and relax. It may be our version of the ideal haven, but wouldn't it be nice if all our havens became heavens. All we need to do is add a few things to our havens. Add the letter E for a bit of eccentricity; exquisite moments; prayerful times where we can let our minds ramble.

*ten*

# Hold Hands With Every Part Of Your Being

**The Good, The Bad and The Ugly. That is who you are. At least right now!**

Looking out of my ocean-view window at the mist-laced forest and islands which vanish and then reappear, as though to tease me, I am reminded of the inter-connectedness of life. The trees would not grow lush and flourish without the mist and the life-giving rain, and if the trees vanished, birds and squirrels would have no home because, ultimately, everything depends on something else to survive.

Similarly, take away part of our inner being; starve it of attention; neglect it, and it will wither and die, affecting all of the other diverse components of who we are. We must be generous with ourselves and hold hands with every part of our essence.

Every now and then, I get a strong desire to work with wood: to cut planks and hammer nails, and create decks; or in extreme cases, to knock out walls and rebuild part of my house. This is not just a random compunction sent to distract me from the more "meaningful" events in my life. I could say, "I need to write to make more money, for that is how I make my living. I do not wish to be distracted from my mission to be the best writer I can be." However, what is happening inside me is that the part of me that is the cutter and hewer of wood is demanding to be acknowledged. "I am relevant," it is stating in no uncertain terms, and unless I accommodate the feeling to work with this creative urge, the other parts of my being will be placed in a sense of disarray.

39

You may say "I don't feel right, or I feel stressed, or I think that something is out of alignment." Listen to the whispers inside and acknowledge their innate wisdom; each in its turn. The physical, mental, intellectual, and spiritual all work in sync with each other naturally, until often unfortunately we dominate our whispers, and become the dictator of ourselves.

We should permit the jigsaw that is Me, to nestle comfortably deep inside, and permit ourselves the luxury of polishing the neglected areas that complement all other parts. When our brains are tired from intellectual activity; instead of hammering away at a problem which seems to be distancing itself further and further from us, simply take a break, and allow another part of our jigsaw to rise to the surface and assume the dominant role for a period of time: like my therapeutic hammering on wood.

Another reminder to me of the interconnectedness of life within us occurs when I think of my maternal grandfather. Here was a man orphaned at an early age, and destined to spend his childhood in a Scottish orphanage in the declining years of the Victorian age; reminiscent of the descriptions of Oliver Twist in Dickens' classic. He survived the horrors of trench warfare in the First World War, but through it all carried a photograph of my grandmother, and the one other treasure he cherished: a silver fob watch which eventually became mine.

This time-piece secured by an ornamental chain, was the type of watch that men used to elegantly wear in their vest pockets. My grandfather would take the watch out of his pocket, press a little latch and the watch case would open. As a child I would stare mesmerized at this magical little "armoured machine" which would tell me the time. But more intriguing to me was another latch which when pressed revealed the incredibly complex intestines of this watch.

Inside was the whirring, ticking interconnected heart and soul of the watch. All of the parts moved independently, yet also collectively; every spring, cog and wheel performed some function in a form of synchronized time-telling ballet. Now, like us, each piece was individually moulded to perform its designated task, yet childishly I thought that the most important piece of this metal jigsaw had to be the largest cog; for surely if this important component was removed from the watch it would cease to work.

The reality was that this was also true of all other components of this watch. No matter its relative size: whether the largest, smallest or the in-between variety, none were dispensable; none were the most important. They each shared the same integral level in the hierarchy of time-keeping. They were all relevant, and equally important: just like the thoughts and feelings that perpetually bubble into our minds throughout our everyday lives.

We should never arbitrarily discard the thoughts, emotions, feelings, or quirky notions that we may have. They all have some relevance on the balancing act we all play on the teeter-totter of life. Their relevance may not be apparent at that specific moment, but we should always invite them into our minds courteously. Permit them to come into our hearts and let them in their innate time-frame formulate something magical.

Don't allow our minds to become steel traps, for we have been trained for years to think and judge always in synchronicity with established norms. Do not hammer the shy, quirky philosophical tidbits into negative formats to suit what you think is "right." Extend a helping hand and allow the cross-fertilization of ideas in our curious minds to pollinate into epiphanies in all moments that may transform our lives in ways never before imagined. Like each component of my grandfather's watch, if we pluck out one piece, the whole process of time and living will cease to exist. The only exception to this rule is to always discard debilitating negativity.

It is time to shake ourselves out of that old comfortable routine, and be willing to form our own fringe group of one, with the help of the Stranger Within who is always willing to step up to the plate. Even when we find that we are in the somewhat uncomfortable position of suddenly finding that we are suspended above others – "out on a limb", be strong, resilient, and smile as we say: "This is where I want to be, and why don't you join me?"

I'm advocating giving every thought, feeling, emotion, and eccentricity, an equal opportunity to sow some seeds. Before we know it, those ideas will germinate and grow into a bouquet of exquisite flowers; and as we stop to smell their perfume, we should not be surprised if we are inundated by solutions to long festering problems presenting themselves to us.

*eleven*

## Minds Like Steel Traps Tend To Rust

**Open the windows of your mind and let the winds of change blow in**

I like all my ideas to have little Velcro hooks. One thing adheres to another in what appears to be a haphazard way, and sends me off on an exciting tangent again. "A magical mystery tour" you say. The process is simple: you sit back, relax, close your eyes and let the sun beat softly against you in this heaven you've made. Hear the words resonate through your being. "OK ideas, come on in. I'm open. My door is never closed to you."

Traditionally, people are proud when they hear someone say "he, or she, has a mind like a steel trap." However, have you ever seen steel as time progresses? It rusts into an immovable object as it literally freezes itself to death. It becomes fossilized, and I believe that minds can similarly become as rigid and entrenched as the steel trap; without the spontaneity and serendipity of our "open door policy." "All may enter this mind, except thoughts which indulge in the realms where I do not wish to be."

If you permit only carefully screened thoughts which have been hammered into shape to enter; if you never permit yourself to daydream – and what is daydreaming? It's certainly not a waste of time. Daydreaming is where ideas flit across your eyelids like sunbeams, becoming as they enter your mind: butterflies and industrious buzzing bees.

Butterflies and bees don't just aimlessly fly from blossom to blossom. They have serious work on their mind. Yes, they're drawn by the allure of nectar, but they're also engaging in the life-giving creativity of pollination. So we should let our brains be like that. If the unusual is expected, the unusual will happen. If we accept the mundane, the mundane is surely going to happen. We must become like bees and savour the bountiful bouquets around us that we never bothered before to explore and enjoy; - never mind even notice.

Now, I'm sure you've all met people who say "nothing ever happens to me; I never meet any interesting people; nothing exciting ever happens to me." They are categorized in my mind as the Blah, Blah, Black Sheep!

I once met a woman who personified negativity. She was entrenched in this armour-plated aloofness; even her eyes looked sealed from the outside world. I remarked to her. "You live in a gorgeous little cottage surrounded by an incredible garden, with the trail from the village passing in front of you. Just imagine what you are missing if your door and your heart are always closed."

People who would love to pass the time of day with you as they pass on their way to the stores; friendly dogs coming to visit; the lilting song of birds as they fly past: the whirling dance of the wind as it plays with dust and petals; the soft murmur of snow- flakes; and the sun slanting through the shimmering trees beside the river. But if you sit in your home all day with the windows closed, the blinds drawn, staring at blank walls, you will miss all that because you've sent a signal out: "my house is closed, I'm closed." I said to her as delicately as I could, "your mind, your heart, your body is closed and you've armour-plated yourself, so nothing can penetrate."

Even if we hide behind closed doors in seclusion, always remember that the incredibly exciting and beautiful moments we spoke about are still happening outside. They are right there. All we need to do is open the doors; open the windows. Smell the breeze that's blowing in from the ocean; hear the sound of the leaves clicking and clacking as they fall through the trees. Hear the barking of the dogs as they play in the meadow; the laughter of people; the chatter of children as they come out of school and head home for supper. The gentle sighing of the breeze as it deposits its treasures on your patio and garden. So, open up, reach out and say, "I am open, I am not closed to anything."

Now, I am certainly not advocating that every single idea; every drifting intrusive thought that comes into our minds is going to change the world as we know it. But, then again, how do we know, unless we give it an opportunity to come in and visit a little while. How can we possibly look at someone and say instinctively "I don't like you" when we have never met them before. When we have never given them an opportunity to speak with us, and reveal their intrinsic inner self. If we make instant assumptions because someone has a certain appearance or "look", hence "I don't like them," it's like discarding or denigrating our ideas. Give them a break and let them work their magic.

Some ideas will seem weird and wonderful when they first wander into our minds, but I bet if we talked to some of the greatest inventors, explorers, or artists of our time, they would say, "some of my best ideas came when I was dreaming; they just slipped into my subconscious and said "what do you think of this?" But remember, if we immediately pull our waggons into the frozen ruts we spoke about and say "no, I'm not going in this direction, I am used to the tried and true," and don't even give the visiting thought the benefit of a second thought, we may lose an avenue to a new life, or at the very least to a fresh perspective.

I'm sure you've all heard the expression "she, or he, is away with the fairies." What do you think that really means? Yes, it indicates that they are daydreaming. It means they're dwelling on things that to the observer are inconsequential; silly. Fairies are mythical creatures after all who fly through meadows, hide under mushrooms, and leave no signs behind. They live in "fairy tales," yet pointedly and happily, in our increasingly cynical age, paradoxically some people still believe in them.

When we do not comprehend something because it is in a realm above our concepts of limited understanding, we often simply toss it into the garbage pile. So, when people say "oh! Her mind's away with the fairies," to them it means she's lost reality: or, she sees something they don't. We should always relish that which we do not understand, for challenge is the stepping-stone to change and comprehension.

What does that mean; how do we define reality - and what is reality? Is it just something that is understandable and tangible? "If I can touch it then I believe in it." The person who veers off in a certain direction; who speaks of things we do not comprehend; whose mind can engage in philosophical gymnastics; who paints in a certain way? Sees life through different eyes. His or her version of reality will be on opposite poles from the rest of us: but whose version is the correct one? Again, as we indicated before, the fringe, as in the tree branch, can ultimately assume the dominant role and become the actual tree.

Think of the legendary Vincent Van Gough! Here was a man who, in his lifetime, sold one painting. The critics of his time looked askance at his flamboyant vibrant canvases which were unlike the current traditional style of painting. "You don't paint like that, you must paint like this," they muttered. Or "we've always painted like this, don't rock the boat." Now, if you wanted to have a Constable-style painting you certainly would not go to van Gough, "oh! No, no, he is too gaudy." For a beautiful, pastoral painting done in the traditional style, you would go to an artist like Constable. But innovators are always initially regarded as slightly edgy, a bit weird; until suddenly, one day, enough people see the light; recognize the merit and worth of what they had been espousing. Your innovative ideas will be like the inquisitive Van Gough's; out on a limb, far from accepted thought But given time; you will be the leader of the pack.

If innovators simply slunk back into the anonymity of the pack we would never have had the exciting, innovative, gorgeous colours of Van Gough, the flamboyance of the other daring artists, sculptors; and the philosophies and visions of other dreamers. So we must always open our minds and let them drift in a dream-like state.

Never ignore what we hear and see, and more important, what we sense; sure, despite ourselves, we will make snap judgements; we will filter some things out, but enough exciting ideas will stay inside our heads: ready with their Velcro hooks to drag us into exciting unexplored realms.

Our minds, bodies and souls should be like a gunny sack. Or like a drawer I have in my kitchen. When it's opened there is a tangled jungle of miscellanea: bits of string, nuts and bolts; coloured plastic tags from containers – just about anything and everything is in there. It's a potpourri of extraneous garbage you might say, but it's all interesting. And although each item has been placed in the drawer independently, ultimately when I try to pull something out, it has coalesced into a mass of intriguing shapes. The Velcro hook philosophy at work.

So give our minds permission to become like my kitchen drawer. Open it up and let it be; the results will be unbelievable, we will become free from inhibitions and the boring highway of the so-called tried and true. And remember, as we arrive at one solution to a problem, our minds will already be moving away to tackle the next issue. Arrivals are also departures.

# *twelve*

# Improvise On Invisible Soaring Bridges

**Learn from the chameleon: adapt to circumstances**

North American First Nations regard their existence on earth and the subsequent continuity in the hereafter, as the Great Hoop of Life. Life to them is symbolized in the completeness of a circle, because there's no beginning and there's no end to its encircling body. When we draw a circle, we start randomly and then continue the line to the left or the right; our line leaves the starting point, but it inexorably returns to its origin. By leaving we are also going back. This concept of the circle and its complete interconnectedness is what I am talking about when I say that everything has a purpose, no matter how obtuse.

We simply must not leave ourselves or anything else behind in the circle of life; walk away, and we will return to our starting place with the same concerns and problems we started out with. The secret is to allow life to shower us with Velcro experiences on our trip, to savour and utilize when we need them. Ultimately we will return to a starting place, but with a huge difference. Simply put: a new you. We start our existence in sublime innocence: let us leave it the way we entered.

I don't know how you conjure up the passing of time. I've always pictured a year as a ladder that's standing vertically – January is down at the bottom and December is at the top, and as the year progresses we climb up the ladder until we arrive at the top. As the next year starts, we start at the beginning of the ladder and start our precipitous climb upwards. We are always being given another chance to be the best we can be. Every year is a re-birth.

49

This is quite a linear image, but it's still circular, with no beginning and no end. The Yin and the Yang; the black and white; positive or negative. The trick is to undergo a metamorphosis as we progress through this journey; improving as we travel along. We don't want to always end up as the same "old me." This is why we are exploring different ways to view our world, and our role in it.

We live in an age where the art of improvisation seems to be a dying art. Something breaks down, and unless we have the exact part to replace it, we are lost. The art of conjuring up a home-made replacement is mostly gone. When you mention the word improvisation now, people think of "Improv." What is that? Well, it's where people stand up in front of an audience and spontaneously make up scenarios. You know the sort of thing; making up anecdotes and jokes "off the cuff." "Improv" artists respond spontaneously to circumstances that are presented to them.

But here I'm talking about improvisation in a different way. I'm talking in terms of fine tuning our ability to act almost intuitively in some ways to emergent issues and dilemmas. We must learn to look on opportunities as sparks that are barely discernible. Blow on them gently until they become a flame. If we leave the myriad of Velcro incidents unattended, they will flicker and die. Everything has a meaning, whether immediate or later.

So often we're told about specific ways to accomplish things; or maybe we are advised that there is just one right way to travel from A to B. We may plod along aimlessly from A until we arrive at B by chance, but what happens however if something happens to block the passage from A to B which prevents our continuing on the journey? In other words, the tried and true is washed out.

Imagine a road that is taking us to our destination. The road meanders along, wrapping itself around a mountain face. It encounters a deep ravine with a thundering torrent cascading down through it. There is a highway bridge spanning the ravine, so as we cross the bridge we scarcely give any thought to the dangers lying beneath us. We just ignore the cascading torrent and cross over. Now what do we do if we are plodding along and suddenly, the bridge is gone? This is when improvisation takes over.

The village I live in is bisected by a couple of mountain streams, which are normally fairly benign, but one ferocious winter day a log jam high in the mountains formed a dam of logs, rocks, mud and debris in one of the stream beds. The pressure of the water eventually exploded through the dam, and a devastating debris torrent came hurtling down the mountain, killing two young men, and knocking some homes off their foundations. In the process, the highway bridge which crossed this once gentle steam collapsed.

I remember driving to work that morning, and at the bottom of the hill instead of seeing the usual bridge, I saw a raging torrent; no bridge, and a crowd of agitated villagers. There's no bridge. What do we do? Improvisation! We can't just sit there because an obstacle has been presented to us and say "oops! I guess I need to wait until someone else fixes it; or maybe if I close my eyes and blink twice and click my heels, the problem will go away; I will pretend that the disaster has not occurred and therefore I won't need to improvise." Problem solved? Think again.

Improvisation is taking a circumstance, frequently something that has never been presented to us before and, quickly and creatively, finding a way to either bypass it, go over it, under it, or go around it – to get on with it; to get on with life on the other side.

In the case of our village's debris torrent and subsequent disaster, someone managed to wade across this torrent to the other side carrying a rope, which he tied around a tree. This form of improvisation now in essence stitched the village together. Some individuals then formed a line on the up side of the rope and using that as a support against their backs helped people to cross the torrent. So, we improvised, and resolved that situation which had seemed insurmountable before.

We have become so wrapped up in our safe little ball of rules and regulations and learning by rote, that we haven't bothered to explore our innate creativity. We haven't given our brains the freedom to explore new ways of accomplishing things. We have never been through a metamorphosis; we have never been like a chameleon that can superficially assume a different colour to suit the circumstances. Just think of the incredible sense of wonder if we could change our mindsets to adapt to unforeseen incidents in our lives.

By saying that, obviously, there's no school that takes every single potential disaster; every single obstacle; every single problem in life and gives it a solution, because the reality is that they would be teaching us spontaneity which we can't really be taught. We have to go with the flow of our inner selves and accept the ideas being presented by the Stranger Within.

Accept the moment and bow to solutions being presented. We must permit ideas free access to roam around in our heads until they present a solution. Never manhandle and manipulate them until they resemble what we feel should be the solution. Let them formulate their own destiny as they humbly come to our aid. It's like taking the path less travelled. Let our inner selves improvise as they select from their Velcro hook collection of possible solutions. Resolution leads to solution.

*thirteen*

# The Art Of Spontaneous Action

**Allow your Instincts to lay out your game plan**

Spontaneity is the act of reacting instantaneously to some sort of situation. Spontaneity is turning right instead of left. As we discover new innovative ways of addressing our entrenched rigid selves, the art of spontaneity greatly enhances this, by allowing action with no perceived dictated thought: all to my favourite mantra of "everything will work out."

An example of spontaneous action occurred some years ago in Scotland when I decided during a visit to my parents, to hitch-hike up through the Scottish Highlands to surprise my brother who lived in a tiny, remote village in the North-east of Scotland.

My mother and father lived in the South west of Scotland so my decision to travel the length and breadth of Scotland was spontaneous– I just decided to do it. I had to combine this action with a touch of improvisation. Because I was dressed for a nice indoor visit with mum and dad, I had no outdoor, heavy weather clothes with me when I packed for Scotland. I borrowed a wind breaker jacket from my fourteen-year-old nephew and with the arms up to my elbows, and armed with a little borrowed school satchel, I set out on my odyssey

Mum and Dad's house was located about thirty miles south of Loch Lomond, which lies on the Highland Line, where above this frontier, the clans used to hold sway. Below this line is the Lowlands. It was pouring with rain as I stood beside the highway with my soaking thumb pointing north. The first vehicle to stop was a small pick-up van. The driver was a carpenter on his way do so some work, and he said "'where are you going?" I smiled "where are you going?" and he said "well I'm heading up north" and he named a village which is Northwest. So I replied, "Then that is where I'm going." Spontaneity!

I decided I would be like a sail boat that tacks back and forth, so I let circumstances dictate where I was going, and the trip was incredibly eventful. Instead of standing beside that road and waiting for a car that was heading exactly in the direction of my destination, I tacked where the wind blew on my voyage of spontaneity.

We drove along sharing thoughts as we headed northwest; well away from where I was actually going which was north-east. But the scenery was creatively stimulating and memorable; incredible people everywhere. I walked through Highland glens in a state of bliss; not in a state of panic, muttering, "I'm going in the wrong direction."

So, as cars stopped to give me a ride and drivers asked me where I was going, I would usually respond by asking them where they were going. I deviated and veered off and took the fork in the road, the road less travelled, until I realized I was far away from where I wanted to go. Then another car came along and, again, "where are you going?" "I'm going north-east," "that's where I'm going." So eventually I was pointing straight to my destination.

Now, all along, my optimism reassured me that ultimately I would reach my brother's village. I enjoyed the improvisation; the spontaneity; the little spark of excitement. I was enjoying the journey. Obviously I was looking forward to seeing my brother and our reminiscences, with the adventures of the journey being an added bonus. All courtesy of the art of spontaneity.

As my journey progressed, the day started fading quickly and eventually I found myself standing on an old stone bridge overlooking a raging river. The torrential rain resulted in some villages being evacuated the following day because of flooding. There I was standing freezing in the pitch black, still trying to get north-east; still trying to get to my brother's village. Passing drivers could no longer see me, so I thought I'd better find some place to hole up for the night. Spontaneity! Improvisation!

Through the darkness of a dripping forest, I saw a light glimmering in a small cottage, so venturing up to the front door, I knocked on it, and when it opened an elderly man stood there. I explained that I was travelling through the area, and were there were any bed and breakfasts close-by; any small hotels; anything of that nature. He said "yes, if you go back down the road five or ten miles." I explained that I was hiking, and he advised me to "go over the stone bridge, turn to the right, go through that little copse of trees beside the river and you'll find a small village; and I think there are few bed and breakfasts there." I thanked the man and headed in the general direction of the mythical village, no flash light of course, across the bridge and through the trees.

I still remember the brooding cold, as the dripping trees hunched over the river which by now was a raging torrent. I arrived at the village which was pitched in impenetrable blackness; no sign of life. There was one main street, off of which a few peripheral roads meandered off into nothingness; into more blackness. I wandered down a few of these little roads and found nothing of interest, until I passed one house; and something made me stop and look up. I saw a letter B. Now, in reality it did not stand for bed and breakfast, it just could have been 120B Avenue or something like that, but I knocked at the door and a lady opened it.

She explained that this was not a bed and breakfast, but, "well, I've got one little room above the kitchen, a little attic room. I'm sure you wouldn't be interested." I said it sounded fantastic as we walked into the house, through a big kitchen filled with delicious cooking smells and finally up a little spiral staircase to the attic right above the kitchen. It was just a tiny room in the ridge of the roof, boasting a little skylight and a single bed. I said "this is marvellous, this is lovely, fantastic."

So, in the space of five minutes I went from being tired, exhausted, soaked; but not really discouraged, because my optimism told me that something positive would happen. The lady also improvised spontaneously by taking me in – one spontaneous act can often lead to a reciprocal act.

After a quick shower I went into the village in search of the perfect pub. Mission accomplished, returned to my cozy attic and had probably the best night's sleep I'd had in years.

I believe that optimism is also a key part of; a keynote of, spontaneity and improvisation. When you're improvising you have to be optimistic and know that there's going to be a resolution to it. My favourite expression has always been "don't worry, something will work out." And I don't just mean that some external force will make it work as a solo act; you will have to assist by projecting positive thoughts. In this particular case I got this fantastic little room for a pittance; and all because of improvisation, spontaneity, and a good solid dose of positive thinking.

The following morning the lady asked me where I was going and on the map I pointed out my brother's village which lay at the bottom of a confusion of obscure country roads. The lady said "look outside just at the corner, there's the main road that goes to Aberdeen. That's the fastest way to get to it. That track up there to the left also leads to your village, but hardly anyone travels along there, it's quiet and I really wouldn't recommend that you take that one."

To make her feel happy, I stood at the corner of the main road until she was out of sight, then I turned and started walking up the little quiet road – the less travelled road, the mountain road, the scenic road. I just knew that something would happen. Spontaneity! Optimism! Improvisation! It worked out – "I'll improvise, yes I'll go this way; I won't go that other way; things will work out," and ultimately it did. I got a series of rides from fascinating locals along the coast, through small farming villages until I eventually got to my brother's. I reached my destination. I'd gone from the South west to the Northeast, but I had gone in a tacking motion. I had tacked to the northwest and had meandered back to the east, back to the west and had eventually reached my brother's home. The interesting thing is that it didn't take me much longer than if I'd tried to go straight there.

# *fourteen*

## "Wagons Ho", Or "Darn We Are There"

**Enjoy the journey, step by step**

I reached a destination. There's that word again "destination." Why does it always crop up? Destination always sounds to me like a cul-de-sac, a dead end. It always reminds me of the Frontier. When the Western pioneers were interviewed about their experiences, most of them described their covered waggon odyssey over the Great Plains as being the most pivotal experience of their lives.

On this monumental trip they discovered, or re-discovered who they really were. They had to reach deep inside themselves and find resources and strengths to keep them going. All of this despite the horrendous hardships; disease and death looming at every step; hostile territory bravely defended by the Indian Nations. And yet, this trip touched them and moulded their future lives.

These settlers found internal strengths that they never knew they possessed; they had to improvise every step of the way. It is fascinating to me that after struggling for thousands of miles to reach their destination, some of them returned back east after setting foot in California or Oregon. Incredulously they retraced their steps. I used to think they were giving up, but they weren't really. They'd experienced a series of epiphanies; they'd explored both the land and themselves and they'd found resources deep within. Enough to last them a lifetime. The destination to them was not so important after all.

There were others, who after going through the same trials and tribulations, settled down, put down roots and built their lives with a sense of relief. They shared a different perspective. They shook the dust of the journey off their feet and said "thank God we're here and that's behind us." Some others, said "damn it, we're here, the journey's behind us." The latter who remained with that mind-set, spent the rest of their lives with the reminiscences of the journey, remembering their struggles and triumphs, and how they had had to massage their souls to find their innate essence.

They had learned to improvise, to be spontaneous and to be really and truly alive. Some of those who drifted back east felt a recurring yearning for the odyssey and ultimately came out West again for the experience, the adventure of improvising day by day. What a challenge! Just imagine, if in our day to day experiences, when we encounter a roadblock or a challenge we have never encountered before, we learn to say with conviction, "bring it on, I am an improviser and I am changing my destiny."

Optimism blended with openness leads to success, as the following story depicts. I arrived in Canada from Scotland into a snowy wintry Montreal, three thousand miles from my final destination; Vancouver on the west coast. With thirty dollars to my name, and dressed more for a Scottish summer than a frigid northern winter, I thrust my thumb into the wind, and five days later drifted into my destination. Trust and we can achieve miracles.

Some of us become bored easily; we enjoy continual bursts of flame; continual winds that blow and stir our souls for a period of time. Just like some of the pioneers. But once we feel a sense of achievement, we look around for new challenges. Some of us are made for the long haul and others for the short haul. Often when we are problem solving, whether in relationships, scientific, technical, artistic, or philosophical dilemmas; or simply trying to untangle the many diverse ways of how to construct a garden fence, the intricacies of improvisation is more exciting than the final resolution. In the final resolution, we may achieve how to do x, y, z, but then think that the actual resolution is merely a stepping-stone to our next challenge.

But think of what we have achieved. We have challenged ourselves, improvised; found a solution, a resolution, and a conclusion. Now on to the next challenge. We should enjoy the different stages of all of our experiences and the resolution will be its own reward.

A new challenge doesn't need to entail crossing a continent in a covered waggon, although that does have a certain appeal. It can be any aspect of your life that reaches out to us. Our own unique definition of what our Frontier is.

Some years ago we bought a piece of land on a little island on the South west coast of British Columbia, Canada. This magical island is six miles long by roughly half a mile wide and is surrounded by white sand beaches. There are no roads on it other than sand trails and very few people. So, with radiant dreams of blissful days to be spent in our desert island, we bought this piece of land on a sandy, treed bluff overlooking a beautiful, pristine crescent beach, with the ultimate plan to build a cottage there.

For a couple of years I intermittently spent weekends there to assess where we would build our cottage. This was to be a family place but I'd initially "pioneer it" on those stolen few days with a little one-man tent. I camped on this place of nirvana, and the highlight of my day was cooking my evening meal over a small camp-fire reminiscent of cowboys out on the range.

Before crawling into my sleeping bag, I'd usually sit on my sandy bluff and watch incredible sunsets which induced a meditative feeling of seeing something profound: just by listening to the dual serenity of the keening wind in the trees and the gently shushing of the surf, which were essentially one and the same, I would find my mind drifting into realms beyond my immediate understanding. I would close my eyes, and lying in my little tent I would listen to this sighing symphony; I couldn't differentiate between the wind in the trees and the hypnotic caress of the surf creeping along the sleeping sand.

These were some of my happiest times. The planning, the thinking, and the raw bushwhacking were my version of the Frontier.

There are several parts to this story, culminating in the actual construction of our cottage. But somehow once the land had been tamed and a cozy cottage nestled on the bluff overlooking the ocean; the land was never the same again. I built the cottage with a great deal of sensitivity to the land; leaving the sheltering trees; crafting the cottage around some of them. But once the challenge of building the small cottage was complete, the spark, the enthusiasm for the venture seemed to be extinguished.

I certainly would not say that I was bored when I would visit the cottage, but the excitement of the whole experience, the spontaneity was gone; I had conquered the Frontier and it no longer existed.

The lesson to be learned again, is that for some, the destination is more important than the journey. The journey is just a means of getting from A to B. For others, like me, getting there is a joy, but meandering along the trail is more interesting. So savour your own perspective.

Even a pleasurable thing like reading a novel reveals the destination seekers and the travellers. My wife for example, is highly skilled at unravelling the various threads of a novel and leaping ahead to the conclusion or destination, while I immerse myself in the feelings, the emotions, and the sense of the literary journey. My wife analysis whereas I experience. She can quickly arrive at the final destination and point out "who did what to whom and why!" I am along solely for the ride, and often the conclusion is its own disappointment.

# *fifteen*

## Plant Velcro Hooks In Your Mind's Garden

Permit your garden to grow a new you: avid gardeners need not apply

If our minds are perpetually closed to the sunlight of optimism and possibilities, we are continually blocking out the prolific generosity of our innate "weeds of interest." But what are weeds of interest? Throughout the ages, botanists have given certain plants or flowers the mongrel, derogatory terminology of being classified as "weeds."

So let's get this straight! At the beginning of time all plants and flowers were equal, had equal status – they grew, competed for sunshine and rain, displayed their unique beauty, and then died. Then along comes man with his fine honed mind and dictatorial need for order and selectivity, and he designates some plants as weeds because he doesn't want them. In his shallow mindset, they have no intrinsic value: they do not fit in to his perception of what "flowers" should look like.

Some trees, like Alders and Poplars, were treated in the same cavalier fashion and became "weed trees." Why is that? Because some people have this great need, this obsession to control and catalogue everything in our universe. They are blind to the unusual; to the unessential they would say; hence they have no place in their world. Cut them out, poison them, root them out before they have a chance to sprout, and contribute to the overall canopy of nature.

They grow their gardens, instead of allowing the gardens to grow them; for I think a more profound way of looking at it is, why don't we let the gardens grow us? Like vagrant thoughts and inklings that dart into our minds. Why do we not allow them to germinate and see where they will take us? Mine the power of your intuitive mind.

I've often said that in our idyllic village, all birds must love me, because any seeds that they drop I let grow. Anything and everything grows in our land: I won't say garden. Fledgling trees shyly appearing, little shrubs springing up; everything living in a wild, disorganized, undisciplined beautiful chaos. Spontaneity rules. The garden is always improvising itself, reinventing itself and it's never the same two years in a row.

Some plants explode, imparting fantastic bursts of colour, maybe a discrete sense of subtlety, a reddish sunset glow, before they fade and allow other shy plants to display their splendour. But to it all there is perfection in its apparent imperfection. There is continual excitement in the "not knowing what will grow next," and what the end result will be.

Year by year, different plants appear in the same area in bursts of serendipity. I don't plant rows of daffodils, tulips, marigolds, rows of whatever – I just let Mother Nature sprinkle her magical bounty and bless the result. It's not through a sense of laziness; it's through a sense of excitement and anticipation. You look at a piece of ground and you see a small spear, like an impudent tongue sticking through the soil and you wonder what it's going to be – a tree, salal, herbs that have blown in from another garden? Who knows! I just allow the garden to indulge in its spontaneity; in continually improvising, reinventing, and going through a metamorphosis. It's never the same. Month by month the garden is always in a state of flux and, for me, it's never boring; whereas if I think of orderliness, rules and regulations, I get bored.

This analogy of my garden applies to all of my philosophies in life: the Velcro principle we have so often spoken about. There always seems to be an allegorical Velcro hook tying one little issue or one little statement onto something else. It's like my garden growing with no apparent rhyme nor reason. The planning is by nature: the result is always stupendous.

Some people may say, "What you're talking about is a lack of discipline, a lack of orderliness, a lack of cohesion, a lack of rules." It's not; it's just a contrary way of looking at things. It's permitting positive events to change us, as opposed to us always dominating events.

By saying that, I'm not advocating running away from responsibilities. That is in itself a discipline; to have responsibilities; a moral code of ethics in which we take care of our loved ones; ensure there's bread on the table, meat and potatoes, and a roof over our heads. I'm just talking in terms of flexibility, not being intransigent, and not being almost moribund in our armour of what society's expectations are of us and for us. Let us give our minds the freedom to design their own gardens, and be amazed at the results.

It's continually amazing to me that through chaotic mayhem, a sense of orderliness descends in a sort of a hierarchical fashion, where nothing really dominates. There really is honest sharing. Some of the plants will tower over others and obviously provide shade which some shade-loving plants love, and these plants will automatically gravitate to the shady areas. Plants that grow low to the ground, graciously allow more sun to penetrate, which encourages sun loving plants to grow in those areas. Other plants grow on the fringe – they like to live in that magical moment between sunshine and shade, light and dark, positive and negative: the fringe. Part of the day they like to be in the sun, other times they prefer the shade. So the garden somehow organizes itself through selective serendipity.

I honestly feel that if we permit our minds to organize our lives through this willingness to allow "weeds of interest" to thrive, exciting innovative things are sure to happen. We are simply tapping into that innate creative well of spontaneity, amply flavoured with great dollops of optimism.

## *sixteen*

# Transform All Your Umbrellas Into Parasols

**Believing leads to achieving once you fire your imposed dictator**

When a child is initially experiencing and exploring life, its eyes sparkle with innocent excitement; everything is new; enticing; everything is magical and to be explored. No judgements are pronounced; everything is accepted. The world is viewed through untainted eyes. Remember the old adage: "innocence is bliss!"

To be in a state of bliss is to truly walk on hallowed ground where joy blends with the appreciation of simply "being." I remember when my youngest daughter saw an oil spill one day, she exclaimed "Dad, a rainbow's fallen from the sky." A can of oil had spilled in the garage. It wasn't a particularly large spill, but when she saw the oil trickling down to the gutter, in her mind, her eyes, in her imagination and in her soul, she saw all the prisms of a rainbow, whereas others would have only seen oil.

This overwhelmingly profound form of imaginative use of our powers, as in a child, certainly encourages poetic thoughts, but when we consider that poetry is the ultimate condensation of feelings or events into its bare essence, then by just throwing our windows wide open, we are screaming for change.

Letting anything blow in, we will find the excitement of a guessing game "what will I be tomorrow; what will my soul reach out for and scream at the sky; what will my heart sing of?" We don't know because for the first time in our lives, we are not the dictator of all that is inside us, or the overseer of our external environment. I'm not suggesting we follow negative paths, and yes, when you leave your mind, heart and soul open, negative vibes will blow in as well as the positive vibes.

However, the negative vibes are going to fade and shrivel up because we will deprive them of interest and energy by simply averting our eyes. This is like staring into the sun until it is impossible to see anything. As we undergo change, our inner glow will blind us to negative influences, like staring straight into the sun's blinding splendour, until eventually, negativity will cease to exist for us.

Remember, if we live in negativity we will end up living in darkness. We will build that armour to protect ourselves against the world; to protect us against emotions and feelings. We will atrophy.

When we let positive vibes happen; when we let our garden grow with all the vibrant sensations, the welcoming plants with their intriguing scents, we will be living in a state of continual excitement and anticipation of tomorrow. We have taken the high road to the openness and childlike innocence of a truly committed and fulfilled life. If we always walk in the shade we will become pallid and dull. We need to get out into the life-giving energy of the sunshine of optimism.

Take a walk one day; decide to go for a walk in the forest, along a beach, beside the ocean, along a mountain trail – somewhere by yourself. Walk along and communicate. How do you do that? Open your mind and if there's no-one around and you feel like talking aloud that's fine, just let the thoughts come in, just let the garden of your mind, your imagination blossom. Let one thought trigger another until there's a cascade of excitement in your brain. Jot down these thoughts even though they may seem disjointed, but then look at them and you will end up saying, "Wow, they make sense."

There is probably going to be symbolism in a lot of the thoughts. Some of those thoughts may appear to be eccentric, unrelated – it doesn't matter – just let everything come in. The negatives: let them fly away; let them wither, you don't want their draining influence. But anything else, give it a try, let it evolve, let it use its Velcro hook to attach to another thought or emotion and see where it takes you.

Sometimes we will go deep into ourselves and we will start to have thoughts; feelings and emotions about the core of our being, our spirit and our soul; that energy, that unique spark that sustains us. Other times there will be a sort of tactile feeling like when we touch a blossom and caress the soft, velvety petals, or the roughness of bark, or the feeling of the wind in our face or our hair; or the sun beating down on us. Sensory thoughts will come into our minds. Other times our brains will be stimulated by endless questions and we will start to puzzle and ponder, "Why am I the way I am?" We will be surprised at the insights that our internal discussion will bring to the surface, by chatting to ourselves.

It is fascinating to me that we can actually debate with ourselves. Debating in our mind is really a form of filtering. An idea comes in and we become our own devil's advocate; we engage in rebuttals; defending positions; make quantum leaps into other thought patterns just by exploring the feelings that come into our minds: the thoughts, problems, emotions and our sense of things. We will start to feel uplifted. We will experience the euphoria of undergoing subtle and gradual change. We are reinventing ourselves. Chameleons do that; the difference is that they return to what they were before when the danger passes. We however are changing into an irreversible being, a quantum leap above our wildest dreams.

Think about it this way. The chameleon can change from its original colour to a temporary colour and back again. This is different from metamorphosis which is an irrevocable transformation; like a butterfly, the pupa, the caterpillar, they look totally different but they're the same. We will undergo metamorphosis into a new us, and the old version will be sloughed off, never to re-appear again.

Like the Trinity of growth; the pupa ultimately becomes a gorgeous butterfly. And there is the cycle again. The butterfly lays eggs and the whole cycle begins again; there is no beginning and there is no end to that.

Just like my garden, there is no beginning and no end. As the trees are growing they're also dying; as the plants are growing they're also fading, but in dying they're re-growing. Walk through a forest and you will see these decomposing hulks of once soaring trees, called nursery trees. These are trees that have fallen, and slowly through the persistent action of the elements, they have started to mellow and decompose and blend their bodies back into the soil from which they sprang.

Gradually the flesh of the tree becomes a nursery ground for seeds to fall into and to grow, with the mothering tree providing nourishment. Through the death of that tree – did I say death? It's not; because the tree is growing again through its ultimate journey into these other trees and plants, by providing the "nursery ground." We may think that when accidents happen and the tree blows over, it's terrible; it's terminal. But it really is not. When the tree blows over it ultimately becomes a nursery tree. From that one accident a positive thing happens; a rebirth of life occurs and, secondly, when it blows over it lets more sunlight through which in turn lets sun loving plants grow again. The circle of life: miracle of rebirth or reincarnation.

Just as the crashing of the tree onto the forest floor is defined as a terrible accident, the reality is that I believe that there is no such thing as an accident: simply a spontaneous shifting of events with a different conclusion. An opportunity for unexpected travels into a path of wonder.

My dad had a pragmatic approach to accidents. As one of six kids, invariably accidents would happen. A plate dropped, a window smashed by a playful stone gone awry; or something similar. We would apologize and say, "but dad, it was an accident" and Dad would say "no, there's no such thing as an accident, it's damned carelessness!'"

But sometimes through accidents miracles happen. We have all heard of cases where scientists who are mixing chemicals together in the hope of making something end up producing some fantastic serum. In many cases it's the result of an accident. A daily example of this is the ubiquitous "Post-it" which originated from a failed adhesive experiment: instead, accidentally it became a sticky substance which would attach, but could also be easily removed.

I remember when I was studying Chinese painting with its exotic aesthetics; I discovered the topic of the "planned accident." I know that sounds strange; what is a planned accident? It probably originated when one of the ancient Chinese artists knocked over his ink while painting, spilling it onto his rice paper and splashing it accidentally over the current masterpiece he was creating. The paint would have assumed forms and shapes which to the imaginative mind were unexpectedly beautiful.

Recognizing the instinctive appeal of these "accidents", the artists would then through spontaneity, introduce the improvisation of "planned accidents" into their bag of artistic tricks. They would purposely spill a small amount of ink onto an area of the painting, and watch the ink assuming just the right complementary shape for the particular painting. When the appropriate shape was just right, the artist would add his perspective to the planned accident, and others would call the result a masterpiece.

Why do we not use the power of "planned," or for that matter, simple accidents to their full advantage, and follow a new direction? It is a positive thing to use an accident to its best advantage, not always to say "darn it's happened, no good will come of that." Look for the best in everything. Explore this unexpected turn of events and tell yourself that this has happened for an inexplicable reason. Accidents are opportunities for dramatic change. Be courageous and follow where the accident leads. The result may be your masterpiece.

A concrete example occurs when we are building something, and in the process we accidentally cut a piece of two-by-four stud a few inches too short. We will probably say, "I should have measured twice and cut once," but we should not throw that piece away. Instead we should keep it, and at the appropriate moment when we need a piece that size, use it.

Do the same with accidents, accept them with the same optimism, forgiveness, and openness, and the understanding that the time will come when this unexpected event can be used to resolve a future roadblock. Fleeting unexpected thoughts will creep into our minds, our hearts and souls at the strangest of times and places. Don't discard them; welcome and keep them until there is a time and place for them. Here is an example – an umbrella, what does it do? It stops the rain from soaking our heads. In sunshine we can hold it over our heads as it protects us from the sun's heat: in its miraculous new role it has become a parasol.

That's like the Yin and Yang thing again; like the changing colours of a chameleon adapting to changing circumstances, or like a metamorphosis from umbrella to parasol. From the driving rain, to the rays of the sun, it is protecting us. Openness, optimism, spontaneity. We can find a use for anything that happens; from everything that happens.

Just like that old gunny sack in the kitchen drawer that I talked about, overflowing with a mountain of miscellaneous, extraneous, and at first glance, possibly useless materials. But there is always a use for them; we can always improvise with these things. The same with thoughts; don't discard them. When we are on our walks thinking about issues in our lives, and trying to resolve impasses; just allow our feelings and emotions to spark off of one another, and in the process of not discarding, resolutions will slip in quietly and resolve our problems.

I carry little notebooks with me at all times, so that when thoughts come to me, I can jot them down. I write poetry, and often times when a complete poem comes pouring into my mind, I pull out my trusty little notebook and write it down. Other times, just a thought intrudes, or a puzzlement, or a why? – Why did this happen? What if? What has? By asking questions, we will invariably find an answer, unexpected perhaps, but at least some sort of answer. We never know where it will lead us.

into our minds. Why do we not allow them to germinate and see where they will take us? Mine the power of your intuitive mind.

I've often said that in our idyllic village, all birds must love me, because any seeds that they drop I let grow. Anything and everything grows in our land: I won't say garden. Fledgling trees shyly appearing, little shrubs springing up; everything living in a wild, disorganized, undisciplined beautiful chaos. Spontaneity rules. The garden is always improvising itself, reinventing itself and it's never the same two years in a row.

Some plants explode, imparting fantastic bursts of colour, maybe a discrete sense of subtlety, a reddish sunset glow, before they fade and allow other shy plants to display their splendour. But to it all there is perfection in its apparent imperfection. There is continual excitement in the "not knowing what will grow next," and what the end result will be.

Year by year, different plants appear in the same area in bursts of serendipity. I don't plant rows of daffodils, tulips, marigolds, rows of whatever – I just let Mother Nature sprinkle her magical bounty and bless the result. It's not through a sense of laziness; it's through a sense of excitement and anticipation. You look at a piece of ground and you see a small spear, like an impudent tongue sticking through the soil and you wonder what it's going to be – a tree, salal, herbs that have blown in from another garden? Who knows! I just allow the garden to indulge in its spontaneity; in continually improvising, reinventing, and going through a metamorphosis. It's never the same. Month by month the garden is always in a state of flux and, for me, it's never boring; whereas if I think of orderliness, rules and regulations, I get bored.

This analogy of my garden applies to all of my philosophies in life: the Velcro principle we have so often spoken about. There always seems to be an allegorical Velcro hook trying one little issue or one little statement onto something else. It's like my garden growing with no apparent rhyme nor reason. The planning is by nature: the result is always stupendous.

Some people may say, "What you're talking about is a lack of discipline, a lack of orderliness, a lack of cohesion, a lack of rules." It's not; it's just a contrary way of looking at things. It's permitting positive events to change us, as opposed to us always dominating events.

## fifteen

# Plant Velcro Hooks In Your Mind's Garden

Permit your garden to grow a new you: avid gardeners need not apply

If our minds are perpetually closed to the sunlight of optimism and possibilities, we are continually blocking out the prolific generosity of our innate "weeds of interest." But what are weeds of interest? Throughout the ages, botanists have given certain plants or flowers the mongrel, derogatory terminology of being classified as "weeds."

So let's get this straight! At the beginning of time all plants and flowers were equal, had equal status – they grew, competed for sunshine and rain, displayed their unique beauty, and then died. Then along comes man with his fine honed mind and dictatorial need for order and selectivity, and he designates some plants as weeds because he doesn't want them. In his shallow mindset, they have no intrinsic value: they do not fit in to his perception of what "flowers" should look like.

Some trees, like Alders and Poplars, were treated in the same cavalier fashion and became "weed trees." Why is that? Because some people have this great need, this obsession to control and catalogue everything in our universe. They are blind to the unusual; to the unessential they would say; hence they have no place in their world. Cut them out, poison them, root them out before they have a chance to sprout, and contribute to the overall canopy of nature.

They grow their gardens, instead of allowing the gardens to grow them; for I think a more profound way of looking at it is, why don't we let the gardens grow us? Like vagrant thoughts and inklings that dart *seventeen*

# Always Be An Inch Taller Than Mile-High Grass

**Experience the most meaningful interview of your life –applying for the job of being the ultimate you**

The early North American pioneers crossing the plains had an obsession to reach the mythical West, but they needed guides and trackers to assist them; someone who had been there before and who knew where the waterholes were; knew where the passes through the mountains were; the safest places to cross rivers; who the most amenable native tribes were. Someone to guide them; to lead them; to coax them and coach them through their odyssey, for it would be a long, arduous journey.

We live in an age in which it seems that every second person you talk to have a life coach, or a personal fitness coach. Hang on! Is a coach someone with a minesweeper that walks in front of you and leads you through a minefield? That's a tracker, a guide. Is a coach saving you from making mistakes, avoiding pitfalls, or purely motivating you?

The answer is all of these things leading you through minefields of doubt, self-doubt, and self-abandonment in some ways; guiding you in a certain motivational way; extending a helping hand when you fall, and coaxing you when your energy flags. However, when you get to your destination you can then decide on the future unravelling of your life. Are you a destination person or a journey person? Only you can decide that.

Another word for "coach" is a waggon. Climb inside it and it will take us somewhere. Do we want to be able to achieve life's goals by ourselves, or do we always want to have a coach with us holding our hands along our unique trek through life? Ultimate dependency makes using the coach a permanent crutch. Until relying on a crutch psychologically make us into a cripple. What we think we become. Ultimately we have to stand on our own two feet.

The coach will help us find a path through the maze of the wilderness in our heart and soul. Clearly, we are trying to achieve something; but we are not sure how to do it. The coach will come along, and by breaking the problem down into manageable portions will show us a path through the maze; show us where the roadblocks are. We will be shown the safest way to get to our destination. A temporary crutch will be available for us. But rebuilding starts with us and ends with us.

Occasionally, once we get to our destination we may need support when we have moments of self-doubt; some new strategy we are not quite sure how to implement. This is only natural, but each time we step forward, the distance covered will be greater.

Right now our daughter is going for a job interview where she laughingly said. "If I get this position, I will be the one with high heels and a hard hat." However if we review the intimidating process, we face the interviewer or a panel of inquisitors on the other side of the table who will ask a series of probing questions to find out who we are, why we are applying for this specific position, what our abilities are, what our work ethics are and what we can contribute to this particular job. The aim of this period of piercing, probing and questioning is to reveal our strengths and weaknesses to the prospective employer.

How many of us have ever questioned ourselves, interviewed ourselves? Here is the exercise. Let us sit back with our eyes closed in reflection, as we ask the questions: Why am I here? What is my purpose? What am I contributing? What am I good at? What are the things I would love to improve upon? What are the highlights of my life? What meaningful things have I done? What have I achieved? What am I happy about? What is my philosophy?

The more questions we ask, the greater our understanding of ourselves will be revealed. Coaches and mentors are helpful in this exercise, however we don't always require someone to sit and ask these questions; we can ask them of ourselves.

This mind-expanding exercise can be practised anywhere we feel relaxed and comfortable. Strolling along by the ocean; through the forest; wherever we feel open and accepting, whether reclining on a couch with a pillow behind our heads, bathed with the sun shining through the windows, illuminating dancing shadows. Anywhere, we feel aesthetically, spiritually, and mentally ready.

By simply taking the first step by asking these imperative questions, we will be amazed at the responses. The point is; if we ask a question and don't have an answer, just stop and wonder why. How can we possibly be content to struggle through life not knowing or caring? The most relevant guide to change is: know yourself first, before attempting to unravel the enigmas surrounding others.

We all know we're on a journey with an inevitable destination at the end of it because physical life is finite; it will end. But our own mind, body, spirit and soul are taking us somewhere. They are reaching out and saying, "Just give us your hand." We can merely drift meaninglessly along, or join hands with our inner self, and start to ask the meaningful questions about our intrinsic worth, and chart a true course of destiny.

Just as explorers and pioneers wandered across wild unknown terrain resolving and solving seemingly insurmountable problems by being spontaneous, they discovered that by improvising and fighting for survival, a profoundly greater understanding of themselves was achieved.

When we reach inside, hopefully there is something there; we are not just a hollow keg with nothing inside. "Hello, is anyone there?" We are going to find out who we are, so we must interview ourselves. Sit there and ask "who am I, what makes me happy, what makes me sad; positives, negatives; the lightness in my life the heaviness in my life; dreams, ambitions, let-downs; trails or pathways I've taken or wanted to take; what makes me tick?"

Remember what we said about my grandfather's watch; all the components being equally important; relying on the other intricacies of the mechanism to work. You couldn't look at one part of the jigsaw and discard it. Everything has to work; don't let's compartmentalize our mind, our spirit, our soul or our heart; our physicality, our deepest dreams and aspirations. We cannot separate all these things because they're all working in concert.

We all know people who concentrate on building their bodies; the "jocks." We know people who are spiritualists, they live in the soul. We know scientists who live in analysis and scientific theory; then there those who live in pure creativity. I'm advocating that we must blend everything in this great circle of life. The hoop as the North American tribes I've spoken about call it. We should not separate it. You know the old cliché, "divide and conquer," I think that's really what happens. Like my grandfather's fob watch, we should never say, "I'm going to devote all of my time on this interesting little piece over here while neglecting the rest."

Like that old steel trap we spoke about, if it is ignored, it will inevitably become clogged, rusty and stop working. Even if of one part of that watch is gleaming and shiny and well lubricated and ready to go, if there are parts that have seized up because they've been ignored: the end result is failure. So we must look upon ourselves as not just one part but as many integral pieces nestling together in symmetry and harmony.

When we interview ourselves, we will deliberate and ask. "How am I doing in the brain section; how are my thought patterns going these days?" Look at yourself in the mirror and say "how am I doing in the physicality part; am I gaining weight; physically how am I doing?" We must reach into our souls and say "I know there's a spark in there; soul, spirit, spark, how are you doing, are you in good shape; are you working in this complex mechanism called me; are you helping me to get along on this journey to my ultimate destination?"

Into another part of our soul we will tentatively explore as we say, "Creativity how are you doing; have you sung lately; have you painted; have you clicked your heels together and danced unrestrained ballets; are you rusty?" Then we go back to our brains and say, "brain, analytically how are we doing, are we sharp, are we good at problem solving, are we getting a little bit stagnant up there; a little bit dull, do we need to polish the old brain cells?"

Through the simple process of interviewing ourselves we are determining if we are ready for the job of being "Me." We are delineating the various parts of our being. We' re finding out if there are imbalances; if some parts need to be polished; if some parts say we're living a lie.

"What do you mean, living a lie?" Well, we've said we have to balance all the components of our being. Weighing and polishing our brain, heart, soul, and getting them in balance. We have talked in terms of leaving our minds open to experiences, to feelings, emotions, to thoughts, to different wave patterns; open to different directions we've never even thought about.

We have talked about interviewing ourselves, "who am I, why am I here, where am I going, what is our purpose? We've done all that. The old expression "hello, is anyone there?" is demeaning in a derogatory belittling way. But think about it! How many of us can truly knock on our doors, our hearts, minds and spirits and say "is anyone there?" We may say, '"yes I'm here, I'm doing well. Look, touch me, feel me, see me, I'm here." But are we truly there? Are we there in a cohesive form where we know our own identity? Come on, we have interviewed ourselves; we have asked all the right questions; we have explored. Right?

Where do we go from there? If we perpetually live the lie, we will be the lie. If someone says "hello, is anyone there?" and we say "yes, I'm here and everything's fine" and it's not, we will slowly climb back into that armour again. We will say "this is me," and the reality truly will be that we will know we are lying to ourselves, because we are not fulfilling why we were put on this earth.

So when we go for an interview we will be rewarded with the position or be rejected. The interviewer is there assessing us and wondering whether we will fit into the organization; whether we have what it takes; "do you have the ability I'm looking for;" do you have the sense, the sensibilities to fit into this organization and contribute in a meaningful way?" If the interviewer feels that we possess the requisite abilities, then we will get it. Remember, when we apply for the job of being "Me", answer truthfully and we will receive the position of a lifetime.

However, there is a scary part here. If we apply for a job that's wrong for us, yet the interviewer says "you've got it," and we take it; here we go living a lie again. We have accepted a role that is not the definition of who we truly are. Yes, I realize that in some circumstances, some situations, we must accept the job to pay the bills, but

I'm talking about being true to ourselves. We have successfully passed the interview. We don't want however to go to Hell's Angels and pass their interview and be accepted into that position. We must be the job and the job must be us.

Ultimately to be totally happy and satisfied we must feel fulfilled. We must feel at the end of the day that we have done a good job, accompanied by a vibrancy which hums and resonates through our whole being.

Tap a tuning fork gently on a table and it will start to hum: it will start its own sonic mantra. It's functioning at its purest level. It is finely tuned. You then go to your musical instrument and tune it according to your tuning fork. A tuning fork is almost like a coach; "the notes over here are a little bit out of balance". So "ding" goes the tuning fork – "ah!"– that's how it should sound, that's what it's going to be like and then you adapt the notes to suit the tuning fork, but if you hit the tuning fork the wrong way "bonk," you will be rewarded by dull soulless sound, there will be no resonance, no musicality, no sense that the tuning fork has reached its full potential of producing the purest sound conceivable.

How does that relate to us? In every aspect of our lives, in our jobs, our recreational pursuits, in our satisfaction. If we strike the tuning fork of our soul and there's a dull bonk, a dull thud, well we're not really in balance, we're not really in tune. There's no musicality. We don't hear sweet music pouring out of our souls; there's not a happy song in there. We better use that tuning fork another way; hit it just so.

We have interviewed us. Are we going to get the job? We are interviewing ourselves to get the job of being the best we possibly can. Being the happiest person we possibly can; being someone who is contributing to the team. The team is the world, the team is life, the team is fulfilment, the team is all those around us. Do we want to flunk that? Let us practice the art of fine-tuning our inner being until we serenade the world with our melodies.

The reality is we may get the job, but maybe it's the wrong job. We have settled for something less than our full potential and we have taken the easy way out. We have found something that's easy to do. We can do it by rote, we produce and punch out those widgets and get paid at the end of the day. We put the cheque in the bank and it buys food, a roof over our heads. Yes, it's providing the basics of life, but what is basic? Is it luxury, is it alpha or omega, is it the nadir or the zenith? Are we going to settle for the lowest denominator of who we are, or do we want to reach to the heavens and make the haven that we are trying to live in, into a heaven by adding the 'e'; by adding excellence.

Why don't we all reach for excellence? Maybe when we interview ourselves we should reach for the ultimate job we can possibly make into the impossible dream; something that is passionate in our hearts and souls and makes us complete. What is that? "I really don't know, I've no idea," we say. "Come on, what do you like to do, what do you feel passionate about, what motivates you, what brings you to tears, what excites you, what fulfils you? What makes you sing and squeal with delight? "I don't know" may still be the response.

Okay, get into the next interview which is digging deeper. Let us go through the filtering process of what makes us happy. The words fulfilled, fulfilment, sound like filling something until it is full. Visualize a beautiful vase sitting on a sun-bathed shelf: that's us! We want to fill it; we want it to be fulfilled. We put a beautiful bouquet of flowers into the vase and contentedly sit back with a profound sense of admiration. We now feel that we are fulfilled; we have achieved.

Hang on! That's a little bit delusional. What's going to happen? Do we think those flowers will live in that vase without nourishment, without water, are they going to be fulfilled sitting in a vase filled with emptiness, filled with air? No, we have taken the easy fix again. We have found something we like and we have achieved it; yes, we have a beautiful bunch of flowers which equates to maybe that job, that function we have decided that we can do easily. We can now sit back and relax and for a while the blossoms will be vibrant, the petals will form perfectly defined halos on the stems; the leaves will be green and silky smooth and a thing of beauty. But what happens if we sit back and ignore them. Take them for granted. The bouquet will start to wither and fade. There has been no true fulfilment there, it's been an easy fix and we have failed to provide nourishment. Just like our body, heart, soul and mind, if we don't give them nourishment like the flowers and water, they will die.

Similarly, we have to nourish ourselves and, as we've said, I don't mean just nourishing our bodies through food and drink. Sure, that would keep the body going, but what about our minds, our spirits? What about the vital spark, the vase of our lives, the ultimate fulfilment?

If we fail to nourish all those components they will fade and die. They will fade at different times, in different ways. The brain may atrophy first – you know the old analogy "if you don't use it, you lose it." Our creativity may dry up first. Physically we may end up needing a crutch and then we may end up not being able to move at all. Our spark, our soul may go first, or they may go all at the same time because there's no life-giving nourishment, no vitality, and no life. We need to nourish all those components otherwise they will wither and die.

So, we must interview ourselves, question ourselves, and find our passion. Nourish the passion but, again, we need to persevere. We need to be willing to work on that journey. If we were one of those pioneers who when they saw a covered waggon or coach just jumped in and said "take me west" and then settled back in seclusion, what would the result be? We would recline in our hidden little world relying on others to forge ahead on the journey. Ultimately we would reach the end of the journey. We would have reached California, or Oregon, the end of the Oregon Trail. We may then say with a sense of pride, "I got here," but haven't really.

We have been on a journey, but we have achieved nothing on that journey, we've learned nothing, experienced nothing, we have allowed ourselves to be carried all the way. We need to personally explore on a continuous basis. The other pioneers and guides who walked the land, were experiencing pivotal events which would mould them forever: savouring the perfume of the prairie winds; witnessing the thundering majesty of the limitless buffalo herds; crossing unpredictable rivers; improvising when the waggon wheels broke.

We didn't however, because we hid in the recesses of the cocoon of the coach. It may appear as though we crossed the plains, but really we didn't, because we were relying on others to provide a crutch for us all through the journey. We lied to ourselves. We were living a lie; we didn't provide any nourishment in the form of assistance to ourselves or fellow travellers. So before we started off we were like an empty vase. We were who we had always been, and at the end of the journey we were still an empty vase. Superficially we crossed a continent, but remained the same through our policy of isolation.

When we interview ourselves, we find out gradually who we are and how we nourish others around us. This is similar to placing a bouquet of flowers in a vase and noticing that they're all at different stages in the cycle of life. Some are in full gorgeous bloom; others are still barely discernible buds waiting for their time to come, but if we provide nourishment to them all, they will all eventually come to fulfilment and fruition in their own time. We must learn to be patient.

As soon as the petals and blooms start to fade and fall off, we shouldn't pick up the vase and throw it out the window, because remember that gently growing buds are still waiting to come to fruition, and impatience will kill the flowers to come. So, similarly, our hearts and minds, bodies, souls and spirits; our creativity, our analytical powers, all the diverse fibres of our being are flowering at different levels. Patience and persistence lead to perfection.

## *eighteen*

# When Is A Rainbow Not A Rainbow?

**Light up your world and illuminate it for others**

It may be that analytically we are right up there with Einstein. Perhaps creatively we are like a Van Gough; physically a Schwarzenegger; spiritually a Buddha. Exaggerations perhaps, but as we have discovered, all the components of our being are probably flowering at different stages. So what we need to do is get a balance with them all. Don't neglect one in favour of another.

So it is with all aspects of our being. Some are in full blossom, some are half way towards fulfilment, some are imperceptible little buds, but we still have to nourish them in all their stages. They will develop in different ways at different times. And through our growing passions, we can watch them develop until they sing their own unique rhapsody.

The same could be said of being prayerful. Our being is like a rainbow. A rainbow is only a rainbow because it possesses a pallet of different colours. In a cohesive display of artistry, all the colours despite their distinctiveness allow their edges to feather out subtly until they blend into each other. If we delete one of the colours, the entity ceases to be a rainbow. We are not going to find a pot of gold at the end because it is no longer a rainbow. A colour has been removed; a prism blotted out. We have sliced off the yellow or the purple. The same with our being; if we slice off part of our being we close the door on our creativity, our soul, our mind, our heart and body. We close those doors and although we are only closing part of it, we are crippling ourselves. We are no longer a true person; we are not being honest with ourselves. We are living a lie, not fulfilling our true potential. We may say "I'm not interested in this or that; I hate exercise, I'm not good at creativity. I don't believe in God and I don't believe in spirituality."

However, remember what we said earlier? We must permit ourselves to be interested in everything; we have to be open minded, not like a steel trap. Advocates of the "mind like a steel trap" philosophy do not realize that through its strict rigidity eventually it is going to rust; so keep the diversity of your being open, viable and fulfilled. Remember the bouquet of flowers that must be nourished like that nursery log in the forest. An accident happens, a tree is blown over and in its appearance of death it nourishes future growth, future trees and forests, future excitement. The same with us as we turn accidents and misfortunes into potential for successful new, exciting ventures.

As my Dad used to say, "There's no such thing as an accident, just plain carelessness." Well! We all get careless sometimes, causing accidents. However as we have discussed previously, ancient Chinese painters who had accidents with their ink used the result innovatively? Like cooking! How do you think some of the fantastic recipes of all time came into being? There had to be an accident, an act of improvisation or spontaneity, there had to be a sense of "what do I have available to use to cook here?" The interesting, wonderful thing is that cuisine throughout the world grew like different blossoms with different flavours, different aromas and tastes. Because of the differences in races and what ingredients were readily available, the excitement of improvisational cuisine grew into an art: accidents can lead to miracles. They can produce magnificent works of art.

However, remember our personal interview? Perhaps we should look at ourselves as a diamond in the raw sitting there in the palm of our hands; the little hammer and chisel waiting for the ultimate orchestration. We're going to make the pure essence of our being into the most fulfilled, perfect thing the world has ever seen. That is the ultimate, but if we're careless and smash the chisel into the stone before we are ready. Boom! we end up with imperfection; we end up with something that really isn't what it should be. Yet, even in imperfection, perfection lives.

In this vein, a diamond cutter must have a really stressful job. A misaligned hammer blow, and the uncut stone breaks and is ruined; relegated as a mal-cut stone to its use as an industrial diamond. Before he cuts, the diamond cutter sits, ponders, assesses and watches. He's visualizing making a cut which will optimize the light that will emanate from this treasure; its intoxicating eye appeal; the facets; the sparkle; the beauty and perfection of that diamond. He's taken immense care and passionate zeal to make that diamond the most beautiful, exquisite thing the world has ever seen which obviously maximizes the ultimate value. We should do that with the uncut diamond that is us.

I learned this lesson years ago when I had a Chinese seal made for my paintings. In order to properly assess the essence of whom I was prior to the actual making of the ornate chop, the Oriental artisan interviewed me for a considerable amount of time. A week later I dropped into the store to pick up my treasure. As I gazed at the subtly carved seal which spelled out who I was, I noticed a chip around the edge. Casually I drew his attention to this "accident." "This imperfection makes the seal perfect," he said.

It took me years to understand what that meant. Which is: Perfection attained takes away the dream of reaching for the stars. We must always pursue the horizon in our evolutionary journey, and not rest on our laurels.

We cannot all be Einstein, Van Gough or Buddha and we cannot all be the ultimate in everything; but what we can be is the ultimate of us; the best we can possibly be. Just think about what we are journeying towards. We're in the process of nourishing ourselves by feeding the various components of our being.

That rough gem longing for fulfilment, has inside it the heart, soul and spirit of a jewel that is the best it can possibly be; it is a million dollar gem as opposed to an industrial diamond. But if we leave the untouched stone lying there, we are leaving our ultimate destinies lying there as a rough diamond forever. We can never really polish it; never bring out the fire, the wonder, the sparkle. We can never bring out that brilliance because we have never taken the time, the interest or desire to fine tune it, to hone it, to perfect it. The potential is there just sitting and waiting for us but we never seize the opportunity, never try to achieve that potential.

However, and there is always a "however;" we need to know how to open our gem of destiny. We need to know in the space of a heartbeat just when and where to put the chisel and hit with the hammer in order to split the raw stone with the correct momentum, the exact velocity, the precise force and angle; maybe even the right time of day in order to open that stone, but what we do need is to have everything set up just right. We need to have all the balanced components of our being singing, "This is it now, this is the time to reach for the best I can be, this is the time to take the chisel and create the jewel called me."

Coaches can help us find and use that chisel to hone in on an area of perfection or imperfection as we interview ourselves. We can find out how to best do that by fine tuning our hearts, souls, bodies, minds, spirits and analytical abilities. When all those things are in balance we will feel like a pendulum.

To get a pendulum started on its rhythmic journey can be pretty heavy going; pushing and pulling, and swinging, but once it starts, once the momentum is going, it's easy, gentle, flowing and effortless. There is perfection in that beautiful curve, in the circle of life, the swing, the to and fro. The same will happen; must happen, when all the parts of the pendulum of our being are in harmony in a perfect flow, moving effortlessly, driven by passion, desire, love, commitment, perseverance and fulfilment.

Once the pendulum of our being is moving in a perfect arc, it takes very little effort to keep it going. Just envision it humming along, fine-tuned and running effortlessly like a space ship sailing through the galaxies. The amount of effort to get a galactic explorer to a certain point through the resistance of the Earth's gravity is enormous, but once it's there and moving effortlessly, it needs very little fuel. With some fine tuning it can drift along nicely – and we have now done that with ourselves. We have fine- tuned every part of our being; we have searched and found what our passion is: Then with ease we have taken a chisel and touched it gently with hardly any effort all and immediately there is perfection, a shining, gorgeous creation that is us.

The incredibly fulfilling thing is that by opening ourselves up with no pretensions, we will help to illuminate others. There is a newfound happiness humming around us with a fine tuned feeling of a destiny attained. Just as we are nourished, we will become a source of nourishment for others. And, it doesn't end there! We have reached a stage now where we have evolved into the best we can possibly be. We are a pendulum, open and optimistic exuding spontaneity with a dazzling sparkle. Our fire is gleaming through our eyes, with vibrancy and intoxicating happiness. We have resolved all our unresolved issues, and others can sense the empowering energy to be attained by being close to us.

Here's another interesting thing. We are on a journey but at the same time we have arrived! We have arrived at a realization of who we are. We have arrived at a resolution to the issues that were inside. We know who we are. We feel happy at the realization of what we have attained. We are nourishing ourselves in our journey of life: but we are voyaging in a coach of our own making.

We have not just climbed into a coach that someone else has created, with blinds pulled down and simply "gone along for the ride." We have designed and built this coach; the coach of our being that is bright, vibrant, shining and it is You, Us, and Me. That is the reality and happiness of you! Once this happens, the effort to polish and fine tune our being should be effortless. The pendulum of our life is now perfectly balanced. Before it was like a teeter-totter, up, down and sideways, but now it's a gentle pendulum swinging effortlessly like a grandfather clock humming away with no effort. There is now total ease and incredible happiness and fulfilment.

We have reached that place because we have nourished ourselves: hence we can now nourish others – it's impossible not to. We produce so much excitement, vitality and, happiness that it exudes; just pours from us in gentle torrents, and others who come in contact with us will benefit from that. If they're in a position where they need nourishment, just by being close to us they will get the benefit of our perfection, and feel the warmth of the fire inside us.

Our sparkle will illuminate the air around us and they will rejoice in the happiness, the humming vitality; the pendulum of our hearts, souls, spirits and beings. Analytically they will pick up on those things because we have, in essence, become a tuning fork. We are finely balanced. If the Great Spirit picked us and just bumped us gently, we would exude this perfect musicality, this lovely lulling humming which everyone else would want to emulate.

To tune a piano, a tuning fork is used to get the notes on the piano to conform to that specific cadence. That's what we are going to be – a tuning fork for those around us. We are going to be a beacon that people will be dazzled by until they say, "Yes, I want some of that light, I like the way he does things, I like the way she achieves effortlessly. What is it about that guy or that girl? They always seem to be upbeat, they really get things done, they never seem to be down, there's happiness about them, they really seem to make things happen."

The funny thing is that at the same time they will also say: "they're not full of their own importance; that person is unbelievable; they can do anything and everything, and nothing is too much trouble, they're willing to share – that's the amazing thing." I guess that is what happens when you have so much love, so much affection, and so much balance. The pendulum is humming along and we don't need to exert any effort at all, as nourishment flows from us.

The bouquet inside the vase that is us is now perpetually filled with nourishment. So much nourishment that it overflows, benefiting those around us from this bounty. We have become a beacon, a reality, a destination. Suddenly we have become a destination and other people want to be like us. They won't want to be clones of us, but they will want to have the sparkle that we have. They will want to feel about life the way we seem to feel about life. Things happen to us, things happen with us. Our visions are coming true; we are filled with exhilaration and happiness only because we kept our minds open and let the winds of change blow in. We let anything and everything grow – we said no to negativity. We let positivity rule.

We used spontaneity, we travelled down roads that were not just less travelled; they were never travelled. Every path that we took was a new one. When our waggons were stuck in the ruts of ploughed fields, when there was frost and ice and snow, we just let the sun warm and soften those ridges so that we could take any path we chose. We have reached a point where we can truly say "I'm on a journey but I'm also a destination for those around me." So as well as heading towards a final destination; the eternal aspect of life which really is not an end, but is a beginning in the cycle of cosmic creativity and of creation: we have become a destination.

The important lesson we have learned is that we need to know ourselves before we can help others. How can we help other people if we don't know who we are or why we are the way we are? If we are imbalanced, if we're living a lie how can we coach other people? We will coach them to be liars. They will see a fabrication of something they think is there, but it's not.

We are going to be like the unscrupulous speculators who took money from Western pioneers to lead their covered waggons across the plains, when they had never really been there before. Yes, we could pretend and act the part with an impressive Stetson, an armament of firearms, jaunty buckskins and a prancing steed. We could look the part of the major coach, ready to guide pioneers across the plains, and sadly the victims wouldn't know any better until disaster struck.

Many of the pioneers came from a place of desperation and poverty which they desperately wanted to leave behind. And we are talking about poverty of the soul as well as of the body. They wanted a renewal of life. So if we look the part of the saviour and take their money with no intention of following through, the people will die because they're lost in the wilderness. Do not play the role, be the real thing!

We want to be the true coach, the authentic guide who does not have to proselytize; we don't have to offer our services. People will come to us automatically. They will detect the pureness. We will have filtered all the dirt of life out and the garden of our being will be filled with the aromatic intoxicating scents of pure growth. It's a balanced garden, there's an excitement about us, happiness. Our journey is cruising along beautifully and people see that and will come to us, and only then will we become a coach. All of this courtesy of the interviewing process in which we asked ourselves if we were in balance.

We have not purposely set out to be someone who nourishes the whole world; to be the guru of all time. We set out to discover who we are, to find our brilliance and what makes it sparkle; to make it as perfect as it can be and to reach fulfilment. The more we reach for perfection the more we can give others, and the more others will see that. All through a simple interview process we have applied for a job and that job is to be the best person we can; the happiest and most fulfilled person; the most passionate person we can be. Is that not exciting! We haven't settled for second best or third or fourth best, we haven't just put a roof over our family; they now have been given a haven. More than that they have been given a heaven by adding that special ingredient; excellence, because we have added that "e".

At one point in our life people may have said that we were eccentric because we were doing things our way, we were out on a limb, on the fringe of things. We were thinking differently and were willing to accept everything, to filter and negate negativity. We were willing to accept that there was an imbalance and willing to get the pendulum of our life moving and swinging smoothly and sweetly. We were willing to nourish ourselves and willing to persevere. We didn't want any flowers dying inside us, we wanted that vase to be perpetually filled with gorgeous flowers to perfume our soul so that people would see and sense and watch the sparkle, and gravitate toward us.

Now, we are not doing that through self-importance; not doing it because we want people to say "wow, here is, the most incredible person I've ever met in my life." I think if we try to do everything we've said with the sole purpose of "Being," as my kids would say "so great", that's not going to happen. We cannot go to school to be a saint: just do everything right and the reward will be sainthood; or just as perfect as we can be. So we are nourishing others now, a beacon; we know ourselves, we have the job we wanted: but the interesting thing is that on reflection we didn't know what that job was. Now we know: The job was to make other people sparkle.

Look at the ocean. On a dull, grey day the water is sullen, but still compelling in a subtle sombre way. When the sun comes out, just the slightest bit of sun, suddenly the ocean sparkles. We want to be like that – the sparkle of our soul gleaming through our eyes.

Before that happens however, the people around us would have only seen a dullness emanating from us, no sparkle. Now, with the prisms of light sparking from our eyes, people are being lit and nourished. They're becoming happy; they will come to us and say "hey, coach me." That is when we can reveal our path to perfection. Optimism, spontaneity, interviewing ourselves, being the best we possibly can and achieving something we never really knew we were trying to achieve – total fulfilment, total optimism because all through this we need to be optimistic, we need to have some commitment and perseverance.

# *nineteen*

## Rambling Beyond Invisible Horizons

**"What! Who me?"  Or the benefits of wandering and wondering**

"Wandering and wondering."  These words sound the same, and in my mind there is very little difference between them. The word wander denotes to me a picture of aimless rambling over a landscape of mysterious mountains and through haunting valleys: just heading toward the horizon where our minds are filled with wonderment at what we are experiencing.  Wondering is the same thing, if we permit our minds to roam unfettered in the exploration of the unknown territory lurking in the wilderness of "why and what if?"

We don't have to travel to the distant, exotic places of the world to wander, to ramble; it can be done internally.  This is all part of expanding the knowledge of who we are by imagining. In the dream-like state of envisioning, the mountains, passes and valleys of the Himalayas are there to relish, or pristine Polynesian islands, to call our own. By envisioning, a state of tranquillity and euphoria is conjured up, as we are wandering and wondering at the same time. Some may say it's escapism but, no, what we are doing is nurturing our spirit and providing sustenance to our soul. When we visualize a place of happiness, we are providing a haven, a heaven, a cocoon to revitalize and re-grow the nature that is us.

I remember years ago in my hometown in Scotland, there was a local club that had a loyal following.  Now, I never have been a joiner of clubs, and I didn't join this particular one called The Ramblers, although I was tempted. In a sort of hypnotic way, the word rambling has always held some exciting connotations for me; rambling was a nomadic word. It was spreading wings and just wandering; similar to the sail boat tacking back and forth, to and fro.

At weekends, the club members would go to different areas of the countryside exploring mountains, valleys, and the pastoral beauty of nature. Wandering, walking and I am sure wondering about all they saw. It was the word "rambling" that captivated me, and that was when the word "wondering," led me through the highways and byways of my imagination.

In colloquial terms, when someone is rambling it is usually used as a derogatory expression, as it means they're off the topic; it means they're not staying focused because their blinkers have been thrown aside and they're digressing. But this is exactly what we're talking about. I am emphatically stressing that we should let our imaginations digress; we should let ourselves wander into areas we haven't been into before. We should ramble; we should get out of the focus-driven here and now and just live for the moment that is being presented on a silver platter.

Let's try something different by thinking about this subject this way. Every day we have a routine in which at certain times we indulge in predictable activities. Obviously we have likes and dislikes; we probably read the same predictable magazines and newspapers, the same sort of books, listen to the same sort of music and watch the same television programmes. A routine has been established, or maybe the routine has established us!

Think about entering a library and purposely closing our eyes. We then walk along blindly, stretching out a hand and randomly pulling a book from the shelf. Spontaneity again! We are doing something different and potentially exciting. Who knows what the mysterious book will divulge; it could be about anything and everything. We are digressing from a routine of analytical choice, and haphazardly reaching into the stimulating unknown. Now make a commitment to read that book and visit a topic previously never thought about. It may change our life, or at the very least help us to understand the joys of random selection: wandering and wondering at its finest.

What does lack of stimulation cause? -Tedium and boredom. Back to that all-encompassing layer of armour that cocoons us by keeping others, events and circumstances out beyond our touch. We cannot grow in armour. "She's put walls around herself; she's withdrawn into herself, entrenched." It sounds dramatically like the middle-ages when people actually did put armour around themselves. The armour around entire societies was called a castle. The people within were protected from exterior assaults and attacks; there was a moat around them as further defence. And when I hear that word I am reminded of the word "remote:" distancing ourselves from others.

In this medieval setting there was always a drawbridge across the moat. This was an entry as well as an exit; again the Yin and Yang. Within that castle the people lived for periods of time in isolation through the inevitable tumultuous times of war and aggression. So, within that walled city the people endured until the danger passed, and then they were free to venture forth again into the wider world.

That may be acceptable for a period of time, but if we stayed in this moated, armour-clad castle forever, we are inevitably going to wither. We require external sources of nourishment, even within the castle domain. We may in our daily lives feel that we can live quite nicely in isolation; withdrawn from the world. How many hermits do you know? We may delude ourselves by thinking that we have found the answer. "I want the world to go away; I want to retreat to my own little place, my own desert island and it won't affect anyone." But it is impossible. Remember the story about the pebble thrown into the ocean and its ultimate effect.

An example on a larger scale occurred at the turn of the 19th century, when the United States president, James Monroe, promulgated the Monroe Doctrine. This was a doctrine; a decree of isolation which saw the United States living as an island. Not influencing others, not becoming caught up in the intrigues, affairs, and the conflicts in mainland Europe, because that is where the centre of power was. Monroe just wanted the U.S. to grow independently in total isolation from the rest of the world. Of course that couldn't happen and the policy failed. Very soon they threw themselves back into the intrigues of the world and into involvement with the rest of the world.

Paradoxically, not too many years later, the United States forcibly forced Japan to enter the 19th century. Japan had lived in isolation for hundreds of years in an anachronistic feudal society. They had chosen to live in splendid isolation. They were living in the past in the industrial age, separated from the outside world, until they were grabbed by the throat and thrown into the 19th century.

Isolation! There is a great danger of living in isolation; social isolation; physical and mental isolation; spiritual isolation. Isolating our creativity in isolation! We need stimulus; cross fertilization of creative ideas. We may say, "If I go to an island, I won't affect anyone; I can withdraw into myself and enjoy being a recluse." But no matter where we are or what we do, we are affecting other people, other things. Just the very act of walking on the ground on this desert island may kill some plants or insects. By blocking the sun, even for a few moments, a particular plant may be affected in some unknown way, or we may step on an insect that through its act of pollination nourishes that plant in some way. So we are causing a devastating reaction.

People who withdraw into themselves think they're not affecting anyone else. But in reality they are. Visualize yourself in a workplace setting in which you never speak to anyone; keep your head down, nose to the grindstone, you have no interaction with people. Yes, you do your job, but you will probably make others feel uncomfortable by this withdrawn demeanour. They might wonder if they have done something wrong because of your isolation. Others may feel frustration or anger at the lack of interaction.

These people who withdraw into themselves may believe that they are merely following their own instincts, but just by their act of withdrawing from society in that limited way, they are affecting everyone; they're projecting their sense of aloofness to others who will suffer the consequence. Feelings of stress are the results of failure to communicate with others and more important: with ourselves.

Even in our chosen "vocation of isolation," people can still be affected in subtle ways. Energy can be projected through our eyes. I remember reading reports of army scouts back in the days of the "Old West," who said that when they were scouting an Indian camp they didn't dare look directly at the people in the camp because the warriors could sense that they were being studied. Again, there was no physical interaction at that stage, but the warriors who were the object of the scouts' scrutiny would know there was someone there watching them.

How that happened, I have no idea. But it demonstrates that others can be affected without physical or tactile contact, but simply by projecting. You know the expressions "he can freeze water with a glance," or "he's shooting daggers at her." That's projecting. Now, isn't it much better to project positive feelings, positive vibrations?

We hear of others who, when they walk into a room, the room lights up; there's an aura of happiness, of positive sunlight around some people. So, if we have a dream we want to reach, a destination which is our dream, we must do everything we can to evolve into a positive thinking person. Throughout this book, we've being opening up blockages in our soul, heart and spirit. We're now thinking creatively, spontaneously, we're improvising and we are not scared to face challenges, not afraid to digress or to deviate. Yes, we'll stand up and be counted and we may possibly continue to be called someone who marches to a different drumbeat. Wear that sobriquet as a badge of honour. "Bonsai not poplar, parasol not umbrella." "Dreams into reality."

I always return to this word "dream." I have some of my best day-dreams at night time just by allowing my mind to wander at will. My old mind is in super-drive, churning away and putting Velcro hooks onto different things; all of which are positive. The sometimes tenuous tendrils of our mind's wanderings will always have a destination as it lead us along. We can play games with our imagination and enhance our dreams as we ramble along intellectual mountains where we can camp beside gentle meadows in the pastures of our soul; we can stroke rainbows on our yonderings along the beaches of our desires.

As we reach for a dream, respect it, as we hold this fragile, throbbing dream like a heartbeat, while we ask; '"is this really what I want, is this where my passion lies?" Respect the dream, say instead; "this is what I want, this is what I need to reach for, this is the horizon I want to get to. This is my dream." Dreams once respected can be realized.

Anticipate some roadblocks, but be willing to climb over them. Go through, around, tunnel under, or simply spread wings and fly high above the impediment. Yes, in our imaginations we can fly over roadblocks. Improvise as the right answers or solutions may not be immediately clear. Say; "I'm going to give different viewpoints a try here in my problem solving." Problems which are broken down into manageable pieces, like the rock we spoke of earlier, will vanish as we incrementally toss them aside.

Just like that castle. Sure, it is made of thick, buttressed rocks with a moat around it, but it has a drawbridge which is the wedge into the heart of the seemingly impenetrable rocky fortress. Despite naysayers who love shooting arrows at us, we will breach the obsolescence of this obstacle. Before our journey into change, the negativity of people would have wounded us, but times have now changed in our new incarnation.

There is an island off the coast where we live, and from our bedroom deck I can stand and gaze at its sleeping bulk. It lies like a huge sleeping whale with its snout facing north up into the Sound. In the wintertime the waves smash against that snout, forming in the icy cold, layers of ice. In the beginning the ice is imperceptible. The splashing water just shines and sparkles, until it in its turn gradually freezes, and another coat of ice forms on top of it. Gradually the complete rock becomes coated in armour plated ice.

This is when subtly through time, we allow a bad habit to form; some negativity encroaches into our new positive thinking lifestyle. However, every little bit of that negativity is like a creeping spray of ice that in the beginning is easy to ignore. Like ships in the Arctic, if the insidious layers of ice growing on the hull are ignored, eventually the ship will roll over and sink being top heavy. If we are not careful; by not thawing seemingly inconsequential bits of negativity as soon as we are aware of them, there is a danger that, again, we will be covered in armour; we will become submerged; losing that positive new- found vision of who we can truly be.

Like the ruts in ploughed frozen fields in wintertime, lying like iron rails and preventing your waggon from digressing, just by gentle thawing of those ruts we can travel in any direction. We can reach for the horizon. We can wander and wonder as we pursue our yondering odyssey.

A word I love is "yondering." I first encountered it in Louis L'amour's writings of the Wild West; the far west of the blue, hazy horizons. I'm going yondering obviously means heading towards horizons, far from the known, and towards distant places. It conjures up an intoxicating sense of spontaneity, a sense of freedom, a nomadic sense of excitement as we head for that magical line in the curve of the earth that we call the horizon.

We sail or march towards it and say, "oops, where did it go, it's vanished? Oh, it's over there now." It is truly a perpetual progression. Incrementally, as you approach the horizon, it moves away again and in some ways becomes similar to chasing our shadows. It's like a nebulous dream. But the positive thing is that it lures us forward, and provides us with continuing incentives to discover the never-ending horizons awaiting us around every bend in our journey.

We should learn to conceive that each horizon may be potentially the horizon of complacency. Like setting goals, there are going to be many horizons to reach; lines of achievement; diverse destinations, and that is just fine. Setting a goal as we have discovered, is breaking the ultimate destination into small achievable pieces: one little step at a time. The first horizon is conquered and we can proudly shout. "I have achieved; I have reached a destination." We have reached a place of achievement where we can rest and re-nourish our souls and your spirits; energize emotions while polishing those different components of our being before moving on.

As we evolve into an ever-changing vision of who we used to be, indulge in always setting new goals towards new horizons. Relish in the euphoria of the spontaneity of simply "yondering." When a goal or dream is set, start immediately towards that magical line on the horizon; however, if something catches our eyes in a different direction, we should not be afraid to digress and assess it. For, we may find out that through our openness to digress, we have, inadvertently arrived at our real destination. Destination is really Destiny; so please do not try to second-guess serendipitous teasing whispers to tack us away from where we think we are heading for.

The destination we thought lay directly ahead or around that easily accessible corner may not be the one we were destined to reach for. It really wasn't our true dream: so be prepared for surprises. Be aware that there can, and will be changes; be aware that circumstances may change and turn on a dime. Miraculously we may discover that through deviating from a set path, and digressing from the norm, we have left our windows open. A new avenue is opened, just like when we enter the library with our eyes closed, and reaching out we encounter unexpected destiny. "What, who me?"

*twenty*

# Destination Calling – Do You Accept The Call?

**Right or left brain? Let the destination find you.**

We live in an age of analytical dissection; where at every level of society individuals and groups, analyze; strategize; engage in all-encompassing planning, prioritizing and a myriad of other intellectual exercises. The goal is meant to streamline corporate or personal lives, or ways of doing business. However in the process, feelings and gut instinct, in which the inner voice says "try this" is generally ignored. We can be a master of efficiency, often mistaken for effectiveness: we can be extremely busy while becoming entangled in the knots of neatness and order, but there is another way to tackle life's issues.

By sitting down and distancing our souls from our intellects and our creativity, and fragmenting our beings into different pieces, we will end up saying, "okay I've thoroughly assessed this issue, and based on logic, here is my dream." However your spirit may be veering in another direction, hand in hand with the Stranger Inside who is no doubt feeling incredibly disillusioned. Trust in gut instinct and reach for the magic horizon beckoning just out of sight.

The following two examples show the extremes between allowing your open intuition, or gut instinct to lead you somewhere you have never been before and the analytical approach in which a decision is made based on extensive mind-numbing intellectual dissection.

The first example of serendipitous decision making involved a young French restaurateur who lived on a small isolated island off the coast of Venezuela. A visitor to the island asked him how he came to choose this particular island: "what drove you to this place?" He replied that at one point in his life he felt disillusioned and knew that he needed a change in his life. What he then did was rather unusual and extremely radical. He took a globe of the world, spun it, closed his eyes and when the world stopped spinning, stabbed his finger at the globe until it hit a random destination. And that is how he came to live on this remote but somewhat idyllic Caribbean island. By orchestrating his life in this unorthodox manner he became the maestro of his own destiny.

When he arrived on the island he realized that "this is my destination." This is where he had wanted to be all his life but didn't know what it looked like, or tasted like, smelled like; but as soon as he arrived he felt at peace. Sometimes, your inner self wants something entirely different from your intellect, but we have been trained to rely on analysis instead of intuition.

If the young Frenchman had just sat down and methodically and analytically written down all the pros and cons of every country in the world; climatic conditions; aesthetics, culture and so on, his intellect may have said "this is where I'm going," but no; there was something – some little spark that was drifting towards a different horizon that was unknown to him until he spun the world on its axis and took the giant step of leaping into the unknown. You may say it was mere coincidence that he found his haven, or, "if he'd touched another part of the globe he would have been equally happy," I don't know. All I do know is that this man felt from the first moment he set foot on that little island that he had arrived; that his life's purpose lay here. It was love at first sight. He had no clearly delineated destination in mind when he spun the globe; he just opened up his heart, mind and his soul and said "take me; take me on a journey to a destination I've never been to before."

An example of choosing a destination based on excruciating research occurred to a family who lived in British Columbia. In the early 1980's they decided to move to the safest, most remote place they could choose. To escape from the chaos of the world, and after great analysis, they picked the remote Falkland Islands off the coast of Argentina. Shortly thereafter the Argentinian army invaded, leading to the eruption of the Falklands War in which the British army ultimately defeated the invading army.

The family had chosen based on analysis and the result was chaos. Intuition or analysis? Both have a place in our lives; but the inner voice should never be ignored. Allow it to debate the issues with you and provide you with new fresh insightful perspectives on your life's journey.

Analysis and research can be taken in my mind to extremes. Some people for example, before they go on vacation develop a regimented mind-set in which they plan every single moment, every single second, and every pit stop. They book a room every single night; they minutely measure the distances they're going to travel each day; they research the sights, the scenes, the attractions of each place; then set their destiny in the rigid tracks they have manufactured, and hurtle down the highway fulfilling their regimented dream and the regimented destinations they have outlined in their regimented mind. Perhaps that is all right for some people, but isn't it more fun if when you decide to go on vacation you just land at point A and spread your arms, spread your wings and let the wind blow you aimlessly? Let the destination find you! It's a neat idea – again, just deviating, digressing. You drive or stroll along, not sure what's around the next bend because you haven't researched every aspect of that trip: as opposed to going on an analytical, organized, strategically planned trip. Your life can be like that, open to surprises and anticipation.

We are carefree explorers, seemingly aimlessly tacking back and forth, encountering and enjoying new and exciting experiences. When we approach the towns on the way, we don't have any preconceived ideas of what they will look like; we don't know all the sights and sounds of the particular area we are going into. We just walk in there with an open mind, an open heart and act through the spontaneity of our souls. We will probably find it more exciting. Strange, exciting things will happen. New people and unexpected vistas will appear as we drive with no blinkers on.

Think of the benefits: if we fall in love with a specific place, we won't have to move the next day because we don't have any pre-registered hotels, motels, or bed and breakfasts previously organized: so we must set our own pace and go!

I think that the most pivotally important part of everything we have said is setting our own pace. It's like driving a car. Some speed fanatics such as racing car drivers are comfortable and competent as they drive at hundreds of miles an hour. Their reflexes are fine tuned for that kind of speed and they probably feel impatient driving slowly. The flag drops and they surge as quickly as they can towards their final destination: the finish line. The strange thing is that a lot of people live their lives like that – they're "fast tracking or "living life in the fast lane." Excessive hurry leads to stress and a blurred view of life.

If you've ever travelled on a train as it hurtles through the countryside rocking back and forth along the tracks, you will probably have noticed that everything outside becomes a blur; the scenery becomes a mismatched haze. You are going so quickly you are missing the vignettes of life you are passing. Like driving at excessive speeds, you really cannot see or appreciate what's outside. You have to slow down, and when you do, when you start to walk, then the blinkers fall away. It's like old "Johnny Head in the Air" we talked about a long time ago; the scales will fall from your eyes; you feel things; you sense things. If this sounds like you; slow down, take it easy. You know the old analogy about stopping to smell the roses? Savour the perfume around every corner.

On our life's journey we must make the trip relevant. Instead of maniacally endeavouring to cram in every possible sensation, allow them subtly to be absorbed into our inner being through an open heart. Travel with uncluttered childlike eyes, and like a sponge, we will become the journey.

We spoke in terms of when we reach the perfection we are striving for, we will sense that we possess so much nourishment within us that we are actually feeding and sustaining others who are gravitating towards us. We have become a magnet without debilitating layers of armour: it's long gone. We are no longer living in isolation trapped in a psychological castle: we are free. Our mind isn't like a steel trap that would have rusted long ago. We have looked after the various components of our being and given them freedom to flourish. Like the parts of my grandfather's fob watch, we have discovered that they're all relevant, they're all important. And we have learned to keep them all fine- tuned so that they will not atrophy.

*twenty one*

# Opportunistic Soup Making

**Life is like soup; you add the Ingredients – Including the kitchen sink**

I love the exciting ritual of making soup as it is extremely creative and lends itself to savoury exploration. I venture into the kitchen with only one plan in mind: to make a huge pot of soup. I honestly do not know how it's going to turn out because I usually don't know what ingredients are available – but I do know what steps I will take.

First of all I will go to the refrigerator and freezer and see what containers and plastic bags filled with leftovers are there. Discards you might say from other meals which I have kept with no rhyme or reason; and often times I don't know the contents of the various containers as they are all unlabelled. But I do know that ultimately when my soup is ready, it's going to be tasty; it's going to have an individual flavour which will be a surprise to me, so that, if someone had said to me before I started, "describe the taste of your soup today," I really couldn't do it. All I know, is my soup is going to be flavourful; that my soup is going to be "souper" and highly individualistic.

Our brains should be like that, filled with leftovers and discards ready to spring into action when we need them. These are ideas, thoughts, feelings, and emotions which pop into our heads uninvited, often at inappropriate or unexpected moments when we are involved in some other activity. We're working diligently on one project totally focused, when suddenly another idea comes in to visit. The tendency, or the temptation, would be to focus at the job at hand and not permit our minds to wander off with this vagrant thought. However, always remember the old focus- blinker thing. Toss the idea into your gunny sack and let it ferment until it is ready to leap into action at a later date.

Embrace that idea which you may not be able to use in the current project, but if you discard it, throw it away; you may never get it back again. It may be a springboard to resolving some major future event in your life. Categorize it as the intriguing variety. Put it in a little box inside your brain somewhere filed under miscellaneous and then when you're working on another project; when you're making another pot of soup in your mind, you can fill it with all the little tidbits, the little leftovers. As you're making your soup you'll think "I remember that idea." Think of projects as making soup: all the ingredients are in your mind waiting to be utilized in their own sweet time.

Now, making soup is an adventure. We know it's good for our well-being when we are feeling decidedly under the weather. When we are suffering from the seasonal flu and we want to be coddled, we take some nice warm comforting soup. Similarly, we should nourish our souls, our minds, our body and our creativity with this melange; this pot-potpourri made out of ideas, thoughts, feelings, emotions that have crept in at serendipitous times. So instead of discarding them, we have learned to file them away in our heads for future use.

When I make my soup, I sometimes buy a soup mix from one of the bulk food stores where there are mesmerizing, brimming barrels filled with ingredients: lentils, peas, beans, split peas, a bit of barley, and other ingredients to add to the eclectic mix. All I know, is that there is a colourful selection for me to choose from; an intriguing bag of soup mix. Individually you could make soup with just lentils or peas or barley, but collectively all of my disparate pieces of the soup puzzle come together to provide my waiting palate with an unmistakable incredible flavour. You might say my soup is opportunistic - whatever is at hand at that moment is added to it.

Again, our ideas are like that: just reach into our idea bank and pull something out and use it. Sticking to the one ingredient is similar to relying on one route to resolving a problem; instead of using a multilayered melange of stored ideas in our memory banks.

A Chinese friend of mine with relatives all over the world once told me that in each country in which they have settled, "Chinese food" is influenced by whatever ubiquitous food is at hand. So, a dish that's called one thing in one country will taste differently from the same named dish in another country because they have used whatever is at hand – their method of food preparation is opportunistic. That is what we must do, be opportunistic in our problem solving techniques.

When we are resolving issues; remember that we have all forms of diverse ingredients in our heads. Each time we reach in to spoon out some soup of resolution, the taste and effect will be different, because the ingredient mix is in a continual state of flux. As I am writing this, thoughts unrelated to the content keep intruding. What I do is allow them to settle in comfortable corners of my mind to germinate, so that when I need a "souper boost," I just reach in and say; "work your magic."

I believe that life should be like that. However, some people talk in terms of their life as being boring, mundane where "nothing ever happens." Well, I guess it's because in the soup of their lives, they're not adding any spice to it. They're just plodding along in the same old way. So we should reach into our rack of spices, of magical leftovers and improvise. Never be scared to add things; to kick it up a notch, as one of TV's cooking show gurus is fond of saying. The ingredients that we are adding may seem totally disparate with no connection between them at all.

Don't analyze the contents of this soup. We may think, "God, are they going to overpower each other and cause an imbalance?" Who cares, "The more the merrier; everything but the kitchen sink." It's exploration; innovation; it's being open to fresh possibilities: so be an innovator. Our vision is to make the most exciting soup possible. Throw everything in; don't be scared, and be amazed at the incredible flavourful direction your life will take. Like soup, life is to be savoured.

## *twenty two*

## Become A Nomad Without Even A Camel

**How to journey to the essence of your core.**

We live in an age of external fitness, where the media bombards us with the quick and dirty way to lose weight, and become a facsimile of our favourite movie star: "thin is beautiful." However, we are talking about honing ourselves by removing the extraneous flab in our inner selves: external fitness is only part of the puzzle. I call this approach "fostering our nomadic spirit." What does that mean? Now, in your imagination visualize a true nomad in his natural environment. Never staying in one place too long; wandering like the wind over the land, and leaving little imprint.

Their life revolved around settling briefly in an area hunting and fishing, gathering berries, grazing their herds of cattle, sheep, camels or goats, and then moving on again. They were not a sedentary people; they were free. Through time, they had honed the necessities of life down to a basic elemental level. Like poetry in motion, they had synthesized, they had distilled and they had produced a fine honed essence, which allowed them to lead a free life drifting before the breeze to beckoning horizons.

They were continually seeking the holy grail of horizons of opportunity. Their very survival depended on them being the consummate opportunists. If they found an area flowing with milk and honey; with good water and grass, they would stay. They would never deplete the bounty around them, but in the cycle of the seasons, they would ultimately pursue the mythical horizon. I am not advocating that everyone should leave their families, their homes and wander the world with sheep and cattle. Rather, foster your spirit of freedom where life is distilled to its ultimate essence; minus the flab of our frenetic existence.

Distillation is the key! Nomads have distilled millennia of data into pure essence. As we have previously indicated: don't throw anything away, any idea, any feeling, any circumstance; everything except negativity. Anything that happens to enter your brain can just stay there to be slowly dissolved into your future evolution.

You may say, "how can I absorb the flood of information coming at me: there's only so much my brain can hold." Well, think back to the dawn of computers when it took several large rooms to house them. But now they have been synthesized, distilled, micro-chipped, and they can give you more capabilities than the archaic obsolete computers of the past. Your brain, at the beginning, will be like the old computer, there will be so much input that you will wonder, "Is my brain too small to hold all of this?" Just think of that computer, think of your brain as those micro-chips that now hold more memory, more detail and more data than ever before. Distillation is the key.

The Nomads wandered across diverse landscapes, but the unique regions that have always fascinated me are the deserts. Now, why is it that when the early prophets and philosophers were trying to discover the meaning of life, and the hereafter, they would wander in a desert. What is it about the desert?

I am advocating making your desert into a dessert; the ultimate sustenance; the utter sublimity. But most people talk about the desert in a derogatory way. "The desert of your soul which means you are downcast when you feel abandoned; nothing is going right for you. The world is filled with negativity; you're wandering in an old sterile desert. But that's not the way it is. The desert is a place of great beauty. It's a raw, visceral environment. To my way of thinking, all the good things in the world have been condensed into that desert to give it an elemental beauty. To give you a sense that you're close to something; close to the centre; close to the centre of yourself; close to the centre of the universe. Maybe close to the heart of creation and eternity.

When you think about it; at the beginning of time when people first appeared on earth, and they started the slow process of spiritual, social, physical and intellectual evolution, they were close – extremely close to the fire and the creator who had produced creation. They could still feel the vibrations; they could still feel the emotions of their birth. Just like when your baby is born; that gut-wrenching excitement.

These people who hovered at the beginning of time were close to the Beginning, close to the spark that ignited it all. Hence close to the creator, or the Big Bang, I would say. But the further and further we have become distanced through time, through desire or lack of interest, that bond which may have become tenuous at times, starts to stretch like a piece of elastic and if you're not careful, suddenly it breaks. The further away you go, the vibrations, the thunder of excitement when time began, are no longer felt at all. We must allow our spirit to soar backwards to the initiation of time, and thus to the inner core of our being.

Just as a Nomad wanders through his timeless landscape, your mind and your entire being will wander through the exciting canyons, valleys, peaks, and river beds of your inner self; exploring, rediscovering the excitement of your birth and yourself. In finding the centre of creativity within yourself, the desert will appeal, and appear to be a place no longer ugly, deserted or a negative environment as you once thought, but a very warm, inviting place.

Like the diversity of desert sands, we are all individuals, although we may appear similar in appearance and our actions. Now think of wandering through desert sands which undulate in ever receding ridges into the far horizons. When you first glance at the dunes, they all appear to be the same: just like those around us, appear to be. The softly shifting sand ridges are sublime creations carved with sensuous flowing curves and as the sun sets behind them, they change like a chameleon into dusky reds and oranges. When the winds blow gently over them like a flautist breathing life into his instrument, you can hear the atoms of the sand vibrating and singing and dancing and changing shape. Just like the ever-changing shape of the desert, so you too will be in eternal evolution: but the essence of you will always remain in your inner core.

So we will be like that evolutionary desert, as we change gradually, subtly, or in some cases dramatically. Although we will look the same in some ways, there will be changes; dramatic changes. As the winds of change blow through us, the sand dunes that were maybe stagnant within us for so long will start to undulate into a new incarnation, until we will experience an epiphany of brightness and excitement. We have transformed our deserts into desserts, by adding the S for serenity. Soon those around us will notice this transformation. In order to be a true nomadic spirit we need to explore deep within ourselves. We need to retreat within, and conversely as we are retreating, we are also advancing into the core of our being, into our waiting spirit. "Welcome home Stranger."

Years ago, Jules Verne wrote the book "Voyage to the Centre of the Earth" in which a party of adventurers were in fact venturing to the centre of the earth through a labyrinth of caverns and canyons to find the throbbing magma mass that is at its core; that is what we are doing as we recede into the core of our being.

But in undertaking our tentative voyage within, take some advice from the cave explorers, or spelunkers as they are named. When they decide to explore the deepest, darkest recesses of the world, they go prepared. They go with illumination and a sense of safety. Safety in their equipment and supplies; so when they go into the darkest recesses, they are not wandering blindly. They advance with safeguards in place, and that is what we need. Our safeguards are simply commitment; trust in ourselves, honesty, and the illuminating glow of optimism.

However, if we try to explore the centre of the earth, or the core of our being, laden with five hundred tons of supplies, we're not going to get too far. Some of these subterranean tunnels are so narrow, that people literally have to squeeze their heads through fissures. They have to deflate their chests to get through, to sneak through these narrow areas. In other words, we have to maintain our courage, for after all, look where we are heading.

No-one said it was going to be easy in our self-exploration, because, think of it, we are venturing to the raw core of our being; the raw core of creation and creativity. We may think: "it's going to be similar going to a dentist when he accidentally hits a nerve." It's painful, and it takes us by surprise because it's unexpected. So, when we start our exploration we need to be in a state of relaxation; we require enough for survival by taking the basics which are synthesized and distilled.

Alcoholic spirits are made through the process of distillation. And what does it do to us? It inebriates us through intoxication. When people are happy and euphoric, they may say they're intoxicated with happiness. When we distill what is really needed in our minds, hearts, souls, spirits and our entire being, we are going to be intoxicated. That intoxication – not inebriation – that feeling of euphoria, will light the way through the caverns and canyons to the centre of our being, and that is our ultimate goal.

Now, at times, during our exploration, we may need "time out;" time to relax. Retreat like the nomad to the desert, and in the "dessert" of our imagination which is a vibrant, visceral, vibrating, raw place we will find a canyon. It can be built of red sandstone that literally gleams and glimmers in the sunlight. We will feel the warmth of the sun, and if it's too hot we can simply slip into the shadows. In a niche in the rocks we will find a pool of cool water surrounded by palm trees. Rustling rushes filled with choirs of birds will serenade us in this oasis until we are ready for our voyage once again. All the basics of life are there in this cool, tranquil environment where the only voice is the silence of nothingness. There will be no necessity to speak because the desert will be speaking to us: meanings of ultimate understanding. Then we will experience a sense of overwhelming peace.

Physically and figuratively, when we are wandering through the recesses of our soul in this exquisite desert, filled with the elemental excitement of being so close to our core of creation, we will discover that the flab of our existence is dropping away. We have become a lean focused nomad in that ever-changing desert which has become a "dessert."

Just imagine spending our lives in a sedentary job; sitting in front of a television; eating an unhealthy diet. Our bodies are going to deteriorate and atrophy. Our vitality is going to be drained; boredom is going to set in; physically, deterioration will set in. And what about our brains? What about our being and our souls? The same thing is going to happen.

If we never question, never explore what's inside, never dream. If we never drift like a nomad through exciting vistas, exploring, taking hidden pathways, trying to enjoy and understand why these things exist, our being is going to become a mass of flab. Our being is going to deteriorate through disuse – hence the cliché "you're losing it." Our being must be explored and exercised so that it can feel and emote. If we spend a lifetime being inscrutable, and showing nothing, accepting nothing, people won't know who we are or what we are, and I'm sure you won't know either. We will not have explored and opened up ourselves to that Stranger Within.

There is a kernel inside us, a spark, vitality and we are the shell. Think upon the kernel as a flame. Now, when we light a fire and remain too close to it, it's going to be uncomfortable just like being too close to a nerve. We are not used to it, it's too visceral and we are too close to the core. But, when we stand back a little way until we find our comfort zone, which is the perfect place to appreciate the warmth of the fire, we can start to understand the life-giving warmth which is not burning us up. We are still intoxicated, because we have never been this close before to who we are: and as we quickly discover: this is where we always want to be.

We have travelled like a nomad: a spiritual nomad. We have ventured to the core of our being stripped of extraneous belongings. We have honed ourselves to the core; we have distilled ourselves into pure Essence, as we journey forward; and that's what the nomads do. They wander, following the horizons through an exciting cycle. They're not sedentary; there is no flab about their existence. They're travellers and they're perpetually on a journey to a dream, to a destination; just like us: to that place deep inside that is the essential me– and we alone can do it

Let us talk for a moment about the timing of our momentous exploration. We may be connoisseurs of procrastination. We may be like St. Augustus, who said: "God make me a Saint but not right now." He wasn't quite ready, he was enjoying himself immensely in the present: his transformation lay in the future, but, not right now. He was having too much fun!

In terms of timing, think back to an age before clocks had been invented; when time was a cycle; sunrise, and the slow play of the day until sunset. The nomads knew exactly what time of day it was by looking at the sky; by where the sun was; how high, or how low it was. They knew instinctively about time. They were living day to day, as we are living, and as I write these words in this present moment, soon they will be in the past, and presently I will be reading them in the future. I find that a fascinating concept. In other words, now is always a perfect time.

As I stared mesmerized at my grandfather's fob watch, the seconds, minutes and the hours ticked away, and I seemed to be witnessing time always advancing. But every day the clockwork routine was the same; the same numbers, the same times. Yesterday, today and tomorrow play the same game: over and over, so the reality is, is that there's no right or wrong time. If you say "I'll do it tomorrow," this actually is tomorrow. If you say "gee, I wish I had changed myself yesterday." Well, this really is yesterday because yesterday is the father of today, and today is the father of tomorrow. So this is the right time!

Years ago I visited a small pioneer gold rush ghost town called Barkerville in British Columbia. It was the dead of winter with drifts of snow towering over me wherever I looked. The entire town had a surreal appearance painted over it, with its boarded-up buildings and sense of lonesome melancholy, and I remember thinking that I wished I had lived here in this frontier town back in those raw pioneer day. If I said that now however it would be for a different reason, but back then when I was a lot younger my statement was based on the rumbustious excitement of that age. The hustle and bustle; the vibrancy of the brawling, sprawling gold rush towns!

When I think back now to that scene, the reality is, I was the only person there. I was surrounded by a scene of total, sublime stillness. Everything was stripped to the core; the houses were basic log dwellings locked in the embrace of winter, with their simplicity of design transformed by the subtlety of snow-drifts. There was no movement; just utter tranquillity. Life at that moment, I think, had distilled to an essence. There were no extraneous distractions, so in reality I was actually living in the past, which, in essence, was the present and the future. Our transformation is our time machine, with no beginning and no end.

We are continually being influenced as we explore our nomadic spirit and we may hear ourselves say; "if I lived in the past or the future, I surely would be a different person. Some people say that the core of your being has always been like that; you won't change who you are, or what you are. Change is impossible! "Or live with what you have been given!"

Yes, we're born with that little definitive kernel that makes us unique; the flame inside sparking with that glow of identity that often times we ignore. "I am an individual," we want to shout, but through time we are affected by the influence of others; by circumstances that surround us, and whether we like it or not, we start to change, often despite our best wishes, and sometimes these changes take us in directions which we don't like.

When we feel overwhelmed by unwanted changes, such as weight gains or overpowering feelings of inadequacy, our self-esteem plummets. If we engage in some activity that we don't really wish to indulge in, but are pressured to do, we suffer. If we are forced to take an occupation which is not a true fit for us, we feel guilty, we feel demeaned. We know we are living a lie. We are no longer the free nomadic spirit following the horizons of our choice. We are no longer fostering the true essential nomadic spirit; the nomadic soul. We have sold, and short-changed ourselves. We are now drenched in that horrendous cumbersome suite of debilitating armour we spoke about.

Can you visualize an Aboriginal in the Australian Outback wandering along drenched in armour; hauling along mountains of supplies, mountains of extraneous so-called necessities? He would not be able to move, he'd be immobilized, and in the heart of the desert which he loves, he would die! But if he throws off the armour, he can travel hundreds of miles without missing a heartbeat. So, fine-tuning is the key. We have to throw away the armour cloaked in outside unwanted circumstances which are trying to change us. If we are permeable, we'll absorb those influences, and in the metamorphosis we will become someone we don't really like.

That is a horrendous thing to say, isn't it? "I don't like myself." If you don't like yourself no-one else is going to like you. It's like the old cliché, "I can see right through that person." That really means they can see right through into the core, and what they see is a fire that's been squelched. They don't see a free, wandering nomadic spirit. They see a dull, sedentary, sad person who is living a lie. A person who has nothing to contribute, who needs lots of nourishing - someone who gives nothing back. Someone who has withered in the desert; they fail to feel the flame of self-sustaining nourishment. They see a spirit like a wild bird that has been caged; a songbird with no melodies, because it's spirit has flown away and atrophied in its imposed cage.

The same can be said of nomads. Take a true nomad and throw him in jail, and he will wither like that songbird and die. Or if you place him in a cage of societal restrictions and subject him to, and open him up to, various forms of abuse called "change of lifestyle;" in this cage without bars, he will also atrophy. He will dry up like the desert sands and wither.

Our spirit is like that; we have to keep vital; we have to let it go walkabout, travel and wander in deserts and plains, in mountains and peaks. We have to explore inside those illuminating caverns, canyons and tunnels that we are wandering through. We have to be prepared for times when we are scared as we squeeze through an area; and we wonder. "Will I get through and will it be safe on the other side?" We must develop trust and optimism. We must be continually fanning the flame that is us.

Now, we don't want to emulate a moth that flies around a candle, and getting too close to the flame, burns up and dies. We may initially singe our fingers when we are experimenting with our comfort zone, but when it is discovered, it will reveal itself to be a safe, secure place accessed only by us. We can travel there any time; we have found our haven, and in our haven, we have found ourselves. We have journeyed and reached a destination, however, just like nomads, once they have reached a destination, they move on again; always following the horizon, and we will do the same. Evolution is never static, so do not become complacent. Follow the horizons of opportunity.

Nomadic change is about accepting incremental destinations, with the realization that the more we explore, and the more horizons we reach and leave behind, the more we will want to leave and travel again. Continual movement, like the ocean waves we will become, like grains of sand in the desert; continually changing. Like the sand which settles in one spot, forming a perfect dune, until a gentle breeze stirs things up. The breeze teases the sand particles until the atoms in the sand start to vibrate in a ballet of dramatic change. They start to journey until they form a new sand dune. So think of our inner selves like that. All these influences are changing us, as we are slowly being transformed.

To retain this fleet-footed nomadic spirit, always remember to prune away extraneous, negative influences, otherwise as we have discovered, what starts as buds become trees. We spoke previously of topping a tree before the topmost branches become the tree in their eternal struggle towards the sun, as they thicken and became entrenched. In each branch there are other little branches trying to reach for the sky and if you ignore those they will also become so strong, they will also require drastic pruning. Just like negativity around us which creates such a thick forest in our souls that it will be impossible to progress through.

## *twenty three*

## On Your Mark. Get Set. Go.

**There is more than one way to run the race of life.**

We must run our marathon through life across oceans, over uncharted lands, and realms we have never before dreamed of. In this book we have spoken in terms of journeying, travelling to ever-receding horizons; arriving and heading towards the next exhilarating destination. In our minds, hearts and souls we are the marathon runners.

Years ago I read a book titled "Flannigan's Run," the theme of which centred around a 1920's foot race from Los Angeles on the west coast of the United States, to New York, 3000 miles away on the east coast. The first runner to reach New York won a prodigious sum of money, and the race rules stipulated that each contestant had to run a verifiable amount of miles per day. This is similar to setting milestone objectives for ourselves; little incremental destinations ultimately leading to the final goal.

They were on a journey; they had a destination, and for me, the pivotal fact was that every single racer ran the race according to their own principles; according to their own desires and their own feelings. This is similar to us and our journey through life as we head to our ultimate destination. There is no right or wrong way for us to achieve that! In Flannigan's Run, for example, some of the people ran independently paying no attention to anyone else. They were totally focused on their destination, so they ran alone; neither relying on, nor assisting fellow contestants, completely self-sufficient.

Others were more gregarious and travelled in groups where they fostered friendship, motivating and encouraging each other on the epic journey. They physically and mentally provided sustenance to each other. They ran collectively as a group. Other people ran in combinations of both; some days they ran independently and other days they ran collectively; whatever worked for those people who were focused on getting to their destination.

Now, the motivation was different for everyone. Some, purely and simply were driven by greed for the pot of gold at the end of the run. Others were seduced by the adventure of travelling the country on foot. Some ran for the sheer physical enjoyment; other people ran because this was a one-off event probably never to occur again in their lifetime. So they ran for different reasons; they had different motivations for entering the race, and correspondingly, the style of their running was uniquely different.

When we are journeying in our nomadic spirit into our being, there are different ways of getting to the final destination. Some of us may do it independently by focusing single mindedly on getting to the core of our being by paying no attention to anyone. Other people will need a lot of sustenance and nurturing. They will need collaboration and encouragement before they reach their destination. The reality is we will all get there ultimately. Some may say, "Hey, this trip to the core of my being is too much to undertake; I can't do it." Think again!

Remember previously we spoke in terms of being incrementalists by solving problems a little bit at a time by breaking the task into bite-sized pieces. It will be the same with the journey – a little bit at a time. Think upon it as travelling into a canal where there are a series of locks like the Panama Canal. The principle is to incrementally lift the boat from one elevation to another through a series of slightly higher locks or pools.

Through this process, the ship enters the lock when the gate opens; the ship waits while water enters, until the level reaches a certain point, at which point the craft sails into the next lock, and so on until ultimately it slides effortlessly into the final lock. In essence the ship has used stepping stones, or stairs to reach its destination - incremental action at work.

Think about problems like that, and say, "Yes I can do it." So imagine sailing into the first lock; this is the first step, the first stage in reaching our destination, waiting in the core of our being. Close the gate and slowly visualize rising to the next level. Now we have total control over how quickly the water level rises.

Some of the stages may take longer than others, but that's fine because we are in control. The most important thing is we have entered the steps; the watery steps, to the final destination of finding out who we are; how we work; the motivation for ourselves, and our total happiness. When we are in those incremental locks as they gradually fill with water, we will feel a sense of euphoria because we are in control of our destiny as we rise to the next level of consciousness.

Again, we can stay as long as we want on each level because we have ultimate control. We are the only ones who can open the lock gate. No-one else can interfere. However, even when we feel that we have reached a smooth flowing river of ease and relative tranquillity, we may encounter rapids or stagnant areas; stagnant times of self-doubt which lead to feelings of discouragement. Just when we thought we had made it to our destination, we may find ourselves stuck in backwaters. Have we lost concentration and are ready to give up and revert to our old selves? The answer must always be no!

Think back to the classic movie of the 1950s, the award-winning "The African Queen", and learn another lesson. Humphrey Bogart and Katharine Hepburn were attempting to take a little steam driven boat down a wild African river to get to Lake Victoria; to their final destination where they hoped to encounter a German warship which they would subsequently sink.

They encountered all sorts of problems including daunting rapids, until eventually they were lost in a swampy marsh. This swamp was a maze of waterways which effectively blocked them from their destination; they felt that they'd wander endlessly in this wasteland. Now, this would have been an appropriate time to feel discouraged; a time to say "okay, look we've given it a good try but we're not going to reach our destination." A time to surrender that nomadic, fine honed, fine-tuned desire and gravitate back to the old flabby us.

In the movie, the camera soared high above the trapped boat and showed the viewers how close The African Queen was to the open waters of the lake. We must also rise above the entrapping issues and look down on the problem from above.

As Humphrey Bogart tried valiantly to pull his boat through this swamp-land maze, he found himself covered by leeches which had to be removed before he could continue his struggles. Sometimes our journey can seem like that. Think about it; we are heading to a destination and suddenly we realize that things are getting sluggish. We also have leeches on us; people who will prey upon us. I'm not talking in terms of dependants, our family who rely upon us; I'm talking in terms of people who basically feed off us because that's what a leech does. A leech sucks the life- giving blood from its host.

Like a mythical Dracula sucking our blood, these human leeches will drain us through negativity, through back biting and gossip, through demeaning behaviour or jealousy; from total negativity. We have all met these types of people who relish the darker oppressive side of life where gossip and negativity is their god, and they perpetually endeavour to make us the same.

These are the leeches that we all encounter at some time in our life's odyssey. Discard them immediately; pull them off whenever they introduce negative thoughts. The best solution is to disengage ourselves socially and every other way from them. The may be co-workers with whom we have to co-exist, or a next door neighbour; or someone we meet by happen stance. Whenever they project a negative thought, we project a positive thought. If they say black, we think white. Discard negativity on this journey, and it is a tough journey, but we are committed. We are doing it. Get rid of the leeches! If Humphrey Bogart and Katherine Hepburn could conquer the dreaded leeches on their journey of make-believe, we can surely do the same, in the most important journey of our lives.

As I have described previously, our home looks out over the waters of Howe Sound. This fjord has a small port at the end of the sound which is the destination for intrepid tugboats pulling their heavily laden barges. I watch these tugboats which are all muscle and brawn, struggling with their heads down as they heave themselves through the surging waves with their tag-along barges. Their job in life is to pull these barges to their final destination; that's what they are built for, that's their job!

Unfortunately, on our journey through life we will encounter people who will throw their baggage at, and on us, and if we are accepting of that, we will end up as a tug, pulling these heavily laden barges filled with others' garbage; which will inevitably slow us down. They will drain our energy, which in turn will sap our total vitality. Just think about it. We are trying to walk along a road pulling behind us an empty cart. At the beginning we can move effortlessly, but as insidious lovers of negativity start to throw their garbage, their personal burdens into our little cart, we will eventually realize that we can barely move. We have become immobilized; we have this horrendous over-flowing burden behind us; this barge with the detritus, trash, from other people. Some of that trash is admittedly ours. But remember our concept of pruning extraneous burdens until we become fine- tuned nomadic warriors moving into the core of our being. The lighter the load, the faster the pace.

There are several ways to get rid of that baggage. One of them is to shout, "Please stop doing that," but selfish people will always try to find a way to burden others. Another way is to go to a quiet area and slowly and systematically empty the baggage a little bit at a time, and keep emptying away until there's nothing left.

Now, that sounds fine until we start to journey once again. If we have simply emptied the accumulated garbage but still possess that aura of vulnerability, people are still going to throw in their problems until once more we can scarcely move. The third and only true way to do it is to uncouple that unwanted cart. Cut the line from those barges and let them drift. Let them become shipwrecked on some rocky, remote island never to be seen again. That is what we must do. We must uncouple the vulnerable barge that we are towing behind and let it drift away.

We have assumed an identity; a persona that says. "You can't dump your garbage on me anymore; I am self-sufficient. I'm on a journey and I don't need your garbage. I don't want leeches on my trip; I don't want to tow these barges behind me. I want to be fleet of foot; I'm on a marathon; I'm running across this life of mine, and all I need is my nomadic heart; all I need are my two legs, my mind, my body, my spirit and I'll get there. I'll achieve it." Believing is achieving. Tangible thoughts lead to tangible results. Remember our visualization exercises.

# twenty four

## Erasable Pencil Or Indelible Ink?

**The art of subtle communication: slippers or steel-toed boots?**

Just imagine that before we had to speak or write anything, we had to first manufacture the paper and the pen. Now, I attended a paper making course some years ago and found it to be a fascinating, but extremely onerous process. The technique entailed using discarded scraps of paper, fragments of leaves, a smidgen of bark, lots of creativity and ingenuity; and after a thin skin of paste had been spread on a screen and dried; you had paper.

Now just think; if every time we had to write something down or speak, we had to make the paper and pencil, I think we would learn rather quickly to synthesize what we were going to say, and what we were going to write, because of the time-consuming effort of physically having to manufacture the tools required.

We are going to become extremely selective in our communications. Irrelevance will be thrown out the window. There will be a newborn relevance and purpose in what we say and do. Our thinking will become fine-tuned, as will our vocabulary. We will have pared down how we relate to the world around us as; just as a nomadic warrior, a nomadic spirit, a nomadic traveller, has no time for waste, or extraneous materials.

So, prior to opening our mouths, we should pretend that we have to manufacture the paper and pencil or pen in which to communicate; and that will certainly slow down the process of thoughtless and aimless passing on of our ideas and thoughts. It's going to be similar to entering a lock in our little boat, and waiting until the water rises to take us to the next level of our journey. The lesson learned is patience; which leads to a more reflective response to life's issues.

Now, the same principle applies to a writing utensil. Are we going to make a pen or a pencil? Or what about a brush? The interesting thing about this is, if we think in terms of ourselves as a pencil, or a pen, or a brush, we are going to react differently. It is going to be similar to the race across America in Flannigan's Run: different techniques and philosophies leading to the same end. By using diverse implements we will start to think differently.

For example; think about an Oriental paintbrush. The brush is dipped into ink allowing the artist to create flowing, sensuous characters on the paper. There is no scratching aggressiveness, no abrasiveness; it is a very gentle, fluid process. If we think of ourselves in these gently flowing non-abrasive terms, our thoughts, speech, heart and soul will become like a fine, soft, subtle Chinese paintbrush. Our life- flow will be smoother.

If we make ourselves into a pen, we will certainly communicate, but in a scratchy, crotchety, aggressive, abrasive sort of way. Yes, there will be permanency in the written word, however the same point can be made with more finesse, and achieve the same end, with the subtlety of the Chinese paintbrush. Subtlety over aggression.

I guess there are other ways to impart life's messages – a pencil for example. A pencil is soft, but however wears down rapidly and requires constant sharpening. It is also impermanent, easily erased, and has a temporary nature. Resolutions written in pencil will fade. Another communication implement is a charcoal pencil. Again there is a decided need for patience here, as we engage in the ritualistic process of making fire, making charcoal and then taking that charcoal twig and using it.

So, there are obviously a myriad of ways to perceive ourselves, and to communicate just who we are. My path has always been the softest, gentlest way; as a Chinese paintbrush, painting delicately, gently and smoothly. In essence; by thinking in these creative ways we help to develop personal rituals which define us. When we are sitting quietly evolving our inner cores; when we are on that internal journey; wandering through the deserts of our souls, there should be a ritual attached to that – but a gentle ritual.

# *twenty five*

# Different Heights: Different Perspectives

**Change your vantage point when resolving issues.**

In the process of changing the way we view life, and ultimately reshaping how we perceive issues, we are basically transforming our responsibility towards ourselves and ultimately towards others. To assist us, why don't we reach deep inside and seek our personal totem. The very act of this internal exploration will inevitably conjure up an image, which will become a totem illuminating our nomadic spirits. The following example illustrates how our totem will teach us valuable lessons.

All too often we view life and its host of issues in the same predictable way. An example of how we can change this viewpoint is when we sit on a beach gazing over an expanse of rippling water at the nebulous line of the horizon. We are seeing it at eye level, just as we often stare head-on at our issues. However think about changing that viewpoint incrementally.

Simply by standing on a convenient rock on the beach, we can easily transform the horizon by extending its distance from us; and allowing more of the world to be seen. We are really witnessing a different horizon; or more simply, a new horizon, or perspective. By climbing an even higher rock we will again have changed the horizon. Ultimately, if we climb the highest mountain and "look," we are no longer gazing across at the horizon, we are looking down on top of it; we are seeing islands beyond the horizon that we would never see looking from sea level. By raising ourselves above issues, we will see the larger picture, and new techniques to resolve roadblocks will present themselves.

So often times when we're trying to resolve issues, define respon-sibilities and relationships or problem-solve, we look at them from the same basic level. Now, by looking at them from a different elevation, new paths will open in our minds. Let's say for example, I choose as a totem a majestic eagle, or a condor, or an albatross, and by visualizing the world from their vantage points what would I see? They survey a wide expanse that we can never see from ground level. Certainly, when they land they can see the same things that we see, but they can put a different perspective upon life because they also have the ability to rise above the line of limited vision that we have and look down with an "eagle eye."

It's almost like distancing yourself from an issue in order to resolve it. So we should pick a totem that means something to us; or better still allow the totem to choose you. I choose an eagle because I can soar high above the world; high above issues and look down almost impartially and see them playing out before my eyes. You may choose to pick a totem of a bear for strength or an antelope for speed. The choice is yours; you choose.

When we try to resolve issues and relationships in our search for self-change, all too often like the instantaneous flame of self-gratifi-cation and immediate satisfaction, we make a big splash. But once the ripples settle what then? What's left? Nothing! We have used the pencil approach to the problem; scribbled the solution, and found that very quickly it is easily erased. To give you an example; we go to the beach with the water rippling in front of us, pick up a huge rock and throw it into the ocean. The rock enters the water with a splash-ing crescendo of sound. Ripples nibble and lap at our feet, but very quickly die away.

Now, all too often and in many ways, we try to resolve an issue without tenacity of spirit, true desire, persistence or perseverance. We tackle it head on, head down, like a musk oxen and hammer at it. We attack it face on by selecting the largest rock around, which we hurl into the ocean with a gratifying splash. There's a momentary sense of satisfaction which quickly fades.

Another way of resolving issues is by using an oblique technique. To achieve that, visualize again standing on the beach, and rather than taking the largest rock to solve an issue, selecting a small, slender sliver of a rock. This time, instead of smashing it headlong down into the water and making a resounding quickly-fading splash, we tackle the problem obliquely as the slender stone is skimmed along the surface; and watch what happens. The wafer of stone bounces along the surface of the water, time and time again. No loud splash, but a series of mini-attacks. Ultimately, when we become proficient we can make that rock travel quite a distance by hitting the problem many times in different places. Nibbling it to final resolution is the aim here.

We are not just smashing a huge rock mindlessly into the problem like we did in the beginning; we are allowing the gentler approach to attack it obliquely. This oblique approach allows the same problem to be tackled many times with the lightest of touch. Just as the slim sliver of rock bounces off the water many times with minimal effort, so we can tackle problems with finesse and not with the proverbial sledge hammer. We are tackling our problems incrementally. The oblique strategy achieves a greater result. There is no "big splash" gratification, but at the same time we reap the reward of achieving success with less effort, but more effect.

Another example centres around an incident which I witnessed on the Spanish island of Ibiza. Of course, being in Spain, ubiquitous bullfights were added to our agenda of touristy things to do, and one sweltering day we attended the local extravaganza. The pageantry although extremely bloody, was impressive in a visceral sort of way, but the thing that sticks out in my mind was the blend of bravery and stupidity on the part of the bull.

In front of this muscular animal stood a slender man taunting the bull by waving a red cape. All the bull had to do was walk up slowly to that man, fix its eyes on him and gore him to death – it would have been easily done! The bull weighed a ton, the man weighed about 130 pounds dripping wet. But what did the bull do?, Similar to throwing a rock headlong into the water, or a musk-ox battering its head straight into another musk-ox, the bull charged headlong at the annoying cape the matador was holding. All the massive beast really had to do was feint, by attacking obliquely to the right or left and impaling the matador on its horns.

This oblique manoeuvre is usually achieved purely by accident, and is inevitably successful. As the enraged bull reaches the cape, instead of impaling the source of its anger, it swings his head to the side and "boom," one of the horns impales the matador. But 99.99 per cent of the time he blindly charges head on at the cape which is not really his adversary, and rarely makes a dent in that issue; rarely solves the problem of that red flag. The only time he resolves the true problem which is the matador, is by attacking obliquely.

This is similar to peripheral vision. We look at something like a problem, face on long and hard, but somehow there is no real connection between our minds and the ultimate resolution; but just by taking our eyes off the issue and glancing to the side, out of the peripheral side of our eyes we experience a different perspective.

So, when we are trying to problem-solve; when we are trying to reach into our hearts to become the best nomadic spirit we possibly can, don't always look at issues at ground level or head-on. Pick a totem to help us; fly above it and look down. Secondly, look obliquely, not straight on, but from the side. Like skimming a stone, an instantaneous splash will not be made, but we will resolve the issue by hitting it in many different places, or attacking it obliquely, and ultimately achieving a more positive result.

The bullfight scenario brings to mind another lesson to be learned. When we are trying to problem-solve and are getting nowhere; could it be that the so-called problem we are attacking is not the real issue at hand? Like the red flag is not the bull's true problem: the matador is the real threat to be tackled. So before we become entrenched in intractable cul-de-sacs of frustration, sit back and reflect, and we will often find that the actual obstacle will present itself.

All too often when we talk in terms of problem solving, rediscovering who we are, patching up relationships, making the best soup we possibly can, we make the same mistake over and over again. We extricate from our bag of tricks the same resolutions and problem solving techniques that have become like boomerangs. We throw them really hard at the problem in an attempt to solve it, and yes, for a limited period of time, that particular problem appears to vanish. However, ultimately the boomerang resolution reaches a point where it starts to revolve and head back towards us.

Before we know it, the problem lands back at our feet – that boomerang problem has returned. So what do we do the next time that problem occurs? We invariably pick up that boomerang solution and throw it into the stratosphere, thinking again that we have resolved the problem; until it's back!

Think about the number of times a recurring problem has crept back into our lives. Despite our best intentions we end up saying the same things, in the same way, and reaching the same impasse. We have thrown out another boomerang solution which has returned to haunt us. The solution seems really simple: change the technique. Forget the boomerang solutions. Make a strong commitment to resolve that impasse in a different way. Teach yourself new techniques using the oblique approach, the skipping stone approach, flying above it; or what your totem offers.

In our society we talk in terms of meeting a problem head on, face-to-face, toe-to-toe; like the Charge of the Light Brigade in the Crimean War. Although this military action was heroic, unfortunately it was total stupidity. Picture a narrow valley with entrenched artillery guns pointing straight down towards you, with a charging group of young, valorous men charging straight into the guns of hell. "Cannon to the right of them, Cannon to the left of them, Cannon in front of them, Volleyed and Thundered".

The doomed cavalrymen certainly made an impact, historians remember the Charge of the Light Brigade to this day. Now the event achieved immortality that particular day, however no-one remembers the soldiers' names. They just recollect the bravery of those men charging into the guns. But if those soldiers had gone at the problem by attacking obliquely, by using a different strategy, they would have been successful. They would have resolved that particular issue and defeated the enemy. So, we must remember to tackle problems obliquely.

# twenty six

## Slow, Slow, Quick, Quick, Fast

**To go from A to Z use all the resources at your command.**

In our great desire to renovate our inner being, we often learn what
we consider the one tried and true strategy. We learn one thing, one
way to change ourselves, so we say "in order to journey to the heart of
my soul, to the heart of my nomadic spirit, I will do it this way." But the
reality is that in any journey there are many different components and
strategies to consider. Again, there are incremental stages towards a
final result.

An example of this occurred years ago when I was working on a
Highland estate in Scotland during the August grouse hunting season.
The nobility hired boys such as me to work as "beaters." We stayed
in the castle sleeping in dormitories, and each morning we would be
taken to the area where the hunt was being conducted. We would
form a semi-circle on the hill-side and tramp through the heather-cov-
ered hillside towards the "guns"; shooters who were sitting in trenches
at the bottom of the hill. The process was simple: the beaters thrashed
the gorse, the heather and the bushes, scaring the grouse into the air
where they were shot by the hunters.

The lesson about incremental steps or diverse stages leading
toward a final solution is as follows. The journey from the castle to the
hillside involved various stages and modes of transportation. Initially
we would be picked up by trucks which would take us to a drop-off
spot where we were then transferred to four-wheel-drive vehicles as the
terrain became rougher. The next stage involved rowing over a loch

to the side where the hunters waited, and finally we had to hike to the top of the hill to start the hunt.

So, when we left the castle, we knew that the ultimate destination was the mountain where the hunters waited. And that there were different, modes of transportation required getting us there. Think of this analogy in your problem solving. If we had relied solely on the truck to get us to the mountain, we would have ended up short of our final destination, as the truck could not traverse the rugged hillside or the waters of the loch.

Now think of some relationship problems which you have unsuccessfully tried to resolve. You have used the boomerang approach, and probably relied on one level of problem solving, instead of implementing several approaches, like our various modes of transportation to the grouse hunting grounds

As you journey towards a final resolution and a new and improved you, think of the different ways of achieving that. As in my trip, we started off at the macro level in a huge truck and then a smaller vehicle, a small boat, then the last part, the micro level, walking on our own two legs. I think often times we forget to do that; we rely on other people to resolve issues for us, to resolve problems for us, that we forget to walk on our own two legs. Ultimately, on my Scottish odyssey, we had to rely on our own two legs, our own stamina and our own determination to climb to the top of that mountain.

Frequently when we're trying to resolve something, we start off with great intentions which often deteriorate into procrastination as obstacles present themselves: and all too often we look around for someone to come along and resolve the problem for us. But all we have to do is stand up, get the kinks out of our legs and start walking towards the goal in front of us. By advancing at different speeds and using different strategies, we will get there faster, than beating ourselves over the head with the old tried and true methods of the past, which we have found are not so tried and true.

For example, in my trip you could sit back in the truck and relax. In the four-wheel-drive which was extremely bumpy, you had to brace yourself, and in the row-boat you experienced the tranquillity of gliding through the water. The actual effort of hiking up the hill on your own two legs required stamina. Each stage evolved at its own pre-determined pace.

The vehicles got us to a certain point very quickly, the row-boat was very slow, and hiking up the mountain was even slower. However, if we had been dropped off at the lakeside and just sat there, we would have fallen short of the ultimate destination while the hunters waited on the other side. If we'd crossed on the boat and sat down, again we'd have ended the journey short of the final destination. The journey was paced, and in our life's journey we must pace ourselves. Sometimes we can glide, but sometimes we must beat our wings frantically.

Recently I was sitting on my deck at my home in a very poetic mood and looking out over the ocean I saw an elegant, seemingly effortless eagle soaring across the islands toward the horizon. I watched this eagle on his epic journey. In my mind I saw my totem flying above the issues of the world below. He would glide for a long time and then frantically beat his wings – at least it seemed so to me – then he would glide again, but always getting further and further away. He was going toward his final destination by using different strategies.

When the eagle was gliding he was relaxing. For me that would be a time for contemplation; a time for looking around – developing strategies! The next stage would be to beat my wings frantically. That would be really working hard on the strategy that I had composed while I was gliding; while I was coasting. But often times we don't do that. Instead, we get on our old roller-coaster going at a hundred miles an hour and don't slow down because our momentum appears unstoppable.

What happens if we are on a train heading toward a small village; hurtling along the track at a hundred miles an hour? If the train maintains the same speed as it approaches the village we will rush through without stopping; yet that village which is quickly receding in the distance was where we wanted to get out: that was the ultimate destination.

As we get closer to our destination, we will feel a sense of subtly developing relaxation. There will be a feeling that we're getting close to something, and instinctively we will want to say pull the reins back a little bit and slow down, because if we do that, we will glide into the station, just as we will arrive at the core of our being. We won't over-shoot it and have to rework the activity to get back to the station. We won't have to go into reverse; we'll be expending just enough energy to get there. When we do get there, we won't be out of breath; we'll still have lots of energy left to tackle the next stage to the alluring horizon.

# *twenty seven*

## Planting Seeds: Harvesting Surprises

**Build a strong foundation with lots of visualization thrown in.**

Do not eat the last seed! What does that mean? It means that we should always leave something in reserve: keep some energy for future projects. Just picture that we are starving, and temptingly lying in front of us is a pile of seeds. In desperation we find an old pot, and throwing the seeds into it we bake them, or crush them into flour and make bread, or possibly we make soup with them. But we eat them all, and sitting back we don't feel hungry any more. But what's going to happen when the pangs of hunger return? What will we do when we reach for the seeds and realize that there's nothing left'.

The lesson is always leaving some seeds to plant; don't eat them all. Always leave a little bit in reserve. We must always leave inner reserves to rekindle the fire for the future. A little leads to more. Leave a little seed. Plant seeds for the future and reap the ultimate harvest.

Think how often we sit in a contemplative mood quietly reminiscing; quietly dredging up good memories of the past, which in essence are really a reincarnation of times gone by. When we close our eyes, we can pick at the net of time, clip that little snapshot of the precise moment we want to rekindle, and bring it back into our minds, our hearts and souls and re-live it. We can smell the wood-smoke from that long distant camp-fire when we were sitting beside the ocean. We can savour that special bottle of cold beer that we had put in the stream beside us to keep cold. We can smell the steak slowly barbecuing; sizzling over the fire; the warmth of the sun; the gentle breeze in our face. A cozy tent just waiting for us to curl up in and the anticipation of sleeping like a log. This is a specific memory that's so evocative we can smell it, we can feel it, and we can actually taste it! It's a blissful moment which causes a resurgence of our spirits when we think about it. We have been recharged. The memory is a seed from time's past, and the harvest is a bountiful rebuilding and renovation of our souls.

Conversely, when dredging up negative memories the opposite happens; we sense sadness, depression, negativity, and bleakness. We experience again those horrendous moments of debilitating loss. Instead of rebuilding or renovating, we're ripping down; demolishing. So for every incremental reincarnation of a positive memory, if we also rehash the negative memories, we will cancel out the positive impact on our lives. We will be taking one step back on our journey.

Do not dwell on the cancers of things best forgotten, but don't wrap them inside a boomerang, otherwise they are going to come back to haunt and hurt us. Instead, we should attach them to the biggest rock we can find and hurtle it into the deepest ocean, never to be found again.

By conjuring up our totem, which is like a guardian angel, we are enabled to view unique memories from a different level; a different elevation. As we have discovered, if we look at them obliquely from the periphery, and visualize the events in a different way, we will gain access into those events which have helped to mould us. Every event is the culmination of many "micro-moments." Even if the total memory has some torn moments of pathos woven into it, in the sifting, the positive segments from the overall memory will overpower the fragments of negativity.

We can also manufacture special memories to assist us in dealing with everyday life, through the magic of visualization. I've never physically been to Fiji, or Polynesia. I've never been to the Serengeti Plain in Africa, but in my imagination, I've been there many, many times. I've cruised into achingly tranquil lagoons in Polynesia with the hot sun playing over and around me. My bare feet can savour the smooth wooden deck of the schooner as I sail into the protected waters of the lagoon. As I moor the boat and jump into the sparkling clear crystal water and swim to shore, I feel the water caressing my skin, embracing my soul, and feel the hot sand curling around my toes as I walk up to the beach.

When I sit at night in a grass shack beside a flickering fire, cooking the fish I've caught in that lagoon, I can sense an intoxicating flood of freedom. In my visualization I have created true euphoria. I've reached my destination, maybe not in body, but in mind and spirit I am there. And the memory I can dredge up is the same as if I had actually lived through that exquisite experience.

I've painted the trees; I've watched the coconuts palms swaying; I've lain on the beach with the sun lulling me into slumber – and I've swam out to the boat surrounded by a myriad of rainbow-coloured fish swimming around me. I've climbed aboard the boat as it swung gently at anchor and felt the warm planking of the deck under my feet.

When it is time to leave this relaxing memory, I pull up the anchor effortlessly and feel the gentle sway of the boat as I set the sails and cruise out of that lagoon towards my next island retreat. I don't have to worry about storms because I'm in control and I can change that part of the memory. I've reincarnated a memory that has never existed in the flesh but it's always existed in my mind, and it gives me a resurgence of spirit. It gives me a positive sense that I'm rebuilding. I can escape from the moment to a place I've always wanted to be and, hey! I'm there.

The constructive qualities of visualization are incredibly important in times of stress when we're on this major journey towards our destination. We've tried all the various strategies and we've chipped away at the rocks a little incremental bit at a time. We've not smashed headlong into an issue, we have looked at it obliquely and we have flown above it. We have used our totem to help us; we've stripped down to our nomadic soul and we have run effortlessly through the deserts.

But there will be times when we still have moments of debilitating doubt; when unresolved problems resurface. There may be a gate we need to pass through, or a chasm may suddenly have appeared in the mountain pass we are crossing. Stop for a second. We should simply close our minds for an instant, and as we open our souls, we will feel visualization powers and energy pouring in. We have turned on a tap of life-giving energy and in the process renovated our souls. Think of being on the other side of the impediment and we will be there.

The interesting thing to remember is that when we start to renovate, we need to demolish first in order to rebuild. We cannot simply walk into a house and start to renovate before an assessment is conducted. Layers need to be peeled away and walls may have to be removed. The wiring and plumbing and a multitude of other construction details need to be attended to. The foundation probably requires reinforcing, and only then, when we are in a position to rebuild, can the actual transformation proceed.

So, in renovating our spirits and reincarnating our souls, we need to knock things down before rebuilding can start. We have to rip that armour off, smash down the walls we have built, open up those dams of discontent that we have built deep inside, and allow the impounded stagnant waters to pour out. We have to tackle problems instead of throwing them aside, because like boomerangs, they will come back. Smash them, throw them into the deepest ocean. Let negativity drain out like that dam behind our souls. Then, in the seeming disarray we can start the rebuilding.

I am sure that many of you have seen a house undergoing major renovation? Like that film, "The Money Pit," in which Tom Hanks decided to rebuild a home. Before the film was over, floors had been ripped up; the roof removed and outside walls knocked down. It was a disaster area. It was like a battle scene from a war zone with hardly anything left of the original structure. Only when the house had reached its lowest aesthetic point; when it looked as though it had been totally demolished, only then could they start to rebuild. Like Tom Hanks rebuilding his movie house, we need to rebuild on a solid foundation.

Some years ago there was a major earthquake in the west coast of America in which some buildings were demolished and many others had crumbled beyond repair. One of the reasons for the extent of the damage was attributed to an earlier period of aggressive building growth when many structures had been built on reclaimed land. This "land" had been artificially made by dredging sand and sediment from the bay. Land, hence Real Estate, was extremely valuable, so the attitude seems to have been. "Let's make more of it," and so developers dredged up more sand and sediment from the bay and artificially extended the shorelines and made even more "land."

Ultimately, this fill made very poor foundations for the homes on the so-called reclaimed land and when the earthquake struck, these houses moved on their foundations, settled, and cracked. Bricks and façades fell off, until with the houses in danger of collapsing, they had to be pulled down.

When we undergo the monumental project of rebuilding ourselves, we cannot do it on top of a faulty foundation; we have to delay peeling away the rotting shakes from our inner roof, and pulling walls down until we have checked the fundamental aspect of all: the foundation! Wow, there's an interesting concept! If we did everything; if we built ourselves into a new version of Us but didn't check the foundation, then the first emotional earthquake, or the first moment of self- doubt; the first time a problem came back like a boomerang, we would probably say, "oh, I meant to change my strategy" as we feel ourselves starting to fall apart. We will regret not having checked that foundation.

The foundation is the support for the new us. When our inner house is up and we have landscaped around it, we will be content and reassured that what is holding us up is firm and well- conceived. Others will see the emerging vital us, like an iceberg on the ocean; seeing only the tip not the bottom. Remember, in the renovation there will be a period of disarray because we are pulling apart something that has taken years to build.

We are designing our nomadic selves, to run like a deer into the future. We are going to the core of our beings, but remember, that only when we are exposed like an x-ray, can we start to rebuild. So do not be too hasty, otherwise pieces will start to fall off through impatient shoddy building practices.

If, when constructing something, we glue pieces together which are supposed to be left for 24 hours for the joint to become really effective, but through impatience after five or six minutes we say, "it looks good enough to me," and we start to build the next part, this causes incremental dissolution. The glue will not set properly and as it loses its grip, it will affect and negate the power of the next component until, like the old proverbial stack of dominoes, the whole thing will collapse. So, step back, review, demolish, rebuild and then move forward. Patience and not procrastination is what we are talking about here.

Again, on our journey, we're going to be inundated by people giving advice. They will notice changes in us and they will dredge up different interpretations of the change they witness, depending on their particular personality, character, their optimism, and often their level of pessimism. But as we have said before, refuse to become burdened by negativity. Some people will even say, "oh you'll never achieve that; it's airy-fairy, what are you trying to prove; isn't the old way good enough for you anymore? You'll never achieve that." Negativity, negativity, negativity!

We don't need this input, and we certainly don't want to dwell on it. Just say: "what I'm doing is positive for me." Sometimes they may say, "You're going off on a tangent, you should be going in this direction." Remember we have discovered that there are different ways to achieve the same end. As the popular pop song said, "I am doing it my way."

Here is an example. Someone walks along a sandy beach and draws a line in the sand. Two people are standing there, and he says, "step up to the line and run forward." The first person goes up to the line while the second person is blindfolded. The first person puts his heels on the line and runs to the left then comes back and sits down. The second person puts his heels on the line and runs to the right. Now they are both going forward, but in different directions. Their perception of "forward" is different.

Or think about circumnavigating an island. Like the great hoop of life, we can pick any point in the circumference and go forward by advancing left, or right, but, ultimately, we will end up back where you started; or as you wish, the destination. So by going forward in different directions we achieve the same end. And there are many different ways of achieving that. Those two people who approached the line in the sand ultimately had at least six variations of going forward. They both could have stood with their heels on the line and run to the left, that's one way; they both could have stood with their heels to the line and run right, that's two ways. One could have gone left and one could have gone right, that's three ways. And so on. We can build on that and say, "Yes, there's more than one way to arrive at a destination."

So, because someone says to us, "the resolution to this is this way," we don't have to accept that opinion, otherwise we will fall into our own morass of negativity and depression. Our self-esteem will die because we want to try something different, do things differently, but we are being told; "no you must try it this way, forward is to the left, of course you can't go to the right."

But we have just proven you can go to the left or the right; right around the island and arrive back at the beginning or the destination, depending on our viewpoints. We have traversed the hoop of life, and pushed deeper into the core of our beings again. So disregard others and be tenacious. Most of all be open to your inner voice and be creative.

Sometimes when we are trying to resolve a seemingly insurmountable issue, it is helpful to view it as something else, as the following example demonstrates. Here, I used visualization to help me in a particularly difficult construction project when I was building our cottage on an isolated island on the west coast, completely without power; pioneer style, or as my wife said "the only way you know how!" One particularly windy, stormy day I was struggling to put the roof rafters in place, and as the waterfront cottage faced the wrath of the wind and the sea, it was a daunting task. Some of the work was tedious: cutting the rafters at the right angle to fit the ridge board; hauling them up an improvised ladder; balancing them on my head so that I could nail them in place; and then eureka!, the euphoria of visualization kicked in.

Suddenly in my mind I was high on the rigging of a square-rigger sailing ship rounding the Horn, because when I was up in the roof-line with the wind in my face and the ocean spray rising high in the air and baptizing me, I felt like I was actually in a nineteenth century schooner, and naturally I started singing sea shanties. I was sailing around the Horn. I was sailing unfathomed oceans to places and islands I'd never been, and suddenly the work became easier. Instead of sitting in a building site methodically plodding along hammering nails into lines of rafters and joints, I was sitting up in the rigging of a sail boat, and amazingly the work went faster and was more enjoyable.

Through my visualization technique I still managed to build the roof, and the bonus was, I had fun at the same time. I had sailed round the Horn; I'd climbed up to the high rigging in a twin-masted schooner. My visualization made the job easier and I got to my destination: completing the roof, just the same.

So, whenever you feel things are not as they should be, and you experience your energy draining from you, allow a feeling of happiness to wash over you; imagine a special place; imagine a helper. Invite your totem to help you, and remember to skim stones obliquely at problems as they present themselves. Determine how many different ways you can devise to resolve the issues and pretty soon you will have the bliss of being someone who was not you before.

You will be reborn. You have gone back to the seed, back to the core of your birth. You have felt yourself bursting out of a cocoon, or pecking through the shell of an egg to emerge as a new person; a lean, honed down person; a nomadic spirit wandering through the landscape of a new existence. We have tackled this journey step by step at different speeds, with time for relaxation and visualization. We have had time to make memories that exist in places we have never been to. To fly like an eagle and run like a deer to the core of our being.

## *twenty eight*

## All In Its Time And Don't Forget
## The Frequency

**Tune into your comfort level and watch miracles happen.**

Often when we make the decision to change because we are no longer satisfied with who we are or what we are achieving, and feel a lack of real passion in our existence, we just leap at this change aggressively like a sprinter trying to run a marathon, similar to sprinting a mile. But, we have to pace ourselves.

Visualize a power boat patiently sitting at the dock, quiet and tranquil, ready for a day's recreational adventures. When the engine is started, immediately the water becomes agitated and boils in turmoil around the waiting boat. The boat starts moving laboriously out into the waters of the bay towards its final destination, pushing, rather than gliding through the water. However, once it is up and running, a smooth, gentle 'V' is projected by the bow and, following the arrow of the 'V, the effortless boat moves into the future – towards its destination.

We are like that when we initially decide to change and undertake our journey of exploration. There is a flurry of activity and emotional turmoil because we've decided to do something new and different. It's like making New Year's resolutions; at the beginning it's difficult to get started, but once the new fresh regime is undertake, we can make the 'V' for victory and cruise more easily into the future.

Another lesson I've learned from watching ponderous tug boats, is that there are times when it's best to sit back and reflect, relax and re-energize ourselves before we tackle the next stage of our journey. Just like a ship going through a series of locks. There is no sense in revving your engine while the water is slowly filling the locks: so relax.

There is an island in front of my house, and in stormy weather when skippers of tug boats realize that they are almost drifting backwards because of the force of the storm, they retreat into the shelter of that island and rest until the storm abates. When the storm ends, they move out again on their journey. They realize that to try to fight the storm would just expend energy and achieve nothing. Likewise there will be times when we will feel drained and exhausted, and that is the time to stop, relax, think and review our plans. When we are re-energized, that is when we move forward again.

On this theme of lessons learned from boats. Years ago I bought a power boat which I spent six months rebuilding. This boat had a fairly small fifty horsepower engine and therefore was sadly underpowered for its size. Well-meaning people would often say to me when I started the engine, "don't worry, when the boat is up and planing you'll use less fuel."

Now the problem was, the engine in my boat didn't have the strength to get me up in a planing position, in which there is less water resistance: this means that you ride on top of the water and are not pushing through it. However, I was continually labouring with this little engine. I was pushing the boat through the water but I wasn't planing, I was forcing the boat through the water.

Similarly, when we make changes, in the beginning we're motivated; we're excited; we're going to become this lean, honed down nomadic warrior; we are going to the core of our being. But then our energy starts to wane and, just like my boat, we start to drag through the water with great effort. We must find just the right amount of energy that we require to move forward. Energy must be rationed; a little bit is all we need sometimes, and we don't have to kill ourselves. Remember, when the journey becomes onerous: stop, relax and sit back and think about the next stage. Again, in your mind's eye, see the arrival before and how we will be when we get there.

Lessons can be learned everywhere, by keeping ourselves open to witness and see, to accept, to understand things. In essence we want to be like a camera: our eyes are the lens and we take in the picture;

we nourish it inside and we can bring it back as a snapshot any time we wish. The vignettes of life, the little snapshots of life, can be filed away to bring out at a time that's really important, and by seeing, by looking, we start to understand.

I've often said, "to see is not to understand: but to understand is to see." Lessons are taught by anything and everything. All of my poetry is the distillation of any situation. We must allow ourselves to be taught by everything around us. It could be a scene from nature, it could be a fleeting vignette of life, a personality profile or an emotional feeling, but lessons are learned and earned everywhere.

Some years ago I was out doing some tentative gardening. I don't meddle much with our piece of forested mountainside because nature does such a great job, but there was a branch hanging low over my driveway which I was rather loath to chop off; so I decided to put a noose around the branch and tie it to the tree to support it. Now, the intention was noble enough, but I made one fatal error. In supporting the branch I almost strangled it. I put the noose so tightly round the branch that when it grew, the area around the knot was weakened by the stranglehold. What I should have done is put a loose noose around the branch so that as the tree grew and expanded, it could grow easily within the loose noose.

The lesson learned here is that there have always been people in our lives, whether they're teachers, peers, siblings or well-meaning relatives and friends, who want to support us; who want to encourage us, but often they do it in a smothering way. They form a noose around us to support us like the branch was supported against the tree. But they end up smothering us with their good intentions. The noose of love and attention is too tight; there is no room for personal growth. A lesson learned gardening in my forest.

You often hear people saying, "I don't get it; that's way over my head," or "you always come up with these great ideas, do you hear something I don't?" Now, what I think we need to do is tune our internal frequency; tune the sensory perceptions in our being.

We go over to a radio, switch it on and start dialling to find our favourite show, yet all we hear are crackles and incomprehensible noises. Sometimes we almost hear something, then just before we can decipher the content, it fades away until suddenly with more adjusting, we get the right frequency and the message comes through strong, vibrant and clear. Only because we have taken the time to very gently change the channel; taken the dial and turned it slowly until that moment when we can connect with our desired frequency.

I think a lot of us are used to listening to the one frequency which exists on a certain level of our complacent consciousness. We don't venture or deviate above and we certainly don't go below. We always channel into the tried and true and listen to the same safe frequency. Occasionally we may have an intuitive sense of something just out of reach; although it's not quite clear or sharp enough. We must make a decision to reach inside the core of our being and find that unique tuning dial which can be tuned to different frequencies. By doing so, we'll open ourselves up to discovery, and to hearing things we've never heard before.

Dial is an acronym for Daring Discovery; Innovation and Improvisation; Arrival, and Loving ourselves. So why don't we do ourselves a favour and dial the Stranger Within.

The excitement of emotional and spiritual growth is acquired simply by tuning ourselves, and being daring enough to listen to a different station. Don't always listen to that same station or boredom will set in. Instead become like others who are always energized, always excited, who have eclectic tastes. That just means that they are open to everything, anything; to new experiences; they're open to change; they're non-judgemental; they're trusting. They are open and trusting, accepting and they're unafraid.

A vignette in my mind takes me back to Scotland when I was working in public health. Some of my duties entailed visiting farms, some of which were fairly remote, and in all of my inspections, I always conducted myself in a very open, accepting, non-judgemental sort of way. Some of my colleagues indicated that I viewed the world through rose tinted glasses, but thinking back, even then I was viewing life in a different way.

I remember one day going with another older inspector to inspect a recent renovation to an isolated farm. We pulled into the farmyard which was like a classic scene from "All Creatures Great and Small". There was the time-weathered 18th century stone farmhouse basking in the dying rays of a rare sunny winter day, and lying on the threshold at the front door was an enormous sleeping German Shepherd.

Now farms are notorious for harbouring dogs whose sole intent in life appears to be in victimizing hapless visitors. Their ritualistic greeting usually entails hurtling themselves either singly or in intimidating packs towards you with spine-chilling growls! At that moment your throat always felt extremely vulnerable until the gruff farmer appears to administer a rapid kick.

In this particular case we pulled the car into the courtyard of the farm, and with my usual optimistic viewpoint of life that everything would be just perfect, I stepped out of the car. As I conducted a quick leap over the slumbering beast on the threshold, a large baleful eye opened, did a quick assessment and then closed. Inspection over, I just smiled, knocked on the door and waited.

The other nervous inspector in the car slowly opened his door and crept towards the house; and ultimately his nemesis, for his sense of dread of the slumbering beast was palpable. His mind was closed to the possibility that this dog would accept him! He was terrified of the beast and he anticipated a negative meeting. As he approached the reclining dog, it erupted into life, leaped to its feet and ran, snarling towards this man who sprinted back and hid in the car. Therefore, he had achieved what he had anticipated.

I stood there bemused. I had stepped over the dog; the dog had looked at me; I had smiled at the dog. The dog had picked up the essence of who I was. When I approached the dog I did it non-judgmentally, I wasn't scared. I stepped over the dog; I didn't intrude. My friend was closed. He knew that dog was going to attack him and through his aura of anticipating the worst, the dog picked up that sense and followed through.

So, if we're open, accepting, and non-judgemental, anticipating a positive outcome, then that is what is going to happen. However if we anticipate a negative response of reaction to everything we encounter, like a self-perpetuating prophesy, that is what will happen. That blanket of negativity will block out the empowering rays of "do not intrude, I am happy."

We are determined not to be like that person who stays isolated in the little village cottage with the doors and windows closed. Shuttered away, crying the blues that "nothing exciting ever happens to me; I lead a dull life." If that is the negative energy that is being expended, then the result is exactly what is being anticipated resulting in nothing positive and exciting.

We must throw open wide the doors and windows to our being. Let them swing in the invigorating winds of change. Feel energy and euphoria blowing in with countless lessons and adventures. Like Johnny Head in the Air, we are flying through life with eyes and a soul that screams: "I am doing things my way because I have learned lessons from everything around me."

## twenty nine

## Trees, Dogs And Spiders Teach Lessons On The Maze To The Holy Grail

**Learn from everything: above, below and in-between.**

In the previous chapter I concluded by indicating that lessons can be learned from the most unusual sources; so do be scared to debate issues with trees, dogs, leaves, and even spiders.

I did have a debate with a spider once! I was on my deck barbecuing a salmon which was searing nicely, and with a glass of chilled white wine in my hand I felt that all was well with the world. Out of the corner of my eye, on a cedar lath railing beside me I spotted a spider which was also waiting for its supper. It sat on the edge of its web filtering the air for its supper – a fly, a mosquito – anything that would land on that web. It was fishing the air; so the poem I wrote was called "Spider Fisher." In essence, I had fished the ocean for the salmon. I spun a web in the ocean. The spider had spun his net in the air and was going to catch his supper. Spider Fisher!

It taught me an important lesson which I have previously talked about. The spider expended its energy initially weaving its net, its web. Then it retreated to its corner and just watched and waited for his supper. Spider Fisher! Expend initial energy, and sit back and wait for the intended result.

Now, my mind always loves to cast Velcro hooks out to link together an incident, a circumstance, a vision, a vignette, a snapshot or a passing shadowy feeling. Years ago in Scotland when I was wandering through the Highlands, I came into a small fishing village where I saw an old man and a young boy sitting on a pebble beach mending fishing nets. As I watched them, I had a vision of these two patient spiders spinning their webs to catch fish in the ocean. They were also spider fishers. Then, all those years later barbecuing on my sunny deck, when I saw the spider, the spider fisher analogy came back into my mind again: back into my being.

The lesson here is that in our gunny sack we store vignettes of life that we think we have forgotten, until our continually searching Velcro hook springs into action. We have stored-away treasures that are just waiting to be re-discovered. And in the discovery will be discovered unthought-of revelations.

If we practice the art of "spider-fishing", images and thoughts will come into our minds at the most unusual times for no rhyme or reason; but as we know, we've filed away some event in our past, which is just waiting to be re-incarnated. It has been jostling around in our minds, our souls and our spirits. Suddenly, just as a sunbeam unexpectedly strikes us in the eye in a sombre forest, a snapshot of our past will hover in front of our eye, and we will witness a moment of enlightenment concerning a current issue which is troubling us. The previous event has taken on a new meaning and has led our mind into a new journey of discovery.

The lesson to be learned is trust and patience: forcing an answer invariably causes a rupture in the genuine honest positive flow that we have been striving for. An example is that there are two ways to "break" a horse to the saddle: gentling it with trust and patience until it comes to trust you and your intention of riding it. The other way is to break it with brutality, which certainly allows you to place a saddle on its back and ride it, but in the process, the animal's spirit has also been broken.

Another lesson of patience occurs as I stand looking out of my window just as dawn is breaking. I witness a very gentle fragmented light filtering over the dark water, sparkling and illuminating a previously dark and dismal world. As the sun rises higher and higher, suddenly the world is bright, and the ocean dances with the wonder of the morning as it revels in light and sunshine. So, just when we have almost given up the search for inner illumination, the sun of realization and understanding will wash over us, all because we waited a few seconds longer. Persistence leads to achievement.

We must learn to relax in the knowledge that sitting patiently waiting with the right intention is time well-spent. Reaching tentatively inside ourselves in the bliss of exploration ultimately prompts and promotes understanding and ultimate change. Initially, if all we see are a few flickers of recognition like the first gently flickering light on the ocean, we may say that nothing is really happening. We want the instantaneous gratification of an enlightened us. However if we just wait a fraction longer, the sun will rise higher, and the ocean of our existence will beam with light. Patience again – we need patience.

We must also learn to amaze ourselves and amaze others. This is to me a play on words, because inside of us there's a maze which holds in its serene centre; a Holy Grail. There's a lamp waiting there filled by our unique understanding; just waiting for us to polish it into a gleaming source of light. If, and when we reach it, all we have to do is caress this lamp and the genie of understanding, the genie of change will appear.

When we first wander into the maze, we will stumble and wander aimlessly right and left; entering cul-de-sacs and dead ends. We are engaging in the dance of advance and retreat. It is unlikely that initially by chance we will find the Holy Grail right where we thought it would be.

What we're patiently learning however, is to be able to enter that maze and subconsciously allow ourselves to drift down the right path, straight to our core each time we need to go there for a resurgence of our trust and love and affection for the world and who we are.

In the beginning, as we have discovered, we will inevitably wander in the wrong direction in the maze until we encounter a roadblock. The dangerous thing here is that in each of these dead ends, there's a little mini prize waiting; there's something there to tease us and encourage us to linger; to say to us, " this is what matters, you've reached what you have been looking for and here's your prize." It could be some sort of instantaneous gratification, some sort of a lure which will detract from the Holy Grail search we are on.

The temptation may be to sit there and relax, and enjoy the shallow reward that's being offered. The danger is that the longer we delay, our will to continue the search for the Holy Grail may start to wane. We may settle for second best. At these moments, we must find a resurgence of our passion for ultimate change by reaching that lamp of illumination. We must learn to leave the tempting fleeting treat of the moment behind, and plunge ahead.

Our determination will drive us on until we hit another roadblock, another dead end and there we will discover another tantalizing treat waiting to slake our appetite; we will need to avoid the hypnotic reason to stay there and must resume our search once again.

These roadblocks that we're going to encounter are not all unpleasant, but some are going to be like saccharine, like sugar; they're going to give us a quick fix which will fade and leave us craving for more shallow gratification, and divert us from our search. However, there will be no lasting achievement, no lasting satisfaction. The reward will be shallow with no depth to it. If we accept the shallow rewards waiting in the dead ends, again we will drift along living a lie. We will not be forcing ourselves to go back into the struggle; the journey to the core of our being which lies in the centre of that maze.

When we do get to the centre of the maze we will find the lamp sitting there patiently and it may look dusty and dull because no-one's been there before. Slowly pick it up and start to polish, and to understand what this is. We will clean and burnish it, and the more we work on it the brighter it will become. The dullness that is the skin of that lamp is going to become a shining, flickering sparkle of light that will illuminate the darkest areas. Rub and polish until the genie of enlightenment appears.

We have found our reward, our manifestation and our true desire. This is what we wanted to do; to journey to the core of our being to find out who we are. To explore, so that we could change our negativity; to fine tune the frequency so that we can listen, hear and understand more. We are going to finally see: we are going to understand.

We are going to say "open sesame" any time we need to go through the maze. We are going to ignore the transitory rewards. We are going to avoid them totally and go straight to the core each time, now that we have found the lamp. And the lamp in there will perpetually shine and be vibrant and will give light. So, even if we initially didn't know the way to the centre, all we have to do now is follow the light, follow the source; follow our rebirth once again. We have entered the maze and we have polished the core of our beings. We have reached our state of enlightenment. We have ignored the lure of the Sirens.

# *thirty*

## Each Moment Is Dessert

**The dessert of perfection is right now [and do not forget the imperfections]**

It has taken me a lifetime to realize that I've never really lived in the moment. I've always been living with the expectation of some sort of reward, a kind of realization that "after the fact" was more important than the reality of the moment.

What this means is, for example: I could never just enjoy a sunset; or a stroll on the beach with the moon shining on the water and the waves lapping on the shore while high above a sea bird serenaded me. I was always living for the reward afterwards that was invariably going to come to me; but I never realized it. I thought that because I was writing poetry it was justification in itself; but it's not. All the while nature played its symphony around me and painted incredible pictures, I was reaching into the future of writing a poem to capture this special moment. I did not simply let the intrinsic beauty bathe me in that moment but instead I leaped ahead.

Another example occurs when we walk into a banquet room and witness rows of groaning tables filled with all sorts of delicacies, appetizers, exquisite soups; savoury entrées and other spicy aromatic delights. Our eye finally sees a table filled with desserts in a far corner. Now, if all through the meal filled with the chef's magical touch, if all we dream about are the desserts, we are missing the moment. We are anticipating dessert and not savouring the moment of the meal, because we feel that dessert is the ultimate reward.

I saw a car sticker once and it demonstrated what I'm saying now. Basically it said, "Life is too short, go straight for the dessert," and at one time maybe I would have thought that was correct. For me the dessert was writing the poem about the sunset, but I missed living in the moment.

We can spend a lifetime anticipating that pivotal moment when we receive a reward, because we have done someone a favour. If the only reason we do something for somebody is to hear them say thank you, or give us some other reward, we are missing the point as well. We are missing the sheer joy of giving. Live for the moment, without thinking about a hoped-for bounty or reward. If we live in a world of continual anticipation, our minds, souls and spirits will wither in "the present moment" while our energy flow is on the far distant dessert.

So, don't live a lifetime greedily anticipating the reward; always poised on the expectation that at the end of something, there will be something better. This moment of our life is the ultimate reward; the culmination of our journey to this point. Enjoy the moment, savour the moment. It has taken me a lifetime to realize this.

Now, when I look at a sunset, or hear the wind sigh through the trees, I can just enjoy that moment of excitement, that moment of beauty and I won't be troubled with producing some monumental bit of poetry, or words or music. If artistry follows, let it be, as I sip the nectar of the current moment.

I am going to strive to live in the moment, in the realization that I have shaken hands with my Stranger Within, and made a friend for life.

# *thirty one*

## Cuckoo Blessings

**Embrace the gift of our uniqueness.**

As I have been sitting intently hammering away at this computer, my mind has suddenly screamed: "time out, time to just sit back Bill and relax. Let me do some work. Close your eyes and let me drift into the canyons of my imagination."

What my mind is saying is simply to allow it to wander at will for a while, with no destination in mind. I guess I have been too focused lately. Forgetting my own lessons. OK where will this take me?

I was starting to forget the sweet bliss of sitting relaxing and allowing random thoughts to drift into my sub consciousness. As soon as I agreed to my mind's dictates, for some unknown reason the word cuckoo leaped into my thoughts. Where now mind? Where is this taking me? No matter where that trail leads, I know that it will honour me with some meaningful conclusions. But is there a link between cuckoos and how will this help us progress in our life's journey? We will find out.

I remember as a child reading about the unusual habits of the cuckoo bird, derided by some as lazy, for its custom of laying its eggs in another bird's nest, yet intriguing to me when I first saw a photograph of a large cuckoo fledgling sitting innocently among its smaller surrogate siblings.

Now in the same family, the cuckoo chick would grow up influenced by the same lessons taught by its unsuspecting adoptive parents until one day an epiphany would occur in which the fledgling would be transformed into its true persona as a cuckoo, and not as a thrush or nightingale. Deep inside it would sense a desire to conduct itself as a cuckoo, and the transformation would occur.

OK mind! I am following this train of thought, so lead on. I'm sure we all know, or have heard of people whose families for generations have always specialized in specific occupations: ministers, doctors, lawyers, stonemasons, involvement in the arts, or some other calling. Then, suddenly, someone is born into that family, who when they get to the age of reason, says "I don't want to be a lawyer, soldier, or a doctor. I don't want to be a minister. I want to be something that is totally different."

Why do these people suddenly have such a unique sense of their identity? Tradition had established roles for their family members for generations yet now a sheep of a different colour is demanding to be recognized. I call it the cuckoo syndrome in a positive way.

Is passionately desiring to forge our own tradition or destiny so bad? Is wishing to honour the spark seething inside us to be ignored? Some may say, "That person is a real black sheep, a square peg in a round hole" You know all those metaphors and analogies. Being ourselves is a blessing not to be ignored!

How does this happen mind? Just think about the cuckoo! Maybe a higher knowledge than us, can comprehend what places special people in families to effect change: to stir life into action where before there was the inaction of "always the same." Yes mind, maybe cuckoos have a place after all. We must embrace our differences, even within the family unit. For remember that the definition of difference is being able to affect someone's life; being distinct. Thank you mind for waking me from my euphoria.

When you think about it, we are like snowflakes with no-one exactly like us. Similarity blinds us to the fact that beneath the surface, the truth lies waiting to be discovered. I realize that now scientists are talking about cloning humans, but the reality will always remain that we are individual creations. We are who we are and there is no-one else quite like us. There may be some people whom we resemble physically, but we're different, we think uniquely. We are snowflakes! Superficially the same: inherently distinct.

I was surfing the Internet one day and found myself in a website dedicated to an unusual man who lived in the frontier age of the 1800's. Born in Vermont, Wilson Bentley devoted his life to photographing snowflakes by utilizing microscopic photography. In an age of axe and gun, he was exploring the frontier within, and developing an art and science that was magic to others. He left the tried and true and threw himself into the unknown. Snowflakes happen! But he had to delve into their differences.

Just like the faces around us, he recognized the distinctiveness of each snowflake. In his age, and maybe ours, some would classify him as a kook, a flake (there you go, no pun intended!) but isn't it interesting? Here was a man who spent his lifetime microscopically photographing snowflakes. He realized that every single snowflake was unique and they all quintessentially were beautiful. Consider that there is no such thing as an ugly snowflake. Their difference and splendour glorifies life. Just as we do.

So, the so-called cuckoo, the so-called black sheep of the family who says, "I don't want to be a minister, doctor, or sailor, I want to do what my heart implores me to follow," is not being selfish. Differences are to be recognized and blessed just like snowflakes which layer the world with the bliss of purity, all interlaced with the diversity of acknowledging similarity and uniqueness.

Just when I thought it was time for me to leap back into action, and take over from my mind, a vision of our grand-children drifted into my consciousness, sitting awkwardly, eyes and face filled with wonder as their tiny fingers probed the world around them. While muttering little incomprehensible peals of excitement, they live in a state of non-filtered acceptance.

As they get older and layer the world around them with play, a magical world will develop. Reality will co-exist with imagination until if we are not careful, external influences will start to drag them towards society's version of maturity and perceived growth: 'here are life's rules and regulations, and oh! By the way, the childish beliefs that you have – forget them. There are no such things as little fairies and gnomes, and grass is always green, and the sky is always blue, and everything has a little box. So forget those childish beliefs you have."

158 | Bill Kimmett

However, there are some of us who pride ourselves as honorary cuckoos who feel a different rhythm; a different drumbeat resonating through the cadence of the uniqueness of our music. We must do things our way in our dreams and our reality. As my mind just shouted. "Remind your readers that snowflakes all eventually melt into the river of life."

## *thirty two*

## Pantomine Problem-Soving Or All-Out War

**Declare war on your problems: don't skirmish half-heartedly.**

There are many ways to resolve impasses in our lives, and I call the following form of problem solving, the "Shakka Principle". This theory revolves around the diverse tribes who lived in Central and South Africa in the 1800's. These tribes lived by their own customs and principles: squabbling with adjacent groups, and living in constant fear and anticipation of skirmishes and warfare. Inherently they were all weak because not one nation dominated the whole area. Their energy was always geared towards protecting their boundaries, which were in a continuous state of flux.

Typically when territorial issues presented themselves, the tribes saved face by adopting an age-old strategy: Both tribes at an appointed time would line up facing each other and conduct a form of stylized, ritual warfare. They attempted to resolve the problem of the moment by thudding their spear shafts against their rock-hard cow skin shields, augmented by hurling howls of abuse at the opposing side.

The next stylized part of the ritual involved a champion from each tribe who would step forward and taunt his opponent. The adversaries would then advance toward each other and engage in a skirmish; waving their spears until blood was drawn. The washing of the spears resolved the immediate issue, at which time both tribes would retreat and celebrate their victory. At least until the next time which would inevitably come? They had pretended to tackle the problem, which of course still existed. Skirmish! As opposed to finalizing the issue by fighting all-out warfare. I am not an advocate of war, but am merely using this as an analogy as to how we can resolve our problems in the following way. The Shakka way.

This formidable warrior was a member of one of these tribes in Central Africa which ultimately become the formidable Zulu nation; and when he first encountered this form of "skirmish warfare" he was shocked, because his viewpoint was that a tribe should tackle an issue by indulging in a war that was "all out", or nothing. He couldn't comprehend this play-acting: this pantomime of war.

Eventually, and inevitably, when he became a recognized warrior, Shakka devised his own form of warfare. Among other innovative strategies, he invented a new short stabbing spear for close contact and by dispensing with the leather sandals which the warriors traditionally wore; he enabled his troops to run quickly towards their enemies unimpeded. If an issue presented itself then it had to be resolved. No play-acting. His form of warfare was to engage the opposing tribe in comprehensive warfare. No pantomime!

As his enemies were inevitably defeated, he then entered the next stage of subjugation and surrender. The question was posed, "do you want to live? If you wish to live, you will live under our auspices and will be assimilated into our emerging Zulu nation." If the enemy said "no" the next step was extermination.

In many ways, when we are presented with problems we take the pre-Shakka route. We see a problem in front of us and become angry; we don't want it to be there. We impatiently shout and paw at it like a kitten pawing a ball. We then contentedly persuade ourselves that we have resolved it and allow the problem to vanish into the back of our minds: at least until it resurfaces.

Deep down in our innermost thoughts we know that this problem will return although we have persuaded ourselves that it has gone away. And we wonder why we are always feeling drained emotionally? Simply because of the gnawing anticipation of that resurfacing problem. We did not resolve it, but just batted it into a corner until the next time.

However, the Shakka way is the final way to tackle the obstacle. We truly want it resolved, not by putting it in the "until the next time" category. We know that we cannot live with it, as it will always be looking over our shoulder. Whether a relationship issue or some other long simmering feeling of discontent in our life, it must be confronted.

In a relationship situation, we may placate our partner and ourselves by glossing over the impasse by a bribe of chocolates and a movie. This is the skirmish tactic by putting off the inevitable.

Adopting the Shakka way of tackling it head on and resolving it once and for all requires a courageous monumental mind shift. His technique was to use a manoeuvre called the "Horns of the Bull", in which by encircling the problem, the inevitable result was problem resolved.

So if we think of our problems like that, we can address them in a similar manner. There should be no hesitation in approaching the issues. As we visualize the various components of that problem, we can mentally break them down into bite-size pieces, as we have previously discussed, and tackle them so they never resurface.

However, sometimes in relationship dilemmas, we encounter the "voodoo doll approach" which is a technique used by one of the partners.

We've all seen caricatures of voodoo dolls in which some evil vindictive person wishes to attack and undermine another person. By inserting needles into the doll in different places, they attempt to injure or eradicate someone.

Some relationships can be like that, in which one of the partners in a relationship uses a symbolic voodoo doll. He, or she, knows the agony and unfortunately not the ecstasy of their partner; comprehends the issues and attacks the areas of discomfort and sadness and emotional upset in that person.

So, what do they do? A relationship is developed in which one of the partners is continually being hurt by the other. Sadly the injured party may be unaware of the reasons of discomfort or sadness, particularly if the vindictive partner presents a picture of happiness, while carrying out the voodoo attacks behind the aggrieved person's back.

In relationships, if we always present a smiling, happy and positive image in front of our partner, but as soon as they're not there we start to think angry, negative, hurtful thoughts about them; what's going to happen? One of the partners will probably think: "there is something wrong, I don't feel good about this relationship but I don't know what it is, because every time I see my partner everything seems fine, every-thing is good." However the voodoo doll principle is in place, and needs to be confronted.

Escaping from a relationship to many people can only be achieved by vindictive behaviour. This is when the voodoo doll situation is crip-pling, as the victim feels the effect of multiple physiological pins. Like Medusa; as one pin is plucked out, another is inserted. You may say, "Why do I wish to remain in this relationship?" Ultimately, if there is no resolution to the mass of issues, an end is called, and both part-ners walk away. However, if we never ask, "why are these impediments here?" Then we will never attempt to resolve them.

Only dialogue will help to unravel the troubled relationship. But, unless we look inside and light up our own feelings first, we should not attempt to lay blame on the other party.

We have all heard the statement, "look in the mirror and who do you see?" The fairy tale life of the Snow White fable does not exist. It isn't like "mirror, mirror on the wall, who's the fairest of them all?" We can kid ourselves, sometimes all through our lives, until we peel back that veneer and really see the person inside.

When Shakka first encountered his opponents, he would be con-fronted by a strong wall of shields, spears and aggression. But he found out fairly quickly that behind that façade there was a real desire in many of the tribes not to fight. In other words, behind that veneer of aggression, of threatening posture, was a body, a tribe, a mass of people who really just wanted to live their lives in as peaceful a manner as possible.

However, through the ritualized, machismo way of living, they had perpetuated the myth of warfare, the pantomime of aggression. So, when you look in the mirror, seek beyond the face and see who really is there. Like most of the tribes, most people do not wish to spend a life in perpetual aggression. The chip on the shoulder gets weary after a while.

Most of us want to live happy, contented lives. At the macro level in relationships with friends, neighbours, the community, workmates and, ultimately, in the micro level with their partners; and in an even more micro way, with themselves. How can we possibly be happy if we are presenting a false image to everyone around us? How can we possibly be happy living the perpetual lie?

I'm not saying that Shakka had the answer, no! All I'm saying is, we can adopt his strategy, his vision, and apply it to our own relationships; our own problem solving. The problem is there; address it and in facing it we may discover that there are some positive aspects that can be assimilated. If it's all negative, exterminate, annihilate it. That's what we must do.

Not everyone is going to like us no matter what we do or act. None of us can expect the whole world to like us. If we try to compromise so that everyone likes us, we will become chameleons. Just visualize it, imagine the stress! In other words, if we try to become the person we think everyone we meet will like, we will destroy ourselves. Ultimately we will become so fragmented that we will have no idea who we really are.

Think about the number of people we encounter in the course of a day; a week; a month; a year, and a lifetime. If we try to change each time we meet a person because we want that person to like us, we will become so disjointed that when the time eventually comes to sit down and present who we are, we will have no idea because we have been playing the "ever-changing game."

Face it. It is impossible to please everyone and, in some ways, we must please ourselves first. I don't mean that in a selfish way. I am not inferring that we indulge ourselves in a hedonistic way. What I'm saying is that we must be true to ourselves; find out who we are; find out what makes us tick; find the happiness points; find the moral points; find pain thresholds; find spiritual relationships. Sculpt yourself, as we said before, and that's the person the world will see.

Visualize meeting ten people in the course of a day, and each of those ten people think we are pretty sharp because of the image we are projecting; and conversely we think we know who they are.

So, we meet that first person and become a chameleon and change, so that person will like us. With the second person, we change again, and with the third, fourth, fifth and so on until we get to ten. What happens when we meet those people collectively, or in groups, or in twos and threes? They've met us individually one day and determined that "we are x,", but suddenly, collectively, all these people are going to be confused because they thought they had us pigeon-holed. We have previously presented a different image, and now x has become y.

Remember that we become what we think. What we think internally, we show externally.

Again, back in Shakka's day, each tribe had a shaman who was the spiritual adviser. He was both feared and revered and people had implicit faith in him. All the shaman had to do was point a finger at someone and that person knew that he was going to die because they believed that it was going to happen; therefore in their mind it would.

Just think however, if we can train ourselves to become what we believe in a positive manner; we can be whatever we really want to be. We can tell ourselves "I am going to succeed in whatever I try; I am destined to become the ultimate me."

In the next chapter we will learn from the flamboyance of circuses.

# *thirty three*

## Foresight Versus Hindsight, And Guess The Winner

**Trust plus variety provides life's lessons**

Earlier we talked of various forms of problem solving, or to be more exact, lessons to be learned from life's experiences and how we can apply them to problems and issues. Which brings me to the magic of circuses, and how the romance of the Big Top can teach us some thought-provoking lessons.

My first "circus class" occurred when I was about 12 years old. The annual circus had come to town, and there I was sitting with my elder brother in the front row mesmerized by the intoxicating atmosphere of sawdust-prancing elephants, and sequin clad acrobats. And then came an epiphany. Lulled into a hypnotic state by parades of lions and tigers emerging to roar their distaste at the audience, I suddenly saw a magnificent Clydesdale horse with a beautiful dream-like girl on its back enter and canter around the ring. The acrobatic girl danced and pirouetted on its massive back like an exotic ballerina. And then came my chance at immortality, or so I thought.

A hush suddenly descended as the Ring Master swept into the arena and in an impressive theatrical voice asked for a volunteer to come forward and attempt to emulate the acrobatic girl. Like a flash I leaped over the rail in front of me and stood in front of the Ring Master. A safety harness attached to a security cable which vanished into the roof of the "Big Top" was strapped around me, and the stage was now set for my circus adventure.

With assurances that as I ran towards the by now galloping horse, they would hoist me onto its back, I raced towards the mammoth beast at an oblique angle to meet it, and ran straight into the horse. Boom! Into this wall of muscle. Of course as I landed on my back on the sawdust floor the crowd erupted into laughter. First lesson learned at an early age.

The lesson of Trust! The Ring Master had played a trick on me – the security line had not hoisted me onto the back of the Clydesdale. I had been made to look like an incompetent fool. In hindsight I learned a valuable lesson in trust. If you always accept things at face value, you may end up on your back. With no foresight, trust can be misplaced. There are those who prey on innocence to better themselves. The worse we look the better they appear.

Ultimately I did leap onto the back of the horse and as I have a fairly good sense of balance managed to sit, stand, and balance on one leg. I started to experience a sense of euphoria, cheered on by the enthusiastic crowd then, again, the rug was pulled from under me, as the security line hoisted me above the horse and swung me around in a circle

Now, I certainly learned from that exciting experience? The first lesson was trust. I had placed total trust in what I was told, and suffered the consequences. In essence I'm really a trusting person, but there are times when we must take control of our own destinies and do things by ourselves. We cannot always rely on safety valves, or "security blankets" like the circus lifeline. Safety lines can sometimes become leashes and actually hold us back.

I learned something else! If I had run at top speed straight at the horse, I would have missed it, simply because nothing in life is ever static. What I had to do was to judge its momentum and run at an angle to meet the horse at a certain point. It was a moving target. The whole thing was an evolutionary process; like issues and problems in life, the horse wasn't static.

We must remember this in our problem solving techniques, and in our own evolution. Sometimes we forget that time really isn't standing still, that we live every moment of our lives in an evolutionary process. By the time I've said this, time has passed. So, if I see a problem, or we have a problem, we usually mull it over and if we are courageous enough, attempt to dissect it; then we throw it up in the air, burn incense and do all sorts of wonderful stuff, but it's still there. We cannot figure it out.

Reason? It's because the problem that we're trying to dissect probably no longer exists in the form we remember it. It's morphed into another incarnation, and progressed in some other way. It hasn't remained still. So, what we have to do is learn to get ahead of the problem and not allow it to overpower us. Look to the future.

Foresight is more meaningful than hindsight. We can all easily say "we should have done x" when y, really was what we did. We should not spend our lives chasing after ever illusive dreams until we collapse exhausted and watch them cantering away; like my circus horse. Anticipate the evolutionary ground in front of the dream, problem, or relationship issue. Do not spend useless hours second guessing why something did not work. Hindsight is wasted time, unless we actually learn a lesson which we can project into our next dilemma. Have you ever tried to ambush a problem?

Life does not exist in a nice neat little box that we can pick up today, a month in advance, or a year from now and expect it to look the same. It will have changed like the seasons. Spend too much time dressing for winter and you will end up sweltering in summer.

I guess I must have the circus in my blood, because one of my great-uncles actually was a lion-tamer and strong man in a circus. Although the photographs of him dressed like Tarzan in a leopard skin outfit are long lost, the indelible memory lingers on.

My next "circus class" occurred years later in Vancouver when I attended a performance of the Russian State Circus with my wife and two elder daughters. This time we were seated in a row of seats right inside the arena, within touching distance of thundering Cossack hooves, and flashing sabres. Again, my chance at immortality came, when into the arena strode an impressive strong man dressed in a leopard skin. This colossus proceeded to demonstrate his prowess by tossing barbells into the air as though they were feathers. And once again, at an appropriate moment it was time for some interaction with the public.

Challenge accepted, I found myself in the centre of the arena beside the Russian Titan. He proceeded to flex his massive muscles before juggling heavy metal balls which he hefted into the air. Now, I'm not a huge, muscular person, so he anticipated as he handed me one of the metal balls that I would drop it. I remember looking at him as I accepted the challenge. He smirked as I pretended that the ball was too heavy for me to hold; made pretence of dropping it, and then lifted it into the air. It was incredibly heavy but adrenalin was my assistant.

He picked up a larger ball; did the same thing several times and each time I managed to muster up the strength to hold it while managing to "ham it up" a little bit, pretending to the audience that I was holding it easily. I could see him becoming annoyed; even perturbed, and then, ultimately, after another ball was thrown to me and I managed to hold that one, he smiled in a strange sort of way, raised my arm in the air and as the crowd applauded, returned to my cheering children.

But what did I learn from this exercise? Of course I was brought out there for entertainment value. This man was going to use my perceived, inherent weakness to his advantage. The weaker I appeared, the stronger he would appear. The name of the game was to humiliate me. His intention was to demonstrate my weakness to the audience by exposing my so-called inability to lift the cannon balls. Unfortunately for him I did succeed.

Several lessons were taught that day. The first is that by using me to extol his own virtues; his own ego and strength, he would appear stronger and I would become weaker. We encounter people like that all through life. They seem to feel that in life the smaller they can make people around them feel, the larger they will appear – and they tackle this in different ways.

They belittle and bully people, and indulge in constant gossip; dissecting a person until they find a weakness and then they put the knife in which they twist; feeling that for them to succeed has to be on the back of others. Our foundation should be solid: built of love and ability, not on the downfall of others.

Years ago I remember reading that in some pre-colonial cultures, when a temple or other edifice was being constructed; some live slaves were thrown into the foundation. In a bizarre sort of way, the structure was built on the pain of others. We must dedicate ourselves to living in a safe, harmonious environment on our own loving foundation: minus the pain and suffering of others.

Another lesson I learned in the Russian circus was that just as the metal balls come in different sizes and weights, so do problems and issues. So, if we try to tackle them and life in the same way, with the same emphasis, with the same problem solving techniques, we will probably not succeed. From the first ball to the last one, I had to escalate my adrenalin and my mind over matter, to combat the additional weight.

Think of your problems like that. Some problems are minuscule. Other problems are monumental. Different strategies mean different results.

have a sense of their internal core; a sense of knowing that this world is a stepping stone to the next. Enjoy this one and you will also enjoy the next one

So, those are the things I pray for; my mantra of serenity, security, spirituality, safety. These are the things I think are really important. It does become like a litany, "dear God please give my family…" And, maybe, it is partly for me. If I know they're happy, then I am happy; if I know they're safe, then I feel safe; if I see them serene, then I'm serene if I know they're advancing in a spiritual way, then I feel good about that as well. Happiness is sharing, and basking in its reciprocity.

But everything in creation has a linchpin which holds the disparate components together: in unison. When the linchpin is pulled out chaos develops as the entity falls apart. It is the catalyst that triggers a reaction, whether in relationships or in the building blocks of our everyday life. But the positive spin on this is that if we can discover this integral linchpin and disable it, then our problems will disintegrate, because there will be nothing to hold them together.

The linchpin can be as simple as a trigger-word in a discussion. Everything consequently builds up against that wall, until it ultimately becomes what appears to be an insurmountable obstacle. Learn where these linchpins are and disable them before monumental issues arise.

We've all seen old movies where someone is trapped inside an eerie room in an old castle; there are no apparent doors to be seen, but we all know that there must exist a secret escape passage accessed by an obscure button, a slightly protruding brick in the wall, or an enigmatic statue. By trial and error the linchpin to safety is found, and therefore if we are ever trapped in that place again, we will know exactly where to find the linchpin to freedom. We should think of our problems like that.

Review situations that make us uncomfortable; positions we have been in where we just want to get out. If we find a technique that works, keep that in our little safety box and bring it out at the appropriate time. Situations although appearing to be different will have great similarities. So, when those circumstances occur, reach into that little magical box and press the appropriate button, or twist the head of the little statue hidden there, then out of that secret room of despair we will escape! We will all find the linchpin to success if we persist.

Finding the linchpin is being able to control the drawbridge across the moat surrounding a castle —of despair or happiness. If we are inside and want to escape, we have the linchpin key. If we are outside and wish to retreat to a place of peace and contentment, again we have the key.

Visualize walking through the countryside on a perfect idyllic sunny day. The sky is impenetrably blue; leaves are rustling with contentment; a stream is laughing beside us and when we glance upwards, the sun gently warms our face. The feeling we experience is one of euphoria. We are uplifted, energized and excited as though we are wrapped in a warm and comfortable blanket. Then a dark sombre shadow creeps along the path staining everything it covers in shadow. Our world cools down in this new grey reality.

Psychologically we feel sad because the sun has gone. In this example, the sky has become entirely covered with sun-obscuring clouds. Now consider this; the same effect would result if just one minuscule cloud decided to sit over the face of the sun. As long as that little cloud sat there it's going to have the same result as if the entire sky was covered in cloud. Remember, all it takes if we let it, is to have a small issue obscure the sunny face of optimism.

Think about that. Sometimes little issues are like that little cloud. They can have the same impact upon us as monumental problems. What we must do is eradicate every little cloud of discontent before it welcomes a myriad of other small clouds to join in clouding our entire existence. Blow every grey smudge in our sky away as it appears, and maintain sunny warmth of optimism.

If we have allowed clouds to gather around us, and then we decide to clear the air and allow the sun to shine around us once again; how do we do that? Do we just huff and puff and hope that the sky will clear, or do we do it in a planned concerted manner.

By flailing around at the cloudy atmosphere valiantly but in a haphazard way, all we will succeed in doing is exhausting ourselves, and when we glance up, the sky will still be hidden behind a solid cloud cover. Remember, all it takes to allow the sun to pour its life-giving bounty on us, is to remove the little cloud that it is covering its face. One small problem; with monumental consequences removed, and the sun will thaw the world around us. Spend a lifetime trying to remove clouds from all across the sky, but leaving the linchpin cloud over the sun, is a lifetime spent in exhausting futility. Choose battles wisely; find the linchpin issue, and the heavens will bathe us in optimism.

Once the sun starts to blossom around us, we will feel our other problems melt away. Remember, too, we are what we desire; we are what we think; we are what we make. We do have choices. We can choose to live in the shadow of the dark side or the sun of the light side.

I remember one beautiful sunny day in Scotland, playing with friends in one of the streets in our neighbourhood. In a nanosecond, it started to rain on the other side of the street. Here we were standing in sunshine, yet a few yards away, the rain was falling; so of course, as children, we ran back and forth from sunshine into rain.

As kids, we ventured into the cloudy rainy side of the street for fun, but in life, how much better if we choose to stay in the light side and not venture into the darkness. Being light-hearted or light-minded allows us to drift and float above the dull drabness of negativity and darkness.

Another weather lesson has just occurred. Out of my window the sky has just become obscured by driving snow. However once I am snug in bed, and the snow has stopped falling, I can ignore it. Right? No! Just when I am about to fall asleep, I will hear the thumping sounds of snow falling off of branches on to my roof. Out of mind, but not out of reality. Just like problems, when we ignore them, we tend to say, "out of mind, therefore if I ignore them they will disappear." However, just like the snow on the trees waiting to fall on us once again when we least expect it, so our problems will reappear at unexpected times.

Simply put, when a problem first appears, don't let it grow and fester; tackle it quickly. In previous chapters we have talked about the various ways of doing that. Whether you tackle it head on or obliquely like stones skipping across the surface of the water, just don't let a small cloud become a major sky-obscuring one until the whole of your heaven is covered by pessimistic dullness. Similarly, do not allow your problems to lie like banks of snow on trees, waiting to drop on you when you least expect it.

Lessons and teachers surround us, and recently I have learned a couple of things from Reba our independently-minded cat. For quite a few years she has been the self-appointed queen of the house. She could sleep where she wanted; she commanded all the attention she needed; and then the unthinkable happened! We became foster parents, you might say, to a kitten. Thomas was a little rambunctious male with an "attitude." Reba suddenly realized that she was no longer the queen of our house and to add insult to injury, this rival also teased, chased, stole her favourite sunny napping place on the couch, and as he is much bigger physically, she started to feel uncomfortable and vulnerable to his attacks.

Now, Reba could tackle this problem kitten in different ways. She could ignore Thomas; she could just say "I recognize you as a problem but I choose to ignore you. I'll pretend you don't exist and whenever I see you or think of you, I'll simply banish you from my thoughts."

Denial solves nothing, because the problem will still exist; but only if we allow it to. Alternately, we can accept that the problem exists and ask "what am I going to do about it?" Reba could state that yes she accepts that Thomas co-exists with here, but her definition of acceptance will mean engaging in continual warfare; she's going to fight the kitten every chance she can get– and Thomas is going to reciprocate. The end result will of course be a continual life of stress and worry with no real resolution to their impasse.

Another way is to say she accepts his presence, but whenever an imminent interaction looms on the horizon, she can climb to the highest ledge she can find, and simply ignore Thomas. Luckily the kitten lacks the ability to reach her unapproachable haven. Sounds familiar? Whenever we feel that we are about to engage in the thrust and parry of conflict, the simple answer is to walk away. Retreating from stupidity is not cowardice, but an act of self-enabling bravery.

We have accepted that a cloud is obscuring our horizons, and we have come to terms with it. By ignoring it, it will still obscure our life-giving sunlight. But by moving above the cloud, like in Reba's haven, the sun will again shine brightly on us. Leave problems in the dust of discontent and rise above them. Fretting and fussing weaves into a blanket of stress.

So, we can choose different paths. We can practice denial and receive the punches; or we can rise higher than the issue and live stress-free without resorting to the punch-bag syndrome, where we will punch an issue for eternity and still find it is there.

Always remember that in life our thoughts become our words, which become our actions. They in turn form our character through the habits we have developed, and ultimately we will design our own destiny. Make it one of worth and quality, love and compassion, where clouds exist only to add character to a flawless sky, and where problems dissolve into ashes and dust through lack of interest.

Earlier we spoke about the voodoo doll syndrome in which an antagonistic partner takes delight in needling us to despair. However if we engage in self-flagellation by repeating the phrase, "I am not worthy" then by using ourselves as a pin cushion of misery, we will in fact become not worthy. Remember, that what you tell your subconscious is what you become.

We will evolve into the essence of who we were born to be by challenging ourselves to fly. By using the magic of word alchemy, we can take the letters VOL out of the words evolve and let them become our mantra as we fly. "Volare." Let's fly….was a sixties song, and by allowing our imagination to fly, we can probe questions like, "how can I paint the wind?  How can I sculpt the wind?  How can I redesign the wind?"

By trying to resolve what appear to be irresolvable questions, it becomes easier to respond to simpler questions which confront us. We should stretch our minds and permit wisdom to flow in on blossoms of understanding. A closed mind is a dark dismal prison where chains of uncaring scream abuse at the sun of enlightenment. Try to sculpt the wind or paint it with the eyes of an uncluttered child.

Society has changed our Age of Reason into an Age of Treason, where we reject our true innocent essence, and fumble with the discord of whittling ourselves into facsimiles of what others expect. If we retain the purity of unclouded eyes, a brighter world will be the result.

Purity or clarity of thought is the catalyst for positive thinking and constructive action. Although I heard someone talking a little while ago about positive thinking and they said "that's garbage, there's really no such thing as positive thinking; it has no effect upon you because everything is pre-ordained."  I disagree, because it has been proven that negative thoughts precipitate sickness and even death.

Think in terms of Shakka's witch doctor pointing his finger at a person and saying "you're going to die." Belief in that negative action led to death. Just as negativity is the forerunner to a cloudy existence, positive thinking and subsequent constructive action leads to sunshine and cloud-free skies.

Apply positive reinforcement to those around you, and also to yourself. Give yourself a pat on the back for deeds well done. Is it wrong to praise yourself? No, as long as it is not conducted in the manner of the Pharisee in the synagogue saying "God, I'm a wonderful person; I'm better than everyone else, look at me, I give more money than everyone else." I don't mean that. Acting in a positive way is its own reward. Light the beacon and illuminate the world.

Jealousy is an impediment to positive thinking and action. How can you sincerely congratulate someone for what they have achieved, if inside you are seething with a sense of "that should be me?" Remember that we are all unique with our own distinct talents and abilities. As long as we remain true to ourselves we will all become stars.

Being true to ourselves reminds me of a story I heard somewhere, in which a man spent a lifetime seething with anger and disbelieve at how everyone but him seemed to have a break, and had risen above their lot in life. The creator called him eventually and said, "the good news is that I am not going to judge you on how you compare to others, but on why you have always been absent from being the best you could have been." So let us shine our individual stars and add to the brilliance of life's constellation.

Now, you might think life would be certainly easier if everyone thought the same way, and if everyone was on the same wavelength. Some ideologies have tried to adopt that philosophy, but no, for each of us there is a separate eternal expectation, and that is our challenge. Evolve and sing Volare as we soar towards success and happiness. VOL, the three letters to remember.

# *thirty five*

## Ocean Lessons And Where Forward Can Be Backward

**Teachers come in all shapes and sizes**

My mantra in this book is that our lives are affected by forces around us which layer us with clues to life's resolutions; that is if we are vigilant enough to see them. For example, as I live facing the ever-changing ocean, I'm affected by the sounds and sights of its diversity; the freighters, tug boats and sail boats that pass by; the waves and the wind. And the eternal interchange between the weather, the sky and the ever-patient water.

Today is a classic blustery winter's day. Outside my picture window the forest canopy is swaying violently back and forth, small branches are flying through the air, and the water of the sound is covered in whitecaps. Careening over the crest of the waves I can see spirals of spindrift. I love that word "spindrift." It means the spray that dances in front of the wind as it charges across the water. As I watched it this day, I thought of my "spindrift principle." It means simply that every action is conducted by something else.

Now, there are many ways in life of travelling on our journey. If we visualize our body as a sail boat, obviously we will need a wind to provide our momentum. The stronger the wind, the faster the speed, the heavier the load, the stronger the wind needs to be. Now, what happens as problems, inhibitions, life's issues, self-doubts, and a litany of other baggage crushes us in daily stress. The more we pile upon ourselves or accept, the stronger the wind we need to give us momentum.

179

The wind is like the adrenalin we need to keep us pumped. The heaviest burden ultimately requires a gale-force wind to move it along.

We start off in life as a child, dancing along like a care-free butterfly requiring hardly any breeze. But the older we become and the more we become enmeshed in the barrage of Age of Treason's immovable problems, we have to conjure up stronger and stronger winds to move us forward. We have not learned yet the magic of VOL, to fly high and fast. So, in order to pitifully stagger through life, we learn to conjure up an adrenalin rush: the energy force we need, until we're perpetually on the point of collapse.

What we need to learn to do is to jettison some of the overpowering burdens that we have accumulated, and what a difference we will find. The more we dump overboard, the faster and easier our trip will become.

Remember I spoke earlier about the old power boat that I spent months rebuilding, and how I learned about "planing'"over the waves, without the bow of the boat pushing through the waves and expending a lot of power? The lesson was that once initial energy was spent on getting the boat on top of the waves, there was less resistance. Likewise in life: the spindrift principle teaches that if we are perpetually head down in the water, plodding through the waves like the tug boats I see from my window, we will be continually exhausted.

So, the two rules of the Spindrift Principle are: expend a burst of positive energy at the start of the journey, and get on top of the "waves of life" and glide effortlessly. Secondly, at the same time, start the process of jettisoning lingering problems and we won't need a gale-force wind to push us along.

The wind also teaches us about trust. I remember reading about the spirit quests among some indigenous tribes in which young men of a certain age would go up into the mountains and meditate, while they waited for dreams or visions to reveal their life's purpose.

One test entailed learning to stand on a ledge while testing and teasing the power of the wind. Ultimately they would stand on the precipitous narrow ledge overlooking a looming chasm below and spread their arms like wings. When they felt the wind was strong enough they would lean forward and embrace the wind with nothing between them and the chasm yawning in front of them.

As they leaned forward into the wind they would learn to trust their instincts, and gauge if the power of the wind at that particular moment was robust enough to hold them, and prevent them from tumbling into eternity. Their trust and intuitive instinct would allow them to assess and judge life's challenges, and embrace them wholeheartedly. To meet challenges we require the commitment, trust and courage to lean into the wind of change at precisely the appropriate time.

In time we will learn to trust our own instincts; to always think positively; to jettison the problems we have accumulated, while expending less energy. And as our commitment to change increases, so will our feelings of self-worth.

Another analogy linked to the spindrift principle centres around how problems come in different guises [or disguises], and how we often try to resolve them in the same way. As an example: a hang-gliding acquaintance of mine used to spend every week-end soaring above local mountains in his fragile craft.

The ritual of attaching himself to the hand glider; running down a gentle slope and then leaping off into the wild blue yonder from a convenient precipice never varied. He'd glide for an hour or so, then land and do the same thing over again. Safety preparation was of course an integral part of the hang-gliding ritual. One day however although it was getting late in the day, he looked at the sun and figured he had about a half hour of light still left. He decided to have one last run.

Grabbing the control bar of the hang glider, he leaped off the mountain, while realizing at the same moment that he had not attached the safety harness to himself! So, basically, he was dangling like a trapeze artist hanging from a trapeze bar in a circus – but without a safety net. And the wind was taking a delight in trying to pluck him from his precarious perch. Now would have been a good time to pray!

Now, hang gliders have a bag at the back, rather like a sleeping bag, that you slip your legs into for support, comfort and the added protection of the additional safety harness. He however was too intent on hanging on to attempt to slip his legs into the safety bag. The other problem he had, of course, was that he had to manipulate the glider so he wouldn't plummet to his death. Eventually he managed to attach the safety harness, slip his legs into the bag and land safely. Needless to say that was his last hang-gliding experience.

Now, the lesson learned here, is that attempting to achieve the same result in different circumstances requires a separate set of strategies. If the hang-glider was sitting safely on the ground in a grassy meadow, it would be easy to manipulate your legs into the bag, because there would be no dire consequences if you failed. However trying the same manoeuvre in flight presents its own challenges, so different strategies had to be implemented.

How often do we figure out how to resolve a problem and say "Great I've mastered it." Again, the same problem arises but this time our previous solution doesn't seem to work as well, if at all. Why? Because the circumstances have changed. We spoke before about the evolution of problems, the escalation and how we have to adapt our problem solving techniques to master the different circumstances.

What do tugboats and huskies have in common? They teach us about gently easing into issues. If a tugboat has to tow a heavily laden barge, the worse thing to do is to throw the engine into full speed ahead. The result will be that the tow rope will spring taught like a spring and pull the tugboat back on its stern. Similarly, with the sled dogs; if they just leap forward they're going to be thrown backwards with the force. Whereas if they both move forward gently, just applying incremental pressure to get the momentum up, they can move forward easily.

We hear people say "God he throws himself into his work, he's like a bull in a china shop, he just charges right in there." If you're trying to resolve an impasse in a discussion and you leap into top speed immediately with no preamble to set the stage, the result very likely will be a rebuff. However, if you very gently increase the discussion to a comfortable level, you both will be able to find a resolution without clashing sabres.

Some years ago I took a trip on a small cargo freighter up the rugged coastline of British Columbia. We nuzzled into isolated coves to drop supplies off at logging camps; visited beach- combing camps and fish farms; Indian encampments and the like. The freighter was a lifeline stitching the communities together. The lesson I learned was in prioritizing.

Before the freighter departed on the trip, the Captain looked at his charts to prioritize which port or destination would be visited first and which would be last on the list. The second task was to assess the eclectic cargo which would be loaded in reverse: so the cargo destined for the final destination was loaded first, and conversely the cargo for the first destination was loaded last. And it worked with great efficiency!

Now, if we can try to prioritize the multitude of issues that continually bombard us, we will certainly lead a more stress-free life. Everything is incrementally stored inside us. Like in the freighter, we have all these "to dos" stored inside us and our task is to arrange them in order of relevance and importance. Some we will realize are not worth bothering about, and they will be tossed overboard. The more meaningful ones will be selected according to their immediacy and consequences.

The wind is still pounding my window panes, but now it has changed directions. Again, just as I assumed that it was coming from the North West, it changed to the North East. Another lesson, in the changeability of life. Prepare for the unexpected, and you won't be surprised. What does this really mean? Well, when we're trying to perfect our sense of things tangible and intangible, we shouldn't always face in the same direction.

Vigilance in life is simply being aware of who and what we are, and what is surrounding and affecting us at any moment. Be prepared to spin around sometimes unexpectedly and watch something different and exciting almost sneaking behind you. What was relevant today may lie on the slag heap of discarded obsolescence tomorrow. As our tastes, desires and sense of who we are changes, so will our ultimate destination. Who said that it is wrong to change direction in mid-stream? You always have to be prepared for different directions. Don't always assume that the direction you're taking is the right one.

This analogy about the passenger ferries that prowl past my window explains this. These ships really don't have a bow or a prow; there's no front and no back. As a friend once said "they've got the pointy bit at both ends." The reason is that when the ferry gets to a dock it noses straight into it. Then when it is time to depart again, the Captain goes to the other "pointy end" of the ship and steers straight out again. This process eradicates the need to reverse in tight spaces.

This all seems like a dichotomy which traps lots of us as we sail through life. Sometimes we are caught in the middle of something and don't know which way is forward and which way is back, because both ways look like the right way. The danger occurs by leaping into a decision we think is right and once again we seem to be going in the right direction – it's the pointy end after all and we are going towards something.

But, suddenly things don't seem quite right. We don't feel a sense of momentum towards a positive destination; 'this really isn't the way I want to go, but it's the pointy end and it must be right." Hey, turn around; don't be scared to go back in the other direction. Don't be scared to backtrack sometimes.

When we start constructing something and right from the beginning we know it's not quite right, so we improvise a little, and it still isn't right but with senseless commitment we just keep building and building. We are busy, active, we are keeping ourselves occupied but we are not building anything that is going to be structurally strong and that will last. Return to Go and start again.

Stop and reflect! Just because we are moving doesn't mean that we are heading in the right direction. Yes we are underway, but is that spot on the horizon really our destination? Always check both "pointy ends." But always remember, when we are trying to rebuild ourselves, it is not always necessary to throw everything away. Retain relevance: discard irrelevance.

An example of this occurred last year when I decided to rebuild my decks. Our house has a thousand square feet of wooden decks and one day I noticed that there were a few rotted boards in different areas. Problem! There were two things I could do. One was to rip the whole deck out and build a brand spanking new sturdy deck. The other was to renovate.

The latter was my choice, and I decided I would remove the rotted areas and other areas of concern: the bad planks, and reinforce these areas with posts and joists. This was obviously a less expensive way of doing it and when it was finished the deck was as strong as ever. So! It cost less, took less time to do it and with less effort.

Now, many times relationships end in divorce, because like my deck with the rotted planks they have problems, and some people just decide to throw the whole thing away and find someone else with whom to build a new life – a new deck; hence a new partner.

The other way is to look at the situation and say "there's a lot of inherent strength still here. The whole relationship isn't bad. Sure there are some rotted areas and other areas we need to work on, so let's tackle those." We can tackle them a little bit at a time, but commitment is needed, and both partners need to work together. Gradually with patience, the problem areas are ripped out, and the entire structure reinforced. When bliss once again descends, the relationship has been given a fresh coat of paint with a new zest for life.

The same applies to our own inadequacies. We may sit and reflect on our perceived the "I am not worthy" syndrome. By saying that, we are really reinforcing this negative viewpoint. Take the other tack. Sit back and in a quiet moment look at what's causing the concern. Our self-esteem isn't as good as it should be because our stress level is high, we don't have any problem solving techniques and our finances are in bad shape. There are many things that trigger concerns. It could be physical ailments, mental problems or spiritual concerns. But the first step towards resolution is the most important one.

Like the tugboats and the huskies, we must just slowly lean into the problem and encourage momentum to develop. Once we're gliding over our barrage of soul-debilitating issues, we will feel energized to reach inside and enthusiastically rebuild. But how do we know we're really improving? How do we know there is some success in all this?

I remember years ago in Scotland on my meanderings along quiet country roads encountering milestones, usually nestling in a fringe of rustling grass. The stones which indicated the number of miles to the next village were typically moss-covered with the name of the now barely decipherable village.

The milestones had been built in a slower age when people relied on their own two legs or a horse and buggy as their main form of transportation, but now with the speed of fleeting automobiles these reminders of the past were obsolete. Lying buried in their nest of weeds, grass and moss beside the highway they however serve as a reminder that times and circumstances change.

The milestones ably served their purpose when they were built, but the current lesson they teach us in their obsolescence, is that objectives must always be relevant to present times and circumstances. We simply cannot resolve problems and dictate our objectives the same way we did years ago. From the halcyon, quiet, countrified milestone days we now live in an age of accelerated lifestyles. So, we have to make objectives that are current, pertinent and consistent with the new situation.

Our goals and objectives must be visible to us as we close our eyes and trace our paths to our ultimate fulfilment. As a child we painted by numbers, and that is still relevant as we work at conjuring up our new life. We need visions in life and if we don't have them, we will end up wandering in a haphazard manner; going in proverbial circles. We may find what we are searching for, but discovering that passionate bliss will be by luck and chance.

Think of a jigsaw puzzle. If we are shown a couple of hundred jigsaw pieces lying on a table and told to assemble them, we may be lucky in eventually assembling them, but the process will be like groping in the dark because we have no idea what the final picture is meant to look like.

Now, the corollary of that is: If we are shown a picture of the jigsaw – even if we don't always have the picture in front of us– we can imprint it in our minds. We will know when we start the puzzle that the image is of the Eiffel Tower, the Leaning Tower of Pisa, a mountain, lake, or a sail boat –and we will have a sense of what we are heading for. Without that clear, pre-determined picture, we could struggle for an eternity without knowing.

We must endeavour to clearly define the direction we are taking and to paint with great clarity what the end result is going to look like; how the final port of call is exactly as we imagined. Define and then systematically refine what we visualize.

## *thirty six*

# The Joyful Paradox Of Going In Circles

**Circles, smoothness, and the perfection of imperfection**

Circles are really meaningful, as in the analogy of the circle of life with no beginning and no end. On the plains of North America, the steppes of Mongolia and in the inhospitable Arctic, the indigenous peoples would build circular houses of hides, felt and blocks of snow. Why? Because they would not blow away. If they had been square however, they would catch the wind like sails and blow towards the distant horizons.

I remember seeing a photograph of an old church on one of the isolated Scottish Hebridean Islands, designed "in the round" so the devil wouldn't have a corner to hide in. Think about that! When there are no corners, there is no place for dust to gather, and it's easier to clean the inside of a circular object than a square thing; think of life like that, our journey; our vision of the future. Think of the picture we want to achieve with no harsh, sharp corners in it. Smooth!

Ponder on the simplicity of worry stones. A friend gave me one once when she came back from Mexico. It was a simple smooth round stone which you could roll in your fingers and feel the sensation of soothing smoothness. Now, if it was a square, an oblong or octagonal shape, if it had edges, it wouldn't have the same relaxing, tactile feeling similar to a pacifier to a child. When you see a baby sucking its thumb it's a pacifier. The worry stone, with its roundness and smoothness is almost like a pacifier for adults.

That is what our lives should be when we eradicate all the rough edges. When a ship's hull is clean and polished with no rough edges, it cuts easily and dramatically through the water and gets to its destination faster. It expends less energy, less power and it provides a gentle ride. If the hull is encrusted with barnacles and weed growth, it labours and struggles through the water. It may arrive at its destination in the end but it will be an exhausting and slow journey.

So, the barnacles and weeds are similar to heavy worries that we carry with us all the time. We have to take our ship out of the water and clean off and jettison the barnacles and weeds so that we can sail again faster and smoother into the future. If we don't do that we will feel we are moving forward and, yes, we are, but we're also draining our energy. Energy will be drained in negative ways. Move forward thinking positively of your vision.

If you sit close to the furnace of your passion and the dream starts to melt, then it's not really your dream. You thought it was but if it melts away into oblivion, it's not. Your true dream, soaring vision, genuine passion, overwhelming desire in the furnace of your heart, soul and being, will be forged into a stronger more dynamic vision. So don't hang onto something because you think that's what you think you need. Because what you think you need, in fact, may be an impostor draining you and inhibiting your final arrival at your rightful destination.

The revelation may come at a time when you're least expecting it so you should always be prepared. Random thoughts may come into your mind, not to be discarded because you feel they have no relevance to you. We must always be prepared for the unexpected because it may be the thunderbolt from the heavens that will define our destination. And, maybe, like the road to Damascus incident where Saint Paul was blinded and had an epiphany, you will find your new way.

As we discussed before, years ago, again in Scotland while I was hitch-hiking through the Highlands, I came into a small fishing village. Two vignettes were being played in front of me. On a pebbly beach a young boy was sitting mending a fishing net. He was weaving the net almost like a spider weaving its web. He was of an age when soon he would be out on the ocean, fishing for his livelihood.

Then I looked further up the beach and saw an old man sitting on a rock also weaving his "cobweb," his net. He was of an age when he could no longer venture out onto the ocean, but what he was doing, in many ways, was weaving that net to catch his memories. I walked up to this venerable fisherman who smiled and said, "I've spent my life fishing, but my creaking bones and aching back convinced me eventually to stop, but now when I sit here weaving this net, I'm fishing again; I'm sifting the oceans, although now it's memories I catch."

What is a memory? A memory is something that has happened in our past that we can bring forward and enjoy, relish and relive. Obviously, there are two major types of memories – a positive memory like a special Christmas morning as a child which fills us with the happiness of an innocent time in our lives. Or there's a negative memory, perhaps of a car crash that we were in years ago.

When we weave our nets and cast them into the oceans of our memories, in many ways we've been made who we are through the negative as well as the positive recollections. The negatives have perhaps made us stronger and forged us in a way that makes us more capable of moving into the future. But if the recollection makes us feel uncomfortable with an inherent sadness, it will drain our energy on a downward spiral. Any time that improper memory approaches us, we should just turn away and let it wither. Forget the negative memory and keep the positive ones.

Be like that old man on the beach. You can sit and fish for your memories, sieving and discarding the negative while reinforcing and building on the positive memories.

All too often when we're trying to achieve some goal we say, "I'm going to strive for perfection." At school, perfection would result in "ten out of ten and a gold star." I feel that the following story is worth repeating. Some years ago I was painting in an Oriental style. I enjoy the moody, misty landscapes resplendent with the signature Chinese red seals called the "chop" you would find on these paintings. So I decided in future when I did any painting I would have my own Chinese seal made that would indicate who I am and what I stand for. We have reviewed this story earlier, but it is worth repeating.

I went to a small art store in Chinatown and advised the proprietor behind the counter that I would like to purchase a seal. He turned round and handed me one of the generic ones on display, obviously mass produced for the tourist trade. Courteously I said, "No, I want one that says who I am, what I stand for, what my vision in life is, so that when I put it on my page it is unique."

The old man then spent some time chatting with me until he finally said, "you can pick up your seal next week." When I returned the following week, he'd made the most exquisite, carved seal for me, but I noticed that although the bottom was perfect, there was a little nick in the edge of it. I didn't say anything but when he saw me looking at it said: "this was too perfect; imperfection is perfect; perfect is imperfection." I wasn't sure what he really meant and I never did discuss it further with him. I think that what he meant was, if we think we've reached perfection, there will be no incentive to carry on.

I think it's similar to a writer, artist or musician who achieves his greatest work at a very early age. He's raised his bar of perfection so high that he may never manage to climb over that bar again, or reach that exalted height again. He may give up or he may think he's achieved perfection so what's the point of doing anything else, whereas, the average person will persist in chasing their vision of perfection. They will keep trying to perfect their art.

We can liken it to some children who are born to eminently successful parents, perhaps a Nobel Peace Prize winner a famous actor; a famous author, painter or musician. They're born to genius and at an early age the child realizes that he's not a genius and he'll never reach the exalted height his parent has. So he gives up. It's almost like "if I can't have perfection, I'll have nothing." So, this seal, this Chinese chop that the man made for me wasn't perfect, but in many ways, to me, it defines perfection because each time I see it I feel I have to do better; I have to advance, to persevere.

Visions and versions of perfection come in many guises because we all look at things differently. I remember a movie I saw years ago about a man who had been badly scarred in the Second World War and who subsequently married a girl who was, supposedly, extremely plain. Nevertheless she saw him as a handsome, dashing partner and he saw her as the most exquisite creature the world had ever made. They saw each other through different eyes and as long as the two of them were together, they were in bliss. They saw perfection in each other.

But others saw simply a scarred man and a plain girl. One day the couple overheard someone describing the "unfortunate couple" and as they looked at each other, for the first time, they saw what others were seeing. However, the strength and overwhelming love they shared overcame that and they realized that what they witnessed in each other was the truth of perfection. They saw the beauty and inner inherent beauty in each other and discarding what others saw, they become once again the perfect soul mates. Perfection is in the eye and soul of the beholder.

We must never permit others to continually belittle our hopes and desires and in so doing shatter our passion. An example occurs when you are a child engaged in some wonderful project. You decide to create something, whether a painting or a special wooden box to hold all of your treasures. Someone states. "Look that's not the way you do that, you should do it this way." Or they make the mistake of asking "what is that you're doing?" Usually the child is simply engrossed in the thrill of discovery as they add a piece here and there. When an intruder says "if you add this, that and the next thing, it will become a really nice car or a boat, or whatever." Someone else has taken control of the vision eliminating the joy of serendipitous exploration and the fun vanishes. Always retain your own vision!

There are always naysayer who enjoy the thrill of deflating others' dreams with "hey what are you doing there, you'll never make a success of that; no-one's going to buy that product, what you're doing is passé. No-one likes that music anymore; you'll never build that without doing this." For them there is perpetual negativity with never a word of encouragement and always a reason why you can't achieve something.

If we hear this negativity enough times it can cast a cloud over us and the sun of our vision will become obscured. The first stage of surrendering is to procrastinate. Before the barrage of intrusive negativity enveloped you, you were happily engaged in a project that you loved. But now if you surrender to their thoughts the end result is that you may end up pulling back from the project and eventually feeling that maybe they're right and maybe the best course is to forget your dream. But just consider that around that next bend your vision is waiting for you to be complete.

When my kids were younger we used to pack up all of our camping gear and head out onto the great summer highways. We had a tent trailer that was a bit long on the tooth, but off we would go heading down the highways along the coast of Oregon; to California or to the sunny desert sandy Interior of British Columbia.

Typically when it got close to maybe 4:30 - 5:30 in the afternoon, we would start looking for a place to spend the night. It had to be perfect; there had to be a swimming pool, shade trees, nice view, and of course we all had a vision of our perfect camp-site. In our minds and imagination we all had different versions of our perfect haven where we would camp for the night. The scenario usually followed the script where I would say with a smile; "let's wait – just around the next bend there will be the perfect one." So we would delay stopping and around the next bend I would smile again and say "let's go round this one, I'm sure it will be the perfect one."

It would eventually get to the point where everyone was getting tired and so we would pull into a camp-site. But every time we did that I always thought that "maybe round that last bend sits the most exquisite, perfect Valhalla of a camp-site we've ever seen." I was always stretching to find that perfect place for us to spend the night. Even when we did get into a camp-site I would drive around looking for a perfect spot within that camp-site.

Now, that is like the journey we are on. Like the vision quest that we're searching for that is going to define us waiting just around that last bend. In life we could almost be reaching an epiphany; almost at the point of achieving that incredible dream – then all these negative gossips come along and end the journey. Sadly we then never really know what that bliss was. All we had to do was take one more step around that corner and embrace our destiny.

When I think of my Chinese friend who made the Chinese seal for me, I think about that lack of perfection in the seal. It's almost like the horizon in many ways; you can never reach the horizon. In other words, if I was writing a poem, or doing a painting, if it was perfect it would mean I had reached a horizon and there was nothing beyond it. But when my friend made my "chop"; he made that little nick in the seal, he made it possible for me to pursue the horizon – even if I run toward the horizon, it's always a step ahead of me. You never can reach it.

That's a positive thing because, for example, if the world was flat you'd get to the horizon, but there would be nothing beyond, it would just end.  Our horizons extend into the inner realms – and I'm not just talking about the physicality of life, I'm talking about delving, exploring, sailing and searching into the spiritual realms.  Always search beyond the horizon.

The horizons are in some ways milestones.  On trips when we reach a milestone there is another and another beyond it until our destination is reached.  In life we have all these horizons to pursue until ultimately we arrive at "destination bliss". But on our trip we have to have belief.

I was sitting here a couple of days ago on a beautiful warm day enjoying the sun beaming in through my window. As I glanced at the corner of the room in a shadowy moment, I noticed that when a cloud obscured the sun I could see a cobweb, yet when the sun shone right on it you couldn't see it- it became invisible. That cobweb can symbolize our dream; ambition; vision: in essence the path we are taking in life.  Maybe we don't always see it in front of us but we must maintain our trust that it is still there.  Just like that cobweb's invisibility in sunlight, yet revealed in the shade.

Paths can be invisible, which takes us back to the analogy of the spindrift principles in the ocean where there are no roads, highways, signposts or traffic lights. The roads to our ocean destination do not visibly exist. When we leave one port and head for another we rely on the magic of longitude and latitude.  Sailors chart their course and follow pathways which are invisible, but they know they are there and trust in the end result.

If we always just rely on things which we can see and touch, well, ultimately our vision may be a shallow one.  But if we build an invisible vision inside that we can truly embrace, then we are experiencing a real vision.

Previously we spoke of the North American tribes and their vision quests.  When the young men got to a certain age, they endured a soul-purifying period of several days fasting. The ultimate goal was to achieve a pivotal vision that would predetermine the course of their lives.  Their totem protector would determine the sort of person they were going to become.

We can do that!  And though we don't have to sit on a mountain top to do that, we must always allow the winds of change and inquiry to blow through us and in its breath we will be reborn into the new us.

I guess there are a couple of ways to build who we are. One is to sit down and pragmatically say "I am going to be x because I think the world needs that, hence that's what I'm going to do." Then we just follow the steps; milestones of education and career advancement until we arrive hopefully at our goal. Some are lucky and achieve happiness and the fulfilment of passion and bliss but usually we just endure our career. However when we explore the cuckoo syndrome we permit our innermost feelings to surface and lead us often in another direction.

When the early explorers set sail, they didn't know exactly where they were going. They were pushing the envelope of exploration. By wandering through nameless, invisible paths through the oceans and exotic lands, they unravelled destiny just as we can.

Explorers, scientists, musicians, artists, writers and dreamers do that. They explore because they are reaching into the unknown. Searching, probing minds find nirvana while others accept their lot in life. Visionaries with passion are not sure what their destination will look like but they just know that they are drawn to pursue something. If we said to them "what will the country you're going to look like, or the final painting you are creating?" They would look at you quizzically because they are going where no-one has been before; they're going on a vision quest which will be unique, just as we are different and must resolve our own destiny.

I feel that we should always be like that. We must always be exploring, always searching. We do it in different ways. Some people do it spiritually, some people do it physically and some do it intellectually. But if we collectively explore all these things in synchronicity, we will build up a gentle breeze behind us until we're flying above the waves. We will not be like tug-boats with their heads down as they expend energy by continually battling through the waves. Our body will be like a very fine, perfectly tuned sail boat that the gentle breeze dances along on gossamer wings: almost flying above the water with no effort.

## *thirty seven*

## The Layering Of Your Inner Fire

**Bonsai wisdom; perpetual Innocence**

There is a candle sitting in front of me with its flame swaying and flickering; ever restless, never still. Through a window in my house, the ocean and trees are moving in symmetry and they seem to know what each is thinking. This morning the perpetual motion to me is like life itself. Ever changing, never looking quite the same as before and the candle in front of me is our body; the outer wax is like the layers of flesh and bones. But without the inner wick there can be no spirit, no spark or no life. We need to find and ignite our own individual spark and once we light that spark we must feed it or we will descend into mediocrity and a passionless existence.

All too often we give no coherent thought to what and who we are. We look into the mirror and see a face, a form and whether we like what we see or not, that's us. Cosmetically we can paint a different picture of ourselves; change our hair style, change the colour; lose weight or gain weight; dress in the latest fashions – but what about the inside? We've changed the colour and texture of the candle, but what we need to explore is the wick of life in the candle. We need to search for the perfect spark of combustion and once we have lit ourselves internally, this inner glow will pour like a waterfall over us and our eyes will speak to the world of what and who we are. There will be a glow about us.

Most people I think drift through life without real purpose or real desire. Yes, I guess they seek employment and security and material satisfaction, but they've sort of lost their child-like enthusiasm and excitement of discovery. Everything about them is replaced by complacency and acceptance. They've grown up. But what does grown-up really mean? Are they suddenly different people, are the lessons of childhood to be demeaned and discarded as not appropriate for adults?

I think the further we go from our source, the deeper we must go for meaning. We were always told that early man was a base, mean, sullen, non-intellectual, coarse being. But the more we learn about early man, the more we find out that he had a really deep spiritual core. Even the much maligned Neanderthal man!

Now, a tree in a dense, secluded forest has only one purpose in life, and that's to grow and reach for the sun; the light giving source of its existence. True, there is majesty in a straight, majestic tree reaching for the heavens, but I like to look at it in another way. A forest of clone-like poplars, I think, can be quite boring in its sameness.

Consider a lone bonsai tree which has struggled to exist in the cleft on a mountain ridge; it revels in its individual soul. The poplar set in a crowd of similar trees grew straight to the sky and was protected from the wind and was not affected by depletion of good soil, but it's sort of a mindless growth; it has no individual spark. Now, the twisted, contorted bonsai has truly lived its existence. It has never taken its life for granted; every moment of its existence has been spent in exploring, swaying to the forces around it. It doesn't sit mindlessly on its rock rich with good soil, but it is perpetually seeking and probing the cliff around it for pockets of soil to feed its soul. Its being drifts with the breeze, ever moving away from the wind yet up to the light. And, in its eternal searching it assumes its individuality and unique form.

The poplar, on the other hand, grows straight as an arrow and it's a mirror image to its fellow forest dwellers. But in the mindless, effortless existence, it is intrinsically weakened. I think that's like a lot of us.

We live in an age of homogenization where food looks the same and tastes the same. People listen to the same kind of music and are programmed politically, in one way. Styles are all the same, homes start to look the same. People are cloned like the poplars, but there is always the so-called eccentric, the individual who seeks his own way; and he's the bonsai.

A bonsai's clinging and contorting aesthetic beauty from a cliff's precipitous face is strong and beautiful and its inner wood is resilient and tough to a woodcutter's axe, while the poplar cuts and splits easily with no effort.

We're like that. If we have to struggle and explore life around us like the bonsai that's probing the cliff and swaying to the influences around it, while maintaining its function and purpose, it's still reaching for the heavens, for the sun, but it does it in an individual body. On the other hand, the poplar is flawed despite its outward appearance of height and strength. It's like the like-minded, complacent people who roll around; mill around like rudderless ships. The bonsai is unique for its eternal zest and non-acceptance of certainty. It places its individual stamp on what it is. If we perpetually seek the truths of what and who we are, and live in non-acceptance of complacency, we will grow strong and resilient, and we'll have a glow that will illuminate all around us.

There will be those who can see only the external image of life and they're blind to what is laying within. To them beauty will always be on the surface. Once their own external image starts to deteriorate, their beauty fades and the bloom is off the flower, their reason for existence ends because they live on the surface. Like the bonsai, those who perpetually seek inner beauty and satisfaction will always glow; they will have a child-like exuberance that will bubble like the spring of life itself.

How often do we hear "come on, stop acting like a child and grow up." What this really means is that the only important reason many people's lives grow is when adulthood is reached. How demeaning that is. Instead, think back to the innocence and naiveté of a child.

Every aspect of a child's existence is encountering strange, new, exciting experiences. Sights and sounds, smells; every nuance of excitement just bombard us. Touching, tasting, feeling, seeing, wondering is an all-pervasive blanket of growth. Nothing is taken for granted. The most mundane thing to a blasé adult is an overpowering adventure to a child. In a child's total absorption to learning, it becomes effortless, it's never boring. Every day, every moment of existence is a journey and it should be a journey for us in our never ending search for truth.

Society quickly paints conformity over a child with rules, and society's perception of what is normal and right is planted in a child. Spontaneity is replaced with routine; creativity is placed in a smooth box made out of society's sense of what is aesthetic and what is not. The outpouring of the child's creative soul is soon placed on a shelf of adulthood and deep inside the child a door is closed never to be opened again.

What we need in our lives is for someone to say "hey, start acting like a child," what's needed in our lives is more innocence, more naiveté; more acceptance of differences and perceptions and more excitement for each day.

To a child a butterfly is a fragment of a rainbow drifting from a fairy castle. To an adult it's an insect grown from a caterpillar. Obviously, there has to be a balance of rebirth into childhood; responsibility still exists; our daily toil is still there. But if we can imbue the daily realities of existence with some of the glow from the child's rainbow, we can paint a more exciting, enhancing existence. I say grow like a bonsai; see like a child.

Once our spark of life ignites the flame it will burn despite us. If I encase the flame in a glass chimney, thus protecting the flame from all external influences, the flame will point straight up. But, again, in its immobile boredom, sameness and complacency will soon occur leaving the flame to be not influenced by the forces around it. In the breezes it will soon dance and sway in an endless ballet of excitement and intrigue; its very existence will be enhanced, it will be ever changing, never still, bowing to all the influences of the universe.

Similarly, if we burn the candle of our existence with no thought or external influence, the potential balletic dance within us will be stilled and our existence will drift to its inevitable conclusion.

In our growing analytical world, we segment our existence into compartments of body, mind, soul, spirituality and so forth. But in dividing our very being into distinct, so-called components, we break the circle of life that we've spoken about and unbalances occur which disrupt our existence. Just as a rainbow relies on multi-coloured prisms to place its stamp on its existence, so we need to interweave all the different, diverse aspects of our lives.

We have previously explored how in our society some people develop into sportsmen, euphemistically called "jocks." Others become intellectuals and are termed "nerds" by some. Still others live solely in the spiritual realm and some people call them "holy-rollers" or people who don't really live in this world. But our being is only complete if we can reunite all the interrelated pieces of our existence.

I've just made a fire downstairs and in doing so, made life. If I had placed a large log in the fireplace and placed a match against it, nothing would really happen. The match may singe a small piece of the bark but true combustion would not occur. What is required is something that will burn more easily but, again, if I filled the fireplace solely with paper, the match would quickly ignite it into an instantaneous blaze. But as quickly as the flames would rise, so they would quickly die.

What is needed is an easily inflammable material like paper, and some pieces of easily-ignited slivers of wood; branches; slivers of cedar, then finally the log which will provide the ultimate continuity of the fire. Like us, each part of the fire is dependent on the rest. Only when there is interdependency does the fire of existence ignite, stay lit and provide continuity.

Some parts of our lives are like the paper in the fire – easily ignited and just as quick to die. Instant gratification – a meaningless spark of passion; a fast food meal; or action with no thought for the future, is quickly achieved and as quickly forgotten. Sad that existence, our society, is like that. It is a society of endless and meaningless gratification: instant gratification!

Our life requires and depends on us providing the fuel for all our endeavours. The more intense and enduring we require the fire to be, the more fuel we must provide. Too often we strive and dream with no results and we put it down to "que sera sera," when in reality the problem lies in us not providing the energy and commitment to achieve. The dream is there but there's no commitment to fulfill that dream; we want it to be easy. Balance is the key to all aspects of our being; devoting our entire reason to improving our bodies, for example, in isolation with no thought or care to our intellect or spirituality, resulting in a cold, meaningless life; a cold, meaningless fire even.

As one spark of our existence blossoms, the other neglected aspects will wither and imbalance results. Feed your body, mind and spirit equally and with the openness and acceptance of an optimist, you will achieve happiness and self- fulfillment. Obviously, we all will, just like the bonsai, growing in our own unique way, but that's good, it's what we should do. We are, like the snowflakes, individuals. Think deeply about what is important and relevant to your existence, whether it's the arts and sciences or just being the best you can be. Then follow that destiny but provide the energy and commitment to that. Procrastination is a perpetual roadblock.

## *thirty eight*

## Find The Stranger Within – Chamelons Need Not Apply

**Become a "dam- buster"**

The beaver dam! Even if we've never actually visited a beaver dam, we've all seen pictures of one. Initially when the beaver starts building the dam the structure leaks and still allows the rhythm of the stream to pass through. The life of the river is gradually diminished as the structure is completed, until suddenly the forces of the stream are stilled and a pond develops behind the dam.

Our lives are like that; our life forces need venting. We need to analyze and we need to allow these forces to dissipate at the appropriate time. Failure to do this gradually, permits the insidious debilitating process of building a dam within us to occur.

Initially, like the beaver dam, the rhythm of our existence will run uneventfully, just like the stream. But as we stifle emotions and unresolved issues, the dam deep within us thickens and becomes less permeable until, without knowing what is really happening, we've built a wall within our inner core, behind which pressures develop as unresolved problems stagnate in the very pool of our being.

A properly constructed dam can be vented by the beaver to release pressures and even stop the entire structure from rupturing. The beaver can pull out some strategically placed twigs and a flow of water can trickle through. A failure to ease the pressure can cause an explosion and rupturing of the dam. Just visualize a log jam developing in a mountain creek – winter rains and snow melts build up behind it until with a groan the uneasy structure just erupts into chaos and disaster.

If we contain problems, emotions and unresolved issues deep in the core of our being, we are constructing our own dams. Initially there are no perceptible effects upon us. However, an insidious, stagnant pool is developing within us. And as unresolved, unfulfilled issues jam themselves into a twisted, jumbled dam, we become a disaster waiting to happen.

If we gradually accept that we need to vent our beaver dam deep inside us; if we gradually decide to discuss problems; if we cease to procrastinate and if we make the decision to tackle issues, then we'll slowly drain the pool of pressure and equilibrium will again exist within us. Contained energy must explode. It's like the proverbial time bomb within us and we must defuse it. The combination of unrestrained anger, confusion, apathy, depression, and a total acceptance of the overwhelming sense of stagnancy, will build and your life will become meaningless.

If we wait until our dam has been constructed, the more sensitive we must be to dismantle it. The first step is to realize that this dam exists and the second step is to devote ourselves to gradually removing it. The third step is to realize that the structure is made of issues of differing magnitudes. With appropriate professional counseling, the problems can be whittled away one at a time. But oftentimes we can do it ourselves. Just as the beaver has built an interwoven wall, we must learn to unravel and slowly dismantle it until the flow and natural rhythm is restored and the stagnancy of despondency and the feeling of being unfulfilled is allowed to drain away.

We must always remember that it is easy to slip into the "manana" syndrome and utter Scarlet O'Hara's classic "I'll worry about it tomorrow." Again, tomorrow never really comes; this moment is tomorrow, today and yesterday all rolled into one. This point of our existence is always the right time to implement change and to confront the dam.

## *thirty nine*

## Knight In Shining Armour Or Princess?

**Yes it can be true**

Compromise, complacency and acceptance are three very important words drummed into us by society and the youthful, unsullied vision of a romantic knight in shining armour or a princess awaiting rescue gradually fades in our relationships. All too often we compromise and accept what is socially acceptable in a relationship. Often we are told that " he or she comes from a good family," or he or she "has a solid or secure job;" or "this is the best to come along so far so I guess I'd better hang on to this one." In other words perfection doesn't exist – and so on and so on.

Relationships that are built on the sands of compromise spend most of their time combating the drifting sands because there is no solid foundation and it leaves little energy for building the relation-ship. It's always trouble shooting; leaping headlong into a passion which is not formed with a proper balance of body, mind and soul, can leave you both swimming in a hazy pool of confusion.

Once the initial sensory gratification has dimmed, the search for mutual ties may reveal divergent viewpoints and desires that differ from your own. True efforts must be made to fuel the flame of your passion, of your togetherness, otherwise separation or dull acceptance of your circumstances will occur and you may say "this is as good as it gets" and you accept it.

As we've said: at the present time we live in a society of instanta-neous results. Every segment of our existence is played out in vignettes

203

of condensed reality. Just think of entertainment; short videos, short thirty minute, or thirty second sequences of television. Love stories are forced into three minute music videos – boy meets girl; boy loves girl; boy leaves girl or lives happily ever after. Writers write increasingly in forms of literary shorthand, I guess, leaving out the true realities of life and instead painting a haiku of meeting, loving and leaving.

Many writers produce a "paint by numbers" version of life; high-lighting the so-called positive aspect and omitting, or diminishing, the negative aspects of the story. So, the message seems to be that every-thing achievable can be had in an extremely short period of time. If you don't like this relationship just switch to another channel until you find what you want. Discard is the word. Don't bother to rebuild or work to strengthen a relationship. You have the remote control in your hand after all, just switch off and find someone else.

We started off by talking of youthful, loving visions of knights and princesses, so why can't we retain that dream? Maybe we should all just delay leaping into the potentially dangerous pool of uncertainly until we know and understand ourselves. Know yourself, know who you really are and retain that dream of the knight in shining armour or the beautiful princes, then when the time is right go for it. Don't compromise.

For a moment think of the fire we discussed. You meet someone and light the paper; passion erupts quickly and then dies out. But unless we dig deeply into ourselves and add the different sustaining layers of the fire, we will never get to sit with the love of our life beside the flickering embers of that fire because we abandon ship as soon as the brightness of the paper fire dies.

Relationships require an understanding of the different depths needed to sustain them. Like the bonsai, we must learn to sway with the breeze around us, but at the same time retain our individuality. Drawing up a matrix of criteria which you would love to see in a partner may seem like a reasonable undertaking; however the spark that burns in each of us is indefinable in many ways. Just as no fire burns alike despite the composition of similar layers of paper, split wood and logs; so people with similar likes, dislikes and various attributes differ as their individual spark flickers to intangible forces making them who they are.

Now the childish questions "who am I, what am I, where did I come from and where am I going and what will I be?" remain unanswered in most of us – either because we've forgotten the questions, or we've never taken the time to seek the answers. So how can we possibly make and develop a relationship with anyone when we remain a stranger to ourselves. And that's what most of us are – strangers! Remember the stranger within us?

Try to think of how we attempt to untangle what makes other people tick. We meet people in many different situations, whether a social meeting, casually or business. The initial, tentative interactions are woven around the name of the person, the job they do, where they live and sort of a superficial reading of their body language. In a short period of time we may actually learn who the other person really is, but we've never bothered to learn about ourselves. Do we know who, what, why and where we're going? Do we understand what our spark, our flame looks like? Are we on a journey of discovery and self-exploration – or we drifting along some ill-defined or even non-defined stream? Do we understand our values; what relevant things fuel our existence; what do we enjoy and why?

The majority of people would stop at most of these questions and say "I'm not interested," or "that's too much trouble." Yet they expect to meet a stranger and develop a relationship. This is a troubling concept! They're taking the trouble to find out about that person yet they still remain a stranger to themselves.

If you remain a stranger to yourself, I feel you will always remain a stranger to your partner. How can you communicate in a deep, incisive manner about the real visceral issues that are critical to your lives if you speak in hazy generalities that are non-defined monotones? How can you build a sustaining fire when you cannot define the composition of it? Are you always going to be smothered by the smoke because there's no fire happening? Are you superficially made of paper, easily and quickly satisfied with life's instantaneous flicker, or do you contain the stuff of bonfires?

Before you take a drive in your automobile you usually have a destination in mind and you ensure that you have all the ingredients for a successful journey. You provide all the fuel you require. If you're organized, you're prepared for emergencies with an emergency kit and you have a road map either in your mind or on paper.

Yet, when we embark on the most complex journey that we can ever undertake; building meaningful relationships with others and amazingly with ourselves, we often enter it with no preconceived notion of where we're going. We haven't defined how we're going to get there; what resources or fuel do we have for this relationship trip? We haven't given that question any thought. As for emergencies – who knows!

When did you last tune up your body, your mind and your soul? Here's a tough question – do you like yourself? You may ask "how can I like myself, if I don't know who I am?" Good question! And one that may start that stagnant pool behind you, which is contained behind a potentially lethal dam, to trickle through and regenerate the rhythm and current of your being. Think behind or beyond the superficial and the obvious. Start slowly with simple questions to yourself and let a natural rhythm re-establish itself. Remember the analogies about the tug boats and jettisoning problems.

How many chameleon disguises are you wearing? This superficial layer is the cumbersome armour which essentially becomes a façade of duplicity which you adopt to assist you through different circumstances. Let's say, for example, you're very introverted and enjoy your own quiet company. In social groups, however, you pluck your costume of gregariousness out of your little survival sack and become Mr. Congeniality!

I'm not saying you should never rise to the occasion, but what if you attend your next function and just portray yourself as you truly are. Gradually slough off those masks and leave them behind, throw them in the fire; burn them and show your true self. In other words, don't force yourself to tell a joke or leap into a deep conversation; if you feel like quietly observing the scene around you – just do it. Don't leap to the bait of "you're quiet tonight" – there are enough voices in the world – if quiet is what you want, don't be afraid to show it.

In your relationship-seeking, imagine that you meet someone who seems intriguing and worthy of meeting again. Hey, so far so good. However, how many masks and chameleon costumes are you wearing at that particular time, and how many might your potential partner be wearing? How can you possibly meet, understand and develop any relationship when you're looking through layers of obscuring masks and staring into another, similar layer. I guess rule number one must be to remove all masks and face the world through the eyes of your true soul. That is if you have really bothered to ask yourself the question "who am I?" and taken the trouble to explore and examine that question.

Initially, when you remove that protective mask which is your armour, you may discover the different personae you have impersonated throughout your life intimidating. Each time you felt backed into a corner, you could always become the consummate actor and reach into your survival sack of tricks and pull the mask of the moment, out and project that as your true nature. Like the "onion syndrome" where you peel away the layers of subterfuge which have accumulated through the years, there will be times when tears will fill your eyes because your real nature will be something that's been hidden from the sun for so long. You will close your eyes because; looking at yourself may be a surprise or a shock at first. But gradually you will face the world around you and it will start to make sense. It does make sense to reveal your true self and understand who you are before you step into sustaining life's relationships.

In our lives' journeys, we design an eclectic assortment of masks to suit all the pressures round us; now if all our so-called friends wish to look the certain stylish way of the moment, we put on a mask to fit in. If they adopt a certain lifestyle, despite our own misgivings we adopt another mask and before we know who we are and how we're going to achieve life's purpose, we're lost! We end up not knowing which mask to wear, so we can never actually answer the question "who are we?" I remember in one of Alfred Hitchcock's movies someone wandered into the "Hall of Mirrors" and asked aloud "which one is me;" it's almost like the multiple personality syndrome. Simply put; just be the real you.

We need to go through a genuine metamorphosis to become the person we were born to be. We paint a counterfeit over ourselves and the thicker the layers the more difficult it becomes to see the original painting. Until, and sad to say, gradually we come to believe that the counterfeit is real and that is how the world sees us – as counterfeit.

So, when someone asks who you are, you respond as the counterfeit because you've tricked yourself into thinking that is really you. We may have become this way benignly. "If I say what I feel I may hurt someone, they may take it the wrong way. If I say this, they may like me more. I think that this is what they want to hear" and so on. But, by lying to yourself, you are tricking others. Be true to yourself.

We live in a chaos of masks and counterfeits where subterfuge reigns supreme. Again, visualize yourself in a social setting of laughing, gregarious, self-assured people. Who are they really and truly? Imagine if someone called out "all masks off please and would the real you present yourselves." Our motto in life should be to explore, reveal and accept. Be more accepting of others and in becoming more accepting of others you will become more accepting of yourself. On our exploration, I suggest we allow the winds of change to blow through and over us. A few minutes in a new environment is a stimulus and will allow a rebirth of fresh ideas and energy to flow.

It takes more energy or fuel for the fires of our subterfuge than for us to live as who we really. Acceptance of who we are does not mean that we cease to explore and expand our being. It means that our foundation is solid and we are now augmenting ourselves; we're not burying ourselves under tawdry lies and deceptions. As we cease to accept the false version of the "old me" we will regain lost energy and all those stagnancies, complacencies and uncertainties will fade away. We will present a new version of ourselves to the world. Ladies and gentlemen please meet the new, vital and improved me. We have undergone a trinity of change in our mind, body and soul.

As we see through clear eyes, we'll be able to see through the layers until masks become translucent and we can witness the real person within. My father suffered from glaucoma and all he had was oblique vision, like oblique problem solving, not tackling or seeming things head-on but on the fringe.

Each and every one of us is born with a distinct personality and distinct abilities. You know; tinker, tailor, soldier, sailor; likes and dislikes, and a sense of what make us happy. It could be a nebulous sort of sense but generally we know the things we like to do, eat and sleep. As we grow, often times, the things which truly make us happy are placed on the shelf titled "unsuitable at this time."

As we enter our scholastic journeys at school, we are continually examined and dissected and, intellectually, we are pigeonholed to society's sense of what we would be good at. This equates into what is popular at the time. In our age computers seem to be the way to go. Now the intrinsic part of our soul makes us happy in doing the things that we enjoy. Often times a particular ability is equated with "because you're good at that, this should be your career choice." But the reality is that because you're good a something doesn't necessarily mean that you should take that as a career.

Tinker, tailor, soldier sailor! How many tinkers would have been happy being sailors? I think you get the picture. Dig deep and explore and hopefully you can devote your existence to being the best you can be – It's your choice. We've spoken before about the cuckoo syndrome; we're all different; we're all snowflakes. Don't be the victim of society or even your family. Don't be what others say; be what you dream of being.

I'm writing in an idealistic way and I realize that circumstances may force us to change our life's path from our true, natural choice. But in order to achieve our true selves and meet ourselves, we need to explore and live our lives in as true a manner as possible. Truth is all that matters

As our world evolves into an ever increasing dispassionate, complex, superficially driven existence, simpler and less technical attributes of life slip into obscurity. I am not advocating becoming a 19th century Luddite and smashing technology. Instead I am advocating respecting a person's choice and lifestyle. Everyone can be what they want and should not dance to the increasingly complex technical age. If you want to adopt a lifestyle which is non-technical, do it.

Now, in our culture, sitting and daydreaming is frowned upon and perceived as being lazy. Being industrious is the key phrase. Philosophizing is only respected if it is uttered by a being who is the owner of a string of letters after his name. In ages past those with the desire to examine and struggle with philosophical concepts did so, minus the mysterious letters.

Is being physically involved equated with the absence of laziness? Yes, I guess some would say that, but is sitting in a rocking chair on a sunny porch being plain idle? Despite the fact that one's mind is wrestling with concepts, playing with words and digging deeper and deeper into the centre of our existence. You don't need a PhD to start to change your life; just desire, and a liberal, dogged persistence.

Obviously seeking and finding are two separate entities. To seek and not to find should be as respected as seeking and finding. The amount of effort can be the same but the end result is different. We should always be seekers. We must always pursue the horizon of curiosity. "Just when I was getting the hang of it" should be our epitaph.

Should we hero-worship a wise man who after all, was born with the raw ingredients of intellect and spirituality? He was given these ingredients. Instead he should be respected for applying them. Similarly, a man who is born with lesser gifts but nevertheless seeks and develops, but never really finds the answer, should also be respected. Like the fire, the different degrees of intensity are based on the foundation. They provide light and warmth in various ways.

For example, candlelight to a pauper is a conflagration but to a king it's an intrusive glimmer. Never surrender to complacency and compromise. Instead, if irrefutable circumstances dictate that instead of becoming a poet, you must support a family; or in the purity of giving, fulfilling another's vision, don't despair. Reach into your core and place your own special dream for yourself in a comfortable retreat you're making, and place it in a private spot known only to you and accessible at any time. Visit your special retreat frequently, allowing the fluctuating winds of change end evolution to mold your dream internally as you grow externally.

Hopes, desires and passions are like fine wine, so when the time comes to open the magic bottle, your destiny, a finely aged sense of purity and heady euphoria will greet you. Avoid the temptation to equate your imposed career with your destiny and, instead, at times when your true nature sinks into a morass of bone-numbing boredom, quickly reach within and feel the glow of your dream permeating your entire being.

# *forty*

## Make Your Haven A Heaven

**A little bit goes a long way**

Passion builds bulwarks against perversity. Always remember, ultimately you are the architect of your destiny. Hermit's cave or princess` castle, you are the maker. Whenever you wish to ease the pressure in your spirit, all you have to do is retire to that specific retreat you have designed. As most of us don't have the required wealth to fly on a whim to anyplace of our choosing, we must develop a retreat within ourselves. I mean, as Dorothy in the Wizard of Oz said "click my heels twice and I'll be in Kansas." Believe, visualize and you can design your individual retreats within yourself where only you may go.

The construction and enjoyment of your retreat relies on your imagination, desire and your individual spark. Just think of the perfect place and moment in time, whether in a different historical age which particularly appeals to you: you will have designed and fine-tuned your own version of security, happiness and fulfillment.

For years I searched in my restless mind until I found my Shangri La for moments of retreat: amazingly almost ready-made. Remember your subconscious is working unbidden and creatively even in your moments of despondency. Plant the positive seed and it will do the rest.

Beside a rocky bay where nature has molded her character into my dream- scape, there is a high pinnacle on top of which I've designed and constructed a special retreat. To access my hermitage, there is a rugged series of steps I've carved out of the rocks; accessible, of course, only to me.  Up this rugged cliff-face I explore until I reach a gentle plateau at the top revealing a small shack; in essence a one room cottage, within which is a fur covered bed and a charcoal brazier where I can cook fish, which I catch in the bay, where of course only I may fish.  There's a natural hot tub in the rock fed by a hot spring where I can soak and dream while gazing over my pristine world – where only I can go.

Remember, your retreat is exactly the way you design it.  My version is not for everyone; yours may be a castle or maybe a quiet stretch of beach where you can pursue your life's issues and develop in stress-releasing relaxation. Just savour the tranquility; design it to complement your character and your soul.

To add to the enjoyment of your hideaway another dimension which you may wish to add is another person. You may have dreamed of being a Robinson Crusoe, or a cowboy, or a space explorer. In your "retreat world" you can be what you wish and be where you want, and if you want someone with you, you invent that person as well.

In order to fully enjoy and appreciate this escape from daily routines and pressure, you must revisit it and continually visualize and remodel it as your circumstances change.  You may remodel and renovate it until one day you say, "I need another retreat"' and you build another one.  You can build as many as you want in your life; as you evolve, so does your visualized retreat.

Visiting your haven should never become a chore.  Instead it should become a mini vacation, even for a few moments or a few seconds.  Remember, no passport is required and no packing!  Later we will discuss how to make your haven into a heaven.

In this retreat deep within the previously inaccessible core of your being, there is another dimension that should be explored and that's how you occupy your time while you're there.  Now, you've designed and built your structure until you're happy with the way it looks and feels, but your next question is "what do I do when I'm there?"  Again, only you can answer that question – and what a pleasurable encounter that should be.

In my hilly hermitage; whether in my hot-spring tub gazing over the bay, or cooking freshly caught fish; or playing a haunting melody on a wooden flute: whatever I do is of my choosing and my making, with no imposed sense of duty or chore. Now, perfect every aspect of yourself; let your being relax and enter into the euphoric freedom of being where you want to be as you simply provide time for the current of your soul to flow as it desires: such peace, tranquility and freedom.

How many times on vacation have we had a dream or expectation of the resort we've chosen before we arrive? The setting will be idyllic; the water will be perfection; the food incredible; the ambiance superlative. Sometimes we may be lucky and some aspects of the vacation will come close to the image of our dream. But the total package invariably falls short of our expectations, yet here's your chance to design your idyllic retreat down to the smallest detail. Conjure up the perfect weather; paint the vegetation in colours you choose; become who you really wish to be and you will be.

You'll forget about the massive crowds of people around you – jostling, sweating and intrusive! Forget long, droning flights; just turn your eyes and vision inward and you will be there, just as you imagined it. No surprises unless you plan and want some surprises: unless you want to have alternative aspects of your retreat to induce happiness.

I am not advocating the hypnotic state of entering a spiritual trance. I'm just saying to ask yourself in times of stress, times of unease or in times when the world seems insurmountable, "where do I truly want to go for peace and tranquility?" Visit your Shangri La as often as you wish and feel the tension slip away; just feel it trickling away through your dam until the current of your tranquility is fulfilled.

Cave or castle? Destiny and fulfillment lie in diverse beds of individual dreams and aspirations. If retreating internally in your vision to the same place becomes an odyssey, that's what it should be. It should be an odyssey to the core of your being in whatever age you wish. The secret is to experience every nuance of your trip or saga.

Let's sail once again to explore a Polynesian island in a classic wooden schooner. Take time to design your craft and soon you'll feel the warmth of the deck beneath your naked feet and feel the tropical breeze on our face, gently caressing your bronzed skin while above you taut sails will surge you towards an exotic island. Ahead you'll watch the approach of a shimmering lagoon fringed by gentle waves and swaying palm trees. You will feel the hot, white sand beneath your feet and the rays of the tropical sun massaging your troubles away. Open your every sense and smell the fragrant air; touch the palm trees and drift into a tranquil sleep beneath the stars. The song of the surf and the lulling breezes bring promise of even better tomorrows. Enjoy the rhythmic lullaby.

You retreat really is a moveable feast, an endless odyssey through areas of the world of your own making in time and place. Open your senses and imagination to the never ending mysteries hidden in your probing soul. Limitations in your imagination do not exist. You are the creator.

Travel within and your destiny and happiness will follow. Travel without and you may evade your destiny as happiness eludes you. Know yourself before you know others. Travel within before you travel without.

# *forty one*

## Sculptor Or Gardener?

**Hands-on with a smile**

A sculptor can visualize the essence of you buried in a block of Carrera marble sitting in his studio waiting to be sculpted into you, into the incarnation of you. In its original state there's a beauty to the coloured veins running through the smooth texture and the way the sunlight plays on its glowing beauty. The block is you - at least you are in the block, and there are two ways to make you appear and assume the true uniqueness and spirit of who you are.

The first step is to sit deep within the marble and permit a sculptor to chip and mold you into their vision of what they see with their eyes; feel with their hands, and so they will methodically carve their vision of you until you stand awkwardly staring around you. Feeling molded by someone else is not truly you; not truly formed by yourself. And as you've been formed and molded, so you will live, molded by others. Their breadth of vision has bonded itself to you and, in essence, you have been sculpted.

Now, the other way to sculpt yourself in your own image is to do it from the inside. Even if you really feel you're already molded in other peoples' eyes and you think it's too late to re-mold, to remake yourself, all you have to do is place yourself back into the block of marble and this time sculpt yourself from the inside. You are saying "I am not content with who I am now, and I am re-creating myself in my unique image."

Think back to the lessons learned so far. We have reached back into the recesses of our being and whittled away the hypocrisies, the counterfeit marble we have laboured under; and the indecisive directions we have taken. Think of those things. In our renewed knowledge of what the essence of ourselves truly is, we have gently sculpted the marble until we appeared; reborn in the image we have always wanted.

Now the layers of marble will seem impenetrable at first and we will feel trapped in this armour as though in a block of ice. But with honesty, willpower and with a resurgence of childlike excitement, we'll slowly emerge.

Sculpting from the inside out is like having a candle frozen inside a block of ice. Just imagine the candle is lit and feel a gentle thawing taking place around the candle. Initially the thawing will be slow but eventually the ice will vanish and reveal the flame of life within.

You are the force within the marble and your desire to rebuild yourself is the flame. The marble will fall away slowly around you and the image which others, and your own acceptance of your previous self, will crumble. You will be reborn in the likeness of your choosing and as you continually evolve and develop, your sculpted image will also change; subtle in some ways, dramatic in others.

We must develop the willpower to foster who we truly are and also harbour the courage to combat the negative moldings of sculpting influences around us. The more entrenched an influence and its effect upon us, the more difficult it will be to chip it away. But remember, if we refuse to accept negativity it will not be there like barnacles on a ship's hull to be methodically chipped away from our self-made image.

Revealing our true selves and acceptance of who we are, are two separate and distinct things. We must pay homage to our intrinsic selves, limitations and all. But, remember, all we can do is search continually for fulfillment and happiness.

Tell me, how does your garden grow? I am the consummate lazy gardener allowing nature to dictate what grows on my land without any forethought to the whys and wherefores. In the wintertime the winds blow blizzards of debris and seeds into my garden and these develop a balance of sorts. I never know what plant is making its way through the soil in springtime, the more the merrier – all can apply!

My form of gardening develops its unique personality unfettered by intrusive attempts to tame and mold it. However, what gratefully survives in my garden, perhaps other people wouldn't like because it's specific to my personality. There is no dominant plant that I wish to see emerging, otherwise I would have to carefully weed away some of the emerging plants. I would become a protector of some and slayer of others. Some may grow a little stunted by the other plants who steal their light and nutrition, but at least they all have a fighting chance.

We are like the hypothetical plants in the garden which are in danger of being starved out of existence. However, the inherent difference is that we grow; but we're continually being crowded by influences which are like weeds and if we're not careful we'll end up being starved and we'll develop into a stunted version of our true potential. In this case we must weed. We're planted and our seed grows until we burst into the light, but already there are influences which are affecting us even before our birth: our parents; where we live, and a myriad of other factors.

If we allow all the intrusive influences around us to smother and mold us, we will not develop into who we are capable of being, but into a stranger. We must learn to weed our own garden; to pull away the tendrils that threaten to smother us and deprive us of the light of our own personal development. Now, some of the weeds will be more difficult to deal with than others: our parents, friends and our immediate environment hold and mold us. We must, however, listen to the vibes coming from our own garden and grow as we wish to grow in accordance with our own drum beat and rhythm.

Once we are committed to a specific cause, we must always be aware of the weeds which surround us and quickly and decisively pluck away the negative influences before they have time to take root. Weeds, like any other organic thing, require nurturing and if we deprive them of that energy they will wither and die.

Negativity needs both an audience and acceptance – deprive it of both! People who are perpetually negative are best avoided or ignored before they can influence you. If we must mingle with these people, avoid being smothered with their innate gloom. Illuminate them with the glow of your own optimism. Pay particular attention to your tap root which connects you to your true self but also stretches back through time to the beginning, to the essence of time.

The continuity of life flows through you in an embrace which started at the beginning of time and continues still in your spirit. Close your eyes and visualize your tap root slowly probing its way back into the dim past of your genes; through your parents and grandparents it goes back to a distant past where unknown people and places fed the tap root that still grows through you.

Now, who were these ancestors? They go back to a cataclysmic age long after the "Big Bang," and the further back your tap root goes, the more complex the work of learning about yourself really is. Think of all the diverse people who have programmed you. Think of their thoughts, their adventures. They're all flowing through you; their desires, their hopes and dreams. Whatever you need to know, think back to them.

Think of the fulfillment which has lain dormant in you for eons and bring it back to life again. Your dream and vision of yourself may be a mirror image of one of your ancestors who stood at the dawn of time with an ill- defined sense of who he or she was, and what they also wished from life.

Obviously, we cannot return to that age but by fulfilling our dreams, our self-fulfillment, possibly we will close the loop started by a distant relative in a time before. In becoming "you", possibly you will fulfill the dream that they had all those years ago.

As your tap root stretches back into the beginning of time, visualize all the networks of other roots feeding into you. Your existence has wound around people and places and onto you sometimes, but the stuff of what you are is made of your intrinsic qualities.

## *forty two*

## Prime The Wellspring Of Your Being And Flood The World

Humble start: heroic finish

We're always learning by experiences which, although they are specific to the immediate chore at hand, can be useful in analyzing future situations. I worked as an environmentalist and one of my tasks was to test the pH of water. Now those of you who have swimming pools will know that the pH is based on a scale of zero to 14, seven being the medium; below seven the water is acidic and above seven the water is alkaline. So you'd know by doing a simple test whether the water was, simplistically speaking, good or bad. In other words "do I have to add any balancing chemicals?"

But in life, when we're trying to judge, evaluate and assess ourselves, and other people, we really don't have a simple pH test. We can't dip a piece of litmus paper in our being, pull it out and say we're good or we're bad. That of course is simplistic, so I guess to equate the pH system with humanity would be to place a Hitler as a zero and a Mother Theresa as a 14 with most of us falling somewhere around the middle. Sometimes we dip into the naughty side and sometimes we exceed our expectations on the positive side. But usually a normal individual in life takes the middle road which Chaucer termed the "Via Media."

One of the problems we have is that we become extremely discouraged when we see someone like a Mother Theresa or an Albert

Schweitzer; someone who is the epitome of perfection in many ways, whether it's in an intellectual, spiritual or a creative way.

Let us say, for example, we want to become a great artist, painter, musician, poet or a philosopher; and we make the mistake of going into an art gallery and we see Van Gough, Monet, Picasso and we think "my God, I could never do that," or we decide to become a writer, a great writer and again, we make the mistake of going into a library and we're bombarded, and surrounded by an avalanche of exquisite writing.

We look around and say "I could never be a Dickens, a Dostoyevsky, a Voltaire; a Wilbur Smith or Louis L'amour; I could never be a good writer." So what's the point? The same with music – You say "I'm going to give up, there is no point."

The intellectual, spiritual, and the creative journey is like a flood in perpetual motion. Now, some of the great artists, some of the great creators, were like the Amazon, Nile or the Mississippi; huge torrents, mammoth amounts of water pouring down as the mainstream. They were the core of that particular genre. Our masters were the flood, the current; they were the dominant rivers.

If you travel along the main arteries you will see little tributaries feeding those floods of creativity, feeding those rivers on a regular basis. These little tributaries are major contributors to the whole. There is a place for different levels of creativity so we should not feel depressed; don't feel there is no point because you'll never equate to a Mother Theresa or one of the major creators. Maybe your destiny is to be the best you can be as a small tributary feeding the creative flow of life, and that is worthwhile. By creating, you're producing a contribution that is beneficial to humanity, something that can be shared by all.

I remember years ago in one of my high school classes, one of my classmates was what I call the creative, intellectual bully. Now, this fellow was very bright, excelling at sports and also excelling at intellectually stimulating courses like mathematics, which most of us struggled with.

Whenever he came out of a challenging class or after an examination, this creative, intellectual bully would look at us all with a supercilious smile that said "that was easy, what a simple exam that was, I've done so well," while the rest of us would crawl out of that examination room with the sweat of depression dripping off us because we'd struggled to answer the basic questions. We'd missed a lot of the answers; we struggled and fought, and instead of this creative, intellectual bully realizing that, and being a bit more conciliatory toward us, he browbeat and laughed at us because of our perceived inadequacy.

The reality is that if you possess a talent and a unique spark of creativity, you must foster and develop it, but at the same time you must share it. Take an example of an exquisite songbird with beautiful plumage – this is your creativity – you catch it and you hide it away, and you don't share it, you don't release it back into its environment; into the world and humanity. The songbird will stop singing, the plumage will become dull and the bird will die and you will be left with a dried corpse.

The same with butterflies! As kids we'd chase these beautifully coloured butterflies which we would catch and place in glass jars so that we could peek at them, watch them and admire their colours. As children would do, we'd touch their wings until gradually their vibrancy would die; they were trapped and would fade away. Like our flame which longs to erupt.

We must never feel depressed if suddenly our creativity which is developing in the journey towards being a 14 on the pH value of quality of life and perfection is not happening quickly enough for you. Don't say: "I don't feel inspired; it's not happening for me, I don't feel I'll ever reach that plateau."

Think of the ocean, the ebb and flow. The inevitability and consistency of its actions should generate a sense of trust in you. The tide advances and retreats; the ebb and flow! So, if you feel that creativity, your spontaneity, your zest for improvement, maybe doesn't seem to be there, don't worry – it will come back again like the constancy of the tide.

Growing up in our house in the countryside of Scotland was idyllic, in many ways, but there was no central heating. In Scotland the temperatures don't vary much at all through the seasons and in our house there were two fireplaces: one in the living room and one in the bedroom, which was my Mum and Dad's room. Now, in order to have heat in the winter you obviously had to have a cozy fire blazing in the fireplace because there was no central heating, no electrical heating, and no hot air heating – nothing except the fireplaces. Similarly, the only hot water to be had in the house was by putting the fire on in the living room, because there was a hot water boiler built into that fireplace behind the wall. So, when you wanted hot water you built a fire and the water would heat up.

In the wintertime when one of us was studying at university or college, to get some privacy and to get some quiet – because there were six children in our home – we would go up to our Mum and Dad's room because that was the only other room with a fireplace. Instead of starting the fire from scratch, we would get a shovel and take some hot coals from the fireplace in the living room upstairs into the bedroom and, using that as a nucleus, we would add a few bits of wood and more coal and the fire would then regenerate and become our source of heat and warmth in that particular room.

Again, that's like our creativity. Don't just keep it in the living room; don't just heat yourself exclusively. Share it, take that small piece of coal that's warm and glowing and start fires in other peoples' hearts. Share the fire! Now, the fire is an analogy for its comfort. It talks to you with its gentle crackling, its warmth and its glimmering. That's your creativity.

That's also your search for being someone better. Don't be a creative, intellectual bully saying "I'm great, I'm wonderful, I have this creative spark in me. I have this intellectually stimulating mind and I can achieve anything - but, hey, I'm not going to share it and I'm going to belittle everyone." Don't build a foundation on others' inadequacies. That's what the creative bully will do. Share what talents you have, don't hoard them. Don't be like that little bird put into a cage until it dies. Do you want to end your life as an item in a garage sale?

You may say, "It's easy for you to talk, you're actually doing something." But, no, I'm struggling like everyone else. With the fire it's almost like priming a pump. If you have a well and just go over and try to dry pump it, sometimes no water will come out because you have to add some water to prime it and get it started. So that's like stimulation, you have to add this little kernel of fire that you're using to stimulate your priming. Invest in a spark and gain a bonfire.

Once when I was building a cottage on an island, I met a man who was a "water witch," dowser! He would determine where water was by the age- old practice of taking a willow twig, or sometimes a piece of wire, and by holding it in his hand he could determine exactly the source of the water. It seems like a primitive way of achieving that but he had an ability and intuition. He had a sense of confidence that he would find it and he wasn't scared to try. He'd say, "If I don't find it, you don't have to pay me." On the island, payment was usually a couple of chickens or a bottle of the dowser's favourite libation.

So, maybe we should try to do that with ourselves. We're trying to decide "do I have a real talent? Do I have what it takes?" We're trying to understand what makes us, euphemistically, tick. So maybe if we can find the pH of our goodness, our intellect and our spirituality, we will become our own water witch; a dowser using techniques of trust and will to find the areas of our being that have to be perfected. "Some of the ingredients of my being are as good as they're going to get," you may exclaim. But by saying that, it's almost like negating the search; almost like saying, "I've reached this point, there's no point in going on"

Consider Jack London who achieved writing success at an early age. After that he wandered the globe and continued writing, but I feel that he was competing against himself. He was trying to reach that level, that Plimsoll line, of supremacy that he reached at such an early age, but he never did. He achieved a lot: he wrote a lot of adventure stories but he never did reach beyond his original success. I guess he had "witched" into his soul or into his creative spark at an early age and found those magical books "The Call of the Wild", "Wolf Larsen" and the like – he found them very quickly and achieved success. Most of us will probably spend a lifetime with this little "willow-witch," or willow twig, trying to find the sparks that need to be discovered and explored within us. Remember, that exploring is the only way to achieve an end result.

When we spoke in terms of the creative, intellectual bully, it reminded me of some people who approach a pot of thick soup which is packed with meat, vegetables and all sorts of wonderful spices and an aroma which is perfection. But some people, instead of taking the soup which includes a liquid, sort of filter it, taking the meat and vegetables and leaving the liquid. Selfishly, basically, what they're doing is stealing some of the goodness from that soup; the liquid is still tasty but their selfishness leaves a consommé instead of a well- balanced chunky meal.

This is similar to the greedy, possessive bully with a spark of creativity who becomes a megalomaniac with a desire to possess and dominate at the expense of others. They want to be the thick of the soup and they want to leave the dregs or the liquid for others. They have developed a selfish personality by doing that, and this we have to fight.

The reality is, when we talk in terms of the soup; in the bowl of soup there's a complementary amount of different ingredients – carrots, potatoes, onions, turnip, corn, peas – different herbs and spices. An aromatic mélange! Now, individually, these ingredients have a spark, an individual taste and aroma but collectively they have a whole new being, a uniqueness of aroma and taste. I guess we're like that. As we said, individually we're like snowflakes, separate and distinct from each other. So that's one identity.

The group setting contains a completely different kind of collective energy and identity; as in the homogenous pot of soup. Sometimes, depending on your self-worth, and self-esteem, your knowledge of who you are individually you feel content, but in groups, which can be overpowering, collectively you can be sucked into the vortex of collective energy and you melt into the group and lose yourself. You must always retain your individual spark and our individual fire: don't lose it in collective suffocation. Do not become a homogenized version of yourself.

I remember as a kid I used to love to play with little plastic toy cowboys, Indians, soldiers and the like. Often when I bought them, and they came in packets, the plastic was a muddy gray or sometimes there were streaks of yellows and reds like veins running through different toys. The reason for this was that lots of different colours of scrap plastics were basically blended together and homogenized to make these fairly inexpensive toys. But the yellows, magnolias, vibrant reds, greens or purples, blended together into a homogenized muddy colour. Just like us their individual identity was lost. Individually we have a bright identity as to who we are but then in a group setting we become muddy and gray.

As a child I used to wander through the Scottish countryside exploring, looking for birds' nests, just admiring the freedom, the

Tom Sawyer freedom, that we had. Now, we were evolving slowly. In my way I was evolving from someone who had been a small child looked after by my parents, playing with friends outside in a protected environment – in a back yard – and now we were exploring a bigger world in the countryside around us. We were evolving and continually mesmerized by the incredible diversity of life in all the little streams and creeks that we explored.

There was a mammoth amount of vibrant life in them from tadpoles evolving into frogs; a complete aquatic microcosm. But the one insect that I remember and was bewildered by was called a stick insect. It was the larva of a caddis fly which when it was born would find a small hollow twig, a piece of straw or something similar and it would use it as its home until it grew larger. Then it would vacate that little home and move into another. So, all through its life it was evolving into a bigger and larger home; similar to a hermit crab. The hermit is a soft shelled crab and it's very easily attacked by predators so it has to find a safe haven. It finds a snail shell and as its body grows it finds another, larger shell and so on, so it's evolving, it's finding a new area, a new place to live and sloughing off the old and finding the new.

Relationships are like that. Think of yourself; of how you've evolved since you were born, the past five years or the past ten years. You've gone from home to school to college to work, to a relationship or possibly marriage. You've possibly been developing your creative spark, your hobby. You're evolving all the time and that is a very positive thing.

The issue in relationships is that there are two people hopefully on the same journey. I guess it could be like railroad tracks, they're going in the same direction. The railroad tracks are evolving mile-by-mile-by mile. The problem is that although the tracks are going in the same direction they never really meet. Look at the railroad tracks on the prairies. They seem to meet at one point, but that's an illusion. So, if you feel that because you're going in the same direction that's great, it's wonderful. You're obviously on the right rack; and there's that word track again. No, you've got to come together, there has to be a meeting place.

Now let's say, in your relationship, you are motivated to go from your pH of goodness of seven and want to equate it up to a 14, but you will compromise up to a nine or 10-. You're going to try to do the best you possibly can, so you work hard and you start to evolve like the caddis fly and the hermit crab. You start to slough off and assume a new persona as you start to change. However, over there your partner is still back at a seven, still back at the point you left a while ago. You are moving down one railroad track at a fairly fast clip but your partner is not.

I guess a couple of things can happen. He or she can say to you "hold on, where the heck are you going; you're leaving me behind, get back here." Depending on who you are you may go into reverse and go back where you were because your partner isn't moving with you. Or you may say "excuse me, this is a two-way track and, yes, I'm advancing, I'm progressing. Although this is a relationship, which is one word, there are two parts to it; there are two individuals in this relationship. It's like a Trinity destination; you, me, us, and then the final destination. Why don't you move along the track to my level and let's go from there?"

Obviously you would use different words, but what I'm saying is that you don't want to be pulled back to where you were before. Once the momentum is going you want to be able to advance and improve; head towards that nebulous 10 or 11 on the scale and PS, take your partner with you.

# *forty three*

## Grandfather's Watch Revisited

**Here it comes again**

Let us travel again to review all of the components of my grandfather's watch which were equally important. They taught us about the importance of inter-connectedness. So, in fine tuning your senses you may say "I'm an artist, hence painting is my God." And you may neglect your other senses. Or you may be a chef and say "I'm concentrating on taste, I'm going to create the most exquisite, aromatic culinary masterpiece the world has ever known, because that is all that matters." A musician may say, "I'm going to compose the most glorious musical masterpiece the world has ever heard."

To have a passion like this may be commendable, however treat the other components of your being with respect and sensitivity and also nourish them otherwise you will get into a situation where, again, you become fragmented. The reality is that what we must do is fine tune all our senses so we can see, feel, touch, taste and hear with a passion, a collective passion.

I am suddenly reminded of that small idyllic cottage I built on an island on the West Coast of Canada overlooking a pristine white beach beside the ocean. Throughout the construction, I wasn't just physically visualizing or seeing something in front of me; all my senses were absorbing it. I could see it, I could see the trees swaying in the breeze, and I could see the waves lapping the shore. I could see the whole world around me. I could hear the sounds as well; the wind, the lapping of the tides. I could taste it, taste the salt water in the air. So, I'm seeing, hearing, feeling, touching, sensing, and every aspect of my passionate being was stimulated. It's like a jigsaw. If one of those components had been removed it would have diminished my enjoyment of it all. I would have enjoyed it but only to a certain level. By fine tuning all those senses, I was alive!

I remember reading one of the Tarzan books when I was a child and one little statement has stayed with me over the years. "When Tarzan awakened in the morning every one of his senses was fine tuned." On a visceral level his hearing, sight, taste and his physicality – his whole being was poised for action. In other words he was wide awake. I've often thought how wonderful it would be to be like that. I don't just mean in the morning to awaken and open your eyes and feel a desire to be one with the day, but I mean in the course of your life to be a vibrant, burning, focused being.

You can learn an encyclopedia of information from animals. When I look at Reba, our cat, even when she's sleeping her ears are twitching, and if you look at her eyes they don't seem to be totally closed. Her nose is twitching as well as she senses the world around her. Now, you can sense in a physical level but what about the spiritual level, what about the sense within you? That can be your inner intuition, or your fire, your spark. We must develop a sense of knowing when the flame inside is starting to peter out; when the glow is starting to fade like the plumage of the songbird, or the butterfly's wings. We need to know when to prime, we need to know when to take the coal from the living room fire, in Scotland, to the bedroom upstairs to start the conflagration again when it's diminishing, when your energy is falling.

For example, and again, years ago in Scotland, I wanted a bicycle and my Mum and Dad could not afford to buy me one and I had very little money. I was still at school and selling newspapers of an evening to try and make some pocket money so Mum and Dad would not be out of pocket on a weekly basis.

One day as I was delivering papers, I saw an old rusty bicycle lying in a garden. To others it was a pile of slowly disintegrating junk, but to me it was a means to my mobility. I knocked on the door and an old man answered. I said "excuse me sir, but could I get that bicycle?" the old man said "I'll sell it to you." So we worked out a price, the equivalent of a few dollars. The bike was worth nothing to him but to me it was worth something, so we compromised and I paid him and took the bicycle home. I rebuilt the bike and scraped off all the rust. I spent some money on some black paint and new rubber grips for the handlebars. It was only a few pennies really, but then the bicycle was functional again.

That bicycle to me is analogous to life. In order to get moving you have to apply some pressure, you have to get the momentum going and expend some energy. Sometimes you have to sit and reflect, relax and rest. You're sitting on the bicycle seat and you can stop peddling and you can coast for a little bit and then you start peddling again. You're steering, you're focused and you have a destination you're going to. So, all these things are analogous to life. We need to exert some energy and we need to know when to stop and rest and put on the brakes. For several years that old bicycle helped me travel around my area delivering newspapers, visiting my friends; sometimes I took the occasional trip.

It wasn't a fine tuned mountain bike, or a ten speed bike, it was an old fashioned one speed bicycle. But that's all we need in life, momentum, energy and an ability to realize when we're tired to take a break and rest a little bit, to break, to steer ourselves towards the future and that is what we are doing.

Talking about energy and depletion of energy; when we were children we were given an old record player. And it was old – from the Victorian era – and we had to crank a handle, put the record on the turntable and lift over a long arm with a needle at the end and carefully lower the arm onto the record and then it would play. It would play to the extent of the energy you expended into it by cranking the handle. In other words, if you cranked it up until it would go no further, the sound that you got back was a normal sound; singers in the correct key, voice speaking in a normal tone.

However, as the energy of the record player started to run down you could hear the voices getting slower, lower and sounding as though they were coming from a deep, dark hollow. Ultimately, if you just left it, it would die and there would be total silence. So, in order for the player to work properly you had to expend energy; just like riding the bicycle, you had to crank it. The records were also extremely old; they were sixty years old and scratched. Some of them were broken and we couldn't use those, but on the scratched ones the record would be playing along and suddenly the needle would start to skip and jump, or get stuck in a groove. Most times when it got to the scratch, it would be like a moment's aberration then it would jump and start again.

Now, that's like life. You start off and expend energy and the record is going; your life is going, then you get to a blimp, a roadblock, a scratch. You have to learn to jump over it. Sometimes in a record there was a major scratch and that's when the needle would get stuck and the song or the music would repeat and repeat until you physically lifted the arm over the deep scratch. In life, little problems present themselves and sometimes it is almost like self-resolution' the problems resolve themselves with very minor effort like the needle jumping over the minor scratches.

When you get to the deep scratches, the deep roadblocks seem almost like trenches, you say "I'm entrenched on this side and I cannot get over to the other side. I can't reach, I'm stuck here." This is when you've got to expend more energy to get to the other side and the record of your life will start again; your life will move again and you will get to a point where you are really reaching for that 10 and you are attaining it.

Another lesson that we could learn from the scratch in the record is that sometimes we must learn to let something go, to move on, otherwise you expend wasted energy. An example is during an examination, and I'll go back to the situation when I was at high school and mathematics was not my topic! If I got to a question I was having trouble with I could literally end up spending the whole two or three hours struggling with that one question and getting a very low mark. Whereas if I left that question and moved on to find one that I could answer, I would get more points and incrementally move through the exam. I still wouldn't do fantastically well because, as I said, math is not my topic. But by knowing our limitations, at times it's more meaningful to move on. You can go back again when you have time, the energy, and the inclination to tackle some of these things.

As we move along this journey of life that we're talking about in our careers, our vocations, avocations, relationships; we go at different places and stages. But all we are truly looking for is a sense of freedom.

Freedom from self-doubt about our direction in life – and freedom needs energy.

One of my favourite books is Papillon. A movie was made of it in the 1960s, staring Steve McQueen. The movie centered on Devil's Island in French Guiana, Central America. This was a hell hole which held French prisoners, including Papillon who was incarcerated there. Although this was a hellish environment of disease, heat and brutality, a soul destroying place to be, he never gave up his freedom.

Physically, Papillon had given up his freedom but mentally and spiritually he always fought for freedom. He was a slave incarcerated there but, from the first moment he arrived on the island, he spent his life trying to escape. Now, the French had a word to describe that and it was "cavale." If you were a cavale person you were a flame seeker; you were someone who was highly esteemed because you would never extinguish that spark of freedom that was within you and, even if it killed you, you would have died for that freedom.

I think that's what we should do. We should never accept slavery. Papillon didn't! He spent his life perpetually escaping and being recaptured, until, ultimately, he was free like a butterfly – he flew away. Now, that was a hard thing to do. Devil's Island was a brutal, intimidating environment where escaping was equated with being tortured, or shot and killed. But he could never see himself just living where there was no freedom, so he spent years reaching for that And I think that the word "reaching" is pivotal.

I mean, if you always keep your hands in your pockets you can never reach for the stars; never reach for a butterfly, hold a Papillon in your hand; you can never fly, you stay entrapped. If you give up your search along this pH line of goodness, or creativity, intellectualism or whatever; if you give that up and stagnate, you give up your freedom and you will stagnate. Always keep your dream alive.

A year ago when I was visiting South Carolina, my brother-in-law and sister took me to an old antebellum plantation. This was down on the coast of South Carolina and it was a classic "Tara" with a grandiose white mansion, little white chapel, brooding magnolia trees, willow trees hanging over little ponds, and an overpowering sense of sorrow. On the coastal side there was a swamp which at one time had been partly drained and made into a rice plantation. But this was now a wild area of alligators and quick-sand - a deathtrap if you didn't know where you were going. I thought back to those days of slavery when they lived in this sort of environment. If they tried to escape they would be brought back and flogged or worse be trapped in the swamp and killed by alligators – ripped to shreds. Yet some did escape, some of them did choose freedom over the soul-destroying chains of slavery and chose to escape.

Many of us, at some point in our lives, feel that we are trapped. Enslaved by circumstances or chained to our workplace. We've no freedom to go anywhere; we have to be home at a certain time to prepare food for the kids; at weekends there are house repairs and a myriad of interminable chores. We are tied to our immediate environment and cannot escape. Now, I'm not saying here that I advocate you run away from your family. I am not saying that at all. What I am saying is that you still can achieve freedom inside. You still can reach inside through the visualization techniques we've spoken about and you can explore, you can travel as far as you want. You can improve your heart, your mind and your soul. You can still do that and attain internal freedom. Once you are no longer enslaved internally, external freedom follows.

You still have to put meat and potatoes and bread and butter on the table, but you still can have that freedom inside; you still can have that gratification of saying "I'm really moving along this scale that we're talking about, I've gone from seven to eight, and by this time next week I'll be an 8-1/2." You are really setting milestones and goals for yourself here. You have objectives and you are laying out the railroad tracks and getting along quite nicely, thank you! You're getting towards the point where you are no longer enslaved because as soon as you start to think of that, you are. If you think in terms of "there's nothing I can do; I don't like myself and there's nowhere I can go, what's the point?" You're going to be stuck in a real morass and you have to move.

Look at it this way. Again, when I was a teenager in an adventurous, romantic mood, I used to read lots of books on high adventure, usually set in Africa and such exotic places. One book I read was "Children of the Mist" by Sir H. Rider Haggard. He also wrote King Solomon's Mines, SHE, and books of that ilk. "Children of the Mist" was set in a high, fog shrouded, and mountainous, fictitious kingdom somewhere in Africa. Now, the Children of the Mist lived perpetually in mist and fog. Think about it! If, from the day you were born until the day you die, you lived in fog, you lived in gloom and you lived in grayness, you would never see the horizon; never see the sun, never see the sky. You could barely see a few feet in front of you – what do you think that is going to do to you?

It's like a lot of people who live in some relationships or social situations, or work environments where they're not surrounded by gray mist but they are surrounded by gray pessimism, lack of optimism, negativity; by people who obviously fall below seven on the scale we were talking about. If you are surrounded by all that and you accept it, the fire that should be glowing inside you and illuminating the world around you, is going to die, is going to wither – it must peter out until there's coldness inside you, only a bleak, unwelcoming place of no love or affection, and a lack of freedom to explore your own being. You will have died inside and you will be smothered by the grayness just like the children in Haggard's "Children of the Mist." They had a sense of gray and, I guess, gray says it all. There was no sun in their lives.

Remember that moment when you look out the window of your departing aircraft and all you see are gray clouds whipping by in a gloomy, grey rainy day. Then, suddenly, you just shoot right through the clouds and you've reached this magical plateau in the sky, and it is sapphire blue with brilliant sunshine and cold, clear air. You look below and you've left the gloom and doom and grayness and sameness behind. You seem closer to your goal; the sky is blue; the sun is warm and you're going somewhere.

We need to remember to do that when we are in an environment that is debilitating to mind, body and soul. Don't socialize with negative people. Any time you hear a negative expression, say something positive! When someone curses, again say something positive. If someone is gray and gloomy, you be bright. Don't be afraid to show that inner glow; show that fire that is glowing inside you.

# *forty four*

## Lay Railway Tracks To The Far Horizon

**Ready steady and fire**

Intensity can also be debilitating. In South Carolina I have a friend who is a black-powder rifle aficionado. He makes these beautiful 18th century replica muskets and, on one of my visits, he asked if I would like to fire one. He'd hung a target on a tree and as the musket was fairly heavy, I found that if you put the 'V' of the sights on the bull's eye and held it there for too long, you'd start to waver and invariably you'd miss. Whereas, if you slowly moved the muzzle towards a point and then when you got the destination, which was the bull's eye, in sight, and just fired, you'd invariably hit it – most times!

Now, in life we are deluged by different levels of intensity. If you're focused on achieving something, if you're focused on resolving something; advancing yourself intellectually or being a better painter, or whatever, you obviously have to do that in an evolutionary way. But if you concentrate so intensely, it's as though you're trying to intimidate the result to come to you.

Visualize staring into the eye of the sun – boom! You'll go blind and won't see anything. So try to achieve what you're aiming for with a lack of overpowering intensity. Commitment and persistence is what you are aiming for, liberally seasoned with optimism and positive energy. Persistence weakens resistance.

This sounds as though I'm negating what I've said before but I'm not. You have a destination in mind and it's in sight; you've a goal to achieve; you've troubles and problems and issues you are trying to resolve and you're moving along at your specific speed. You are achieving; you're moving incrementally but if you hold that vision too long and stare too long at it you will start to waver. In other words, there is a time for action and a time for delay.

When you get that goal in sight you must move. You have to move otherwise you'll be like the muzzle of that black-powder rifle focusing on the goal; it's going to start to waver and shake and is going to drop. Whereas if you get it in your sights and you fire you'll hit the goal. A lesson learned in South Carolina!

Another thing we must learn about ourselves is what I called our Plimsoll Line of security. It's basically knowing yourself and knowing your limits; your strengths and weaknesses; knowing your likes and dislikes. All through this odyssey we're been talking about, we have been exploring those issues; trying to find out who we are. But in our evolution we must be aware of our Plimsoll Line of security which dictates that you've reached the limit – maybe just for that particular moment; that particular day, that month or year. You've reached an incremental point, a milestone that is safe and secure. It's comfortable; you're fine tuning and polishing that particular objective. Once that's reached it's another piece of your foundation laid in place and you can jump along, you can move ahead.

But if you get too greedy and act with no forethought, problems will arise. Let's say you're building a brick wall. In order to build a brick wall everything has to be lined up evenly; you have to use the right type of bricks for the job at hand; the right consistency of mortar to adhere the bricks together. If you try to jump ahead too quickly the mortar will be weak possibly, and the wall will start to crumble.

Although sometimes you think it would be great to jump on that train and just fly along on those railroad tracks that you built – wow, fantastic! Yes, but you may get to a point when you suddenly realize there is no railroad track ahead and the train is going to crash. You always have to be ahead of the game in this exploration of yourself. You always have to be aware that in order to go forward you are laying some sort of foundation.

The pioneers and early explorers, who were wandering across the wastelands of North America, had no railroad tracks to go on. But what they did have were rivers to follow. They would follow the tracks of animals and, of course, they had the indigenous first nation's peoples to help them. You are pioneering within and becoming your own path finder.

So, just be aware of that Plimsoll Line of security. You have a plan, you're on this journey and you're on your way; you are heading towards becoming a ten or an eleven – possibly you'll become a Saint when you're fourteen – who knows! Just know your own limitations. Like going along on the old bicycle! When you go along and you're going too quickly you can just put the brakes on and slow yourself down a little bit. We've all heard the expression "I'm going so quickly I can't think any more."

You must give yourself time to think, just put the brakes on very gently and if need be, just stop. You can go back a little bit; there's no disgrace in going back to check something. It's not like surrendering or retreating. All you're doing is going back to review, to assess, to reaffirm that what you have done is right. Then you get back on that track because it's already there and you get to that milestone and with that you start to move progressively again.

I remember an incident when I was working on a movie set. I was employed as an extra; euphemistically termed "moveable furniture." This particular setting lay in a beautiful sunny meadow fringed by trees and bordering a grassy river front.

When we had breaks it was interesting to see how the groups broke up into almost three distinct areas. One of the groups would huddle under the shade of the trees; that was their choice. Others would sit broiling in the middle of the lawn with the full intensity of the sun on them. The third group was interesting! It was as though they couldn't decide which they were, the shadow people or the sun people, so they would sort of flit between the sun and the shade.

Maybe that's a bit more reasonable, but I'm a sun worshiper so I was sitting out in the sunshine. That's like life; we have choices that we can make and the choices that we do make. You can choose the light or you can choose the shade, or you can go back and forth.

But when I say dark or shade, I'm not talking in terms of negativity, the blackness, the bleakness. I'm talking in terms of shades of your being. There are some people who just love to be in the limelight because they're extroverts and that's their true nature. They're not wearing any masks when they're in front of an audience or in the limelight, as we would say. Other people are quite happy to be in the background for that's their role and they're quite content in the supporting role. As extras that's what we were; we were not even supporting, just moveable furniture, but we were supporting the overall film.

Then there were the stars and those with minor roles who drifted between the shade of the extra and the star limelight. That's o.k. As we've said before, not everyone can be a Dostoyevsky, a Dickens, a Gauguin, Van Gough, We all have different limits; we all have different strengths and some of us are going to be floods of Mississippis, Niles and Amazons. Some of us are going to be gentle, possibly unnamed, tributaries, but we are all essential to the overall good of the world in general through our own unique contribution.

I love the word incremental, but incrementally we are all feeding that flood of life. Whether people are looking for art works, or music, or books, whatever; they all have different likes and desires. They may want to pick up a light- hearted novel to read in the summertime – which is almost like disposable literature in some ways – you read it quickly, it's enjoyable and it's as quickly forgotten. Some may want to immerse themselves again in the classics that may prove to be indecipherable to others. The same with music; you can go from highbrow classical to the new rap, country or whatever. There are different degrees, different variations and sensitivities in the music; the same with painting and art.

So, we have different levels. We should never be embarrassed or we should never feel flawed because we're not a Mother Theresa, a Gauguin or Paul McCartney. As long as we've achieved the best we possibly can then our ego and our self-worth is satisfied. As long as we feel that have justified to, I guess, our creator that we're the best we possibly can be, that is good. But don't deprecate yourself; don't get embroiled in the guilt situation.

Guilt! One of my faults is procrastination. Sometimes I have really good intentions of doing something but I delay and say "I've got to get around to that." A practical example is: for a long, long time the shower door in our master en suite bathroom was an ongoing irritation. It had never been properly installed which caused it to jam. Each time it was opened or closed there was a clunking or clanking and a pulling and shoving. I procrastinated and said that I would fix it but I delayed and delayed until the guilt got on top of me and I fixed it. Suddenly the door opens and closes easily!

How often do we do that? We know there is something we can achieve and sometimes it's very easily achievable; it's something that takes very little effort. The shower door, for example, was not a monumental thing – I took a few screws off and, as my wife would say, I made a meal of it, but it wasn't a major thing.

So, procrastination leads to guilt and we've talked about that before in the beaver dam situation where you build things up until they are ready to explode. You have to learn to pick your time, ease the pressure and do the job – achieve!

# forty five

## Off The Beaten Track

**Peek through the curtains**

Last weekend my wife and I decided to take a trip along the Sunshine Coast, which is a rural waterfront area just north of Vancouver, British Columbia, Canada.

We've been there many times before on this Peninsula, which is accessed by ferry boat only. So, in essence, you arrive at the bottom by ferry and drive along one road to the top then leave again by ferry to go to another place. Because we've always been going to our cabin, which is on an island at the top end of the Peninsula, we catch the ferry, nip off the ferry then drive straight up the road onto the other ferry and we'd never really seen the Sunshine Coast. We were on one main road; we were focused; there was no meandering because of time limitations; so we never saw the Sunshine Coast.

Now, I've always been a great admirer of the blank spaces on maps. To me the most exciting word I ever saw when I was a kid, and even to this day, was the word "unexplored." I'd look at a map of the world with all the beautiful colours of its rivers and tributaries. Along the coast, the main cities were clearly defined and you could see mountain peaks; but sometimes you could see a little area, or a bit area, that was white, and across it in black letters would be the word "unexplored."

To me that one word meant an unknown area where the world as we see it did not exist: where anything was possible. The hubbub, the trials and tribulations of our modern age would vanish; there would be more trials and tribulations of a different sort, but there would be peoples who had never seen the horrendous mistakes that we've made; there would exist flora and fauna that we've never seen before. That was the most exciting thing! To me, looking at that one word and that white area was more exciting than looking at the rest of the map.

So, on this specific trip on the Sunshine Coast, for the first time we decided to explore – and it was mind blowing! We spent two days just meandering down side roads along the scenic coastline; finding little coves and quaint ocean-side restaurants and inns; little bistros. We had a stimulating two days off the beaten track, revitalizing our lives and relationship.

Life! Just think about your life like that. We start off child-like and adventuresome until we're programmed by society. We've left school; we've gone to university; we've selected a profession; we've taken a job and moved to the suburbs with a wife and 1.2 kids, blah, blah, blah. We are now on a focused highway and we're not meandering at all.

Yes, there are some justifications for that. We may convince our-selves that we are living good lives filled with happiness. We have lov-ing partners, children, the benefits of where we live and the life we have created. But we're on this highway and in many ways it's like the railroad tracks that we're zipping along. You may think "one day I'm going to do "X" or I'm going to become an opera singer; I'm going to become a painter; I'm going to make furniture out of driftwood" – whatever! You have this little dream and, like the railroad tracks on the prairie, you say "when I get to that point I'm going to start doing this."

It's like looking at the horizon while you're zipping along this men-tal-tracked highway and watching that little point continually evading you and moving further away. Not really further away; it's always the same distance away from you, like the horizon, which of course you can never reach: or can you? So, what do you do? Often times you say "well, I guess I'm too old." You know that stupid expression "you can't teach an old dog new tricks" and all the rest of it.

Just last week I read in the paper of a woman, a 108-year-old Sardinian woman, who was the oldest woman in the world. At this incredible age she had a really strong desire; a passion, to go back to school and take some lessons. And apparently she did! She went to school with some teenagers at that incredible age. She was an old dog but she learned some new tricks: so, it's never too late.

You can actually get to that point that we have talked about, the convergence of the lines. You can pull it towards you; just use your will power, your imagination, your visualization powers and bring it to you and say "world, as of tomorrow I'm going to do this," or "my game plan is to do the following…" Again, you do it incrementally. I'm not inviting you to give up your job, abandon your family, and escape to the South Pacific. No, I'm saying there are different levels to your goals depending on what they are. As we've said before, some of the goals may be unrealistic or appear to be unattainable. If you suddenly say when you're 70, "I'm going to be a fighter pilot;" then the likelihood of that is not too strong. But if you make realistic goals; and by saying that do I mean compromise; possibly. But one little step is better than no steps at all. That's what we must always remember.

## *forty six*
## Tinker, Tailor Or What?

**Dream your destination**

Traveling, moving along roads; reaching and leaving destinations, endless journeys! Earlier I wrote of my memory of hitch hiking in the Highlands of Scotland, a rough romantic land, filled with soaring peaks, moorlands, quiet fishing villages, sheep, deer, castles, ruins, crofts, and picturesque villages. On one of my trips a small vehicle stopped and the driver, who was a tinker, smiled and said "jump in."

Traditionally, Tinkers are like Gypsies, itinerants, who roam through villages and towns repairing pots, pans and assorted metalware. This man was filled with the milk of human kindness as he told me his life story.

His great sense of pride was that he was beholden to no-one, except, perhaps, the Creator. He had a small patch of land, maybe one or two acres, of rough land that was pretty well worthless to anyone else, but he had a goat; a cow for milk; some chickens. He lived close to the coastline so he would go with his children down to the beaches, in season, and gather shellfish, cockles and mussels and the like. He would go fishing, and he smiled as he said that, because "fishing" was his euphemism for poaching. He would catch salmon and sell them door-to-door, and he would do handyman repairs. From the viewpoint of monetary assets, which were negligible; his land was worthless and his vehicle was held together with wire and string basically; but he was a very contented man!

Superficially many would say that this man lived a poor, threadbare existence, but here was an individual who had achieved a sense of perfection through adversity and variety. He didn't just say "I'm going to be a farmer, or a fisherman or a handyman." He did it all. He had a cow for milk and a few chickens for eggs, which he could also sell; he could pick up shellfish and fish; in the meantime he could do some repairs. He did lots of things. Some people would say reluctantly that he had a sort of freedom. To others, he was a slave to the so-called hard life that he had. He was tied to an unforgiving piece of land where growing crops was impossible - the main crop would be rocks. The vagaries of nature and time had waited until this light- hearted tinker had transformed these un-tillable acres into a haven.

Some people would say he was burdened with the drudgery of a hard life. But he was a happy man and he was beholden to no man. He didn't owe any money to anyone; he had achieved happiness. Again, there are different levels of happiness.

We've talked in terms of trying to become the greatest author, painter or whatever, in the world and you may have to compromise and say "well, look, I'm going to be the best tributary that I possibly can. I may not be a great river but I'll be a small tributary and I'm happy with that." If you become discontented with your role then that's where your negativity starts to develop and that's when your self-esteem starts to fade. This man had simple goals on the journey to happiness. Remember not all goals must be atom splitting; not everyone is going to discover how to split the atom; discover the intricacies of DNA; how to paint a van Gough; or how to be the best film star, a superstar.

Often when I'm lying in bed I look through the window at the sky and when the sky is clear the heavens are filled with a multitude of stars. They're all shapes and sizes and of different intensities; some are clustered together, some are isolated and some are barely visible and you have to look at them obliquely to really see them; but they're all stars and they're all in the heavens and all have a special place there. That's us, we're all stars but with a different, specific place in the constellation – the constellation of this odyssey called life.

From the vibrant to the barely flickering, to the medium, again in the pH scale of life a lot of the stars are a seven with some so low that

they are barely discernible. But they're still there serving their purpose of illuminating the heavens. Our own luminosity will increase as
we stoke the fires within.

Maybe I spend too much time looking out of my window. I can witness the subtle flow of the seasons just by sitting there by my window. I
am privileged to see the sun setting and the sun rising. The trees moving, tug boats passing, the tides ebbing and flowing. The cornucopia
of life! I can also see the predatory storms when they launch their
attack.

But, some people spend a lifetime of pessimism anticipating the
worst. An example is that where we live we get battered by storms
called "Squamish Winds" several times a year. These winds are of
the steroid variety, whipping the trees back and forth and throwing
branches onto the roof. And you think "we're going to be killed or
end up in Kansas like Dorothy in the Wizard of Oz." Now, think about
it this way. If you hear four days in advance that there is a huge, major
storm with gale force winds advancing towards the West Coast, towards
your area, you could spend those four days in anxiety, stress and worry.
You're going to be depleting your energy moment by moment until,
when the storm eventually hits, if indeed it does hit, you may be too
exhausted to tackle it.

Whereas, someone who is out working in his yard and has missed
that particular storm warning on the radio or T.V; and he doesn't read
the papers because he's happy doing his own thing – he doesn't hear
about it, so when the storm hits he has the resilience of his energy, his
passion, to accept it, to tackle it, to combat it and come to terms with it.

Now, in life, as I say, a lot of people are perpetually anticipating
the negativity of that storm. They become paranoid, they become passionless, stressed and anxiety ridden because they are always anticipating the worst. They're saying "there's no point in doing this because
the consequence will be that." They're always looking at the negative
aspect; they're not looking toward the positive aspect until they're
exhausted. They're always looking for that storm to hit them and they
become ill, sick in a self- perpetuating cycle. They say "see I told you I
was going to become ill." Yes, because you made yourself ill.

Whereas, if you think optimistically you still can know that there's a
potential for storms out there, but if you spend every moment of every

day sitting looking out there, waiting for the first breeze, you're going to become sick. You will reap your own storm wind.

Probably close to 20 years ago I decided I'd like to have a boat so I bought a 22 foot wooden cabin cruiser which I rebuilt inside and out. I then sunk a mooring buoy in front of our house. I went through the passion of rebuilding the boat with a vision, a dream. Then I went through the labour of sinking engine blocks chained together off our shoreline, as an anchor, with a line up to the buoy which the boat was tied to. So far so good! The problem was that from my house I could look through the trees that fringed the ocean and I could see my boat sitting at the buoy.

But, as boats will do, it would gradually move from side to side, back and forth. Now, when it went behind the trees I'd wonder "has it broken its moorings, has it drifted off?" And then it would come back into view. I found I was expending nervous energy, sitting at that window looking out at the boat waiting for it to come back into focus.

If we do that in life; if we continually sit looking for problems – as people might say "nitpicking" – looking for negative things so we can jeer "I told you that would happen." Like the practice of telling someone they're no good until they become no good. But if you nitpick, if you're always looking for those negative things, yes, you may find them.

I always remember this anecdote. A wise man was sitting one day in a little dusty village in the desert, when a traveler approached him and said. "Excuse me, I'm looking for a new village to move to. "Would you please describe the type of people who live here? The wise man answered. "Well, what were the people like in the village you left?" The traveler replied. "They were backbiting, stabbing, vicious; a thoroughly nasty bunch." And the wise man replied. "Well that's what you'll find here." Another man came along – same scenario – and again the wise man responded to the man's question. "What were the people like in the village you left?" "Oh! They were generally understanding; caring, gentle and sharing." And the wise man smiled. "Well, that's what you'll find here."

So, you reap what you sow, you really do. If you exert negative vibes, you're going to get that back again. It's like throwing a rubber ball hard against a wall and as it bounces back and hits you in the face, you say "what happened there?" Well, you provided the impetus and it just rebounded. Like a boomerang, you throw it and if you're not careful it will come back and hit you as well.

In life, as we go along, a lot of people say, "I need to see, feel and touch it to believe it. There's no way that's going to happen, I don't understand that." We've talked before in this book about visualizing; we've talked in terms of where you make your special retreat where you go to internally. But, you know, visualization should always come before action.

When we bought our house, it had many windows which took advantage of beautiful ocean views. But here was one wall, an angled wall, a solid wall with no windows, and when you stood on the deck in front of that wall you looked towards the most gorgeous view. You saw the village in the distance, the boats, the ferries, the music of the world; this exquisite maritime wonderland in front of us. Yet this was a solid wall so, for a couple of years, I would look at that wall and visualize the view through it. Then one day I decided to put a window in there.

So, I did what I do best, I measured it up and hoped there were no electrical cables; cut a huge hole, put a window in it and the world suddenly opened attain. Let there be light and views! Visualization!

Visualization is, I guess, the ability to see something that isn't there at that particular time. Now to some people that may seem ethereal, but the analogy of the window is that when I looked at the wall before the window, I could visualize the panoramic view through it and once I installed the window; voila, just as I imagined!

I remember years ago in the mini-series "SHOGUN" starring Richard Chamberlain as the English sailor who was shipwrecked in Japan, there was a sequence that had a huge impact on me. It concerned Richard Chamberlain sitting with a Zen master archer in a room discussing weapons. Chamberlain, of course, with the Western mind set had his black powder pistol and the Samurai Zen master archer had this exquisite bow and arrow. Chamberlain was talking on a purely superficial level about his weapon; about the mechanical aspect of the weapon and shooting. The Samurai was talking about his weapon in a more spiritual, visual way.

To prove his point the Samurai, who had become irritated with Chamberlain, turned and suddenly said to him "do you see a wooden gate post at the front of your house?" He answered "yes, I know where it is." The Samurai just closed his eyes and fired three arrows in succession through the Shoji wall and the arrows hit the wooden gate post. Chamberlain walked over and the three arrows were identically in top of the post. Now, this transformed the Englishman's way of thinking. Visualization had taken the arrows there. The Samurai had visualized the wooden gate post through the wall and hit it; he didn't have to physically see it, but his mind did.

So, that's what visualization is. It's almost like a supreme confidence in your ability to see through something, or to see the end result. The Samurai warrior, by looking at this solid wall, even with his eyes closed, was able to see his arrows piercing the wall and hitting the post. Most of us tend to think in terms of achieving and doing something by thinking "if I start, that's the main thing; give me that hammer, or give me that pencil." That may work sometimes, but the reality is if you visualize something before you undertake the task, it makes the end result easier to achieve.

Before I start any project - like when I was building the cottage – in my mind I was hammering nails, trimming the trees, cutting boards and doing all that so when the time came to actually construct the cottage it was easier. A lot of athletes do that; they visualize themselves running the most perfect race of their lives: beating everyone; their breathing is perfect; their leg muscles are fine- tuned and they win a gold medal before they actually do it.

If you learn to do that, learn to visualize things, be the best you possibly can and witness the end result before it is actually done. Visualize that you've reached the end of the race; visualize that you've reached a 14 on the scale that we talked about. You are seeing the picture of the best that you possibly can be. Visualize your perfection and taste it, feel it and sense it. As we spoke before about fine tuning your senses, when you visualize, savor the senses as well.

Visualize the impact on the sentient aspects of your body. If you're building something, like when I was building the cabin I could smell the sawdust. I could feel the hammer hitting the nails; I could hear the sound of the saw. I could hear all those things. I could smell it and taste it and feel it. All through the magical power of visualization!

Some people think: "what is the point of doing this; what's the point of visualizing myself becoming the best artist, writer, person, relationship builder, when there's nothing original left. Originality has all gone; there are no more new words to be said; no more truly original paintings to be done; there are no more intense relationships to foster. Anthony and Cleopatra; Romeo and Juliet had loving, passionate relationships so there's no point in me attempting to emulate them. There is no originality left."

Now, if you make the mistake of submerging yourself in negativity and surrender, nothing will ever happen. The world will grind to a stop and evolution will not progress. Yes, originally there must have been an original thought; multiple original thoughts to devise the wheel. Yes, originally someone invented the wheel. Everything since that time is premised on the wheel.

Take my Grandfather's watch. Look inside the watch and witness how all the wheels and cogs are premised incrementally on something else. The same proposition applies to music. The first musical sound would have been achieved by banging a branch against a tree for a drum; blowing through a reed or a piece of grass to make a whistle. Everything subsequently evolved; there was an evolutionary process. So, when someone says there's no originality, no original thoughts left in the world, think of a sunset: they may all appear to flood the horizon with the flamboyance of vivid sameness, but like a snowflake they are all intrinsically different. Original in fact!

# *forty seven*

## Variations On A Theme

**Creative piggy-back**

When Einstein formulated his theory of relativity, surely he was building on the more mundane, scientific innovations of the past. Some people quote "there's nothing new under the heavens." Yes, when you go to any movie you will notice that they're all variations on a theme. Granted there are only so many words, but it is how those words are assembled that give meaning. Yes, there are only so many musical notes. I didn't invent them; great musicians didn't cry "'Eureka" one day; but, by interspersing and changing the positions of those notes you get an original work of art.

Is it plagiarism to use a wheel because someone else invented it a long time ago? Is it plagiarism to use notes; to use words; to use paints? Only if you copy what someone else has done. That is plagiarism. In other words, you have not built incrementally on someone else's discovery. Invention and innovation are processes; the building blocks of new creations, but for someone to say "that's been done before," that may be an incorrect statement.

For instance, if someone living on a little isolated island simultaneously invents something that has been invented in another place, that is not plagiarism; it is not copying. It is his original thought. But because we live in a world of homogenization with the global village concept, communication and ideas that happen simultaneously can be broadcast instantaneously.

Don't be afraid of your idea; of expressing your thought, of exploring what you think is right. It may be just a slight variation on that theme, but it may be all that really matters.

You know the expression "going off on a tangent." I once met a man and I asked how he earned his bread and butter. He said he specialized in the incomprehensible world of differential equations, or differential analysis. And I said, being a stunted mathematical mutant, "what does that really mean?"

He said, "An example is a space ship leaving earth to go to a planet; we have to work out the speed that is required to leave earth to get through gravity; we need to work out the position of the planet at a specific time, and get the trajectory of the space ship to coincide with that moment in time when the planet is at a certain spot."

I voiced the thought that it was all beyond me so he said "differential analysis, or differential equation, is a way of working all these things out so that the space ship will be in the right spot at the right time, if it isn't it will go off on a tangent. Remember school geometry and all the puzzles around circles. If a line just touches the edge of the circumference of the circle it's going to go off on a tangent and miss the whole thing totally."

So that's what this man specialized in, with his differential analysis; to be finite in his calculations and be able to hit an "invisible mark" in the vastness of space.

When you think about it, that's such a complex concept, at least to me, to hit something millions of miles away; eons of years away, and here we are trying to resolve an issue without going off on a tangent. Surely it must be easier to do that.

Now this scientist has spent a lifetime studying one little component of his complex endeavor. He has prepared all the equations and theorems and the theory of how it should go; plots it all then gives it to someone else who designs the space craft until, collectively, the space ship arrives at the space station or the planet.

When we're trying to resolve issues or set ourselves goals, oftentimes we do that ourselves. I mean we're trying to aim for a certain point and we don't want to go off on a tangent. We want to make sure we hit it accurately. Yet how often we make premature decisions with no prior planning or forethought, and become overwhelmed when we fail to "hit the mark." Apply your brakes; visualize what you hope to achieve and do not always go for the quick fix. Successful endeavor requires a strong dose of optimism liberally seasoned with the creativity of positive visualization.

Self-sufficiency is a tough concept in our modern age. The closest most of us get to the concept is through T.V, shows like "Survivor" with its pathetic groups clinging to alliances. We spoke in terms of the scientist collaborating in a team effort to reach space, but individually when we are left to tackle problems ourselves, how do we do that?

There is a small craggy island off the coast of Scotland, connected by a causeway to the mainland. The people who live on the island are extremely self-sufficient in many ways, but they always know in the back of their minds that all they have to do to get to the mainland is cross over the causeway and they're there. It's almost like an insurance policy: "no matter what happens on this Island, I can always get in my car and drive over the causeway."

Even if they don't use that causeway, it is still there as a last resort. Inherently they rely on that as a crutch for the unexpected eventualities of life. Now, what will happen if suddenly the causeway is washed away, demolished and they can no longer have it. Even if they don't use it they'll want to rebuild; they'll want that umbilical link to the mainland.

This is analogous to us. We're individuals, we are islands, yet we have various causeways that we have access to. Let's take an example: when you go home you may believe you are an individual and you can pretend you're self- sufficient, but you go home to a multitude of causeways to the world. To friends, family, business associates, department stores. For example, the telephone – it's a causeway. It is a lifeline, but it's a causeway connecting you with other people.

Basic electricity in the home is a causeway providing heat and all the comforts you rely on. You switch on your television or the radio, and you have a causeway to entertainment or learning. You switch on your computer and you have e-mail, you have the internet; you've access to the world through that. Even when you travel outside your house, you have your cell phone which is a causeway linking you again to people and places. So, although we're all individual little islands, we have all these causeways.

Now what happens when the causeways vanish; they're displaced; they're ripped out and they no longer exist. How are we going to tackle living with no support systems? Are we going to become self-sufficient? How do we do that? How do we reach into ourselves and find internal causeways to give us support – are we going to panic?

As I mentioned earlier, probably 20 years ago in our village, the main bridge which was a causeway from the village to the big city, was washed out by a flood. The people who drove down to that bridge just parked their cars and stared around in awe, despair and wonderment; with a pervasive sense of dislocation and isolation. This major causeway was gone. The issue was resolved by a temporary bridge which then became a permanent bridge and the causeway was renewed again. But for the space of time when people realized that their causeway was severed, people responded in different ways.

Similarly, in our village, we get ferocious winter winds which hurtle down the Sound. When the power is knocked out the whole village is plunged into blackness and living in your homes reverts to inhabiting little dark caves. The first thing we always do is light a fire.

Symbolically, the flickering of the flames provides comfort, warmth, light and companionship. A fire dancing in a fireplace is a friendly reminder of all the things that are relevant to us. And what we normally do in our house is sit round the fire with a blanket around us; stare into the flames and talk. For a limited space of time we can forget all the causeways; the telephone; the hydro which provides the heat in the house, the movies we're missing on T.V., our favourite shows, the radio. All those things we can forget for a period of time because we're play-acting. We know the power is going to come back on again – that support system is going to renew itself and be given back to us. So, for that short period of time, we're self-sufficient.

The classic image of someone becoming a castaway on a desert island comes to mind – but what happens when there's no causeway, no lifeline or support system? We have to rely on ourselves, and that's usually when you hear people saying "I dug deep into myself and found resources I didn't even know I had." And that's true: when we have all these support systems provided to us on a platter we really don't have to dig deep inside ourselves to support ourselves.

I'm certainly not advocating we all become hermits and move into a cave and grow our own crops – become the classic hewer of wood and hauler of water. What I am saying is, at least we should be aware of the so-called lifelines that you have; these so-called causeways. Use them if you wish, but do not totally depend on them. And, like the islanders on that little island with the causeway in Scotland, don't become so reliant on it that when it goes, you panic.

If you provide your own internal supports; if you have been following the process so far, and you've been rekindling your fire, your passion, your optimism, your sense of positive thinking; if you've been fine tuning and honing your talents and abilities, and you are progressing along that trail that we spoke about, you won't feel the same panic. You won't be as anxious as other people would be.

Some people throughout their lives pride themselves in giving to other people, and that is a wonderful thing to do, but the reality is that a lot of people often give with an expectation of something in return. So, it's really like a barter system; people will say things like "if you scratch my back, I'll scratch yours." Now, that's not giving, that's bartering, that's selling a commodity.

True giving; and we spoke in terms of the creative bully who hoards his talents until he sells them, belittling people who he thinks do not have the abilities that he does have. And we spoke of creativity like the shovel of coal that you can take from one place and prime and kindle in another person. So, the more you give, the more you receive.

On New Year's Eve in Scotland we would wander through our immediate neighbourhoods with a New Year bag. In that bag were usually a bottle of Scotch whisky, which is the ubiquitous drink in Scotland, a bottle of Port and a bottle of Sherry. You would visit your neighbours and walk into their homes, where there was usually a nice Ceilidh (a singsong) going on. You would pour a glass of Scotch, usually for the man of the house, and a glass of Port or Sherry for the lady of the house. This was a gift for them. They in turn, always gave you a drink back; but there wasn't an expectation of that. You were not giving them a drink so that they would reciprocate. Otherwise you could have stayed home and drank the bottle yourself.

258 | Bill Kimmett

So, if you give, and you twiddle your thumbs and wait for the person to reach behind them to give you something, you're again relying on them to support you. You are saying "I gave you X therefore you must give me Y." The more you develop; the more you balance your life; the more you fine tune your optimistic streak, the more you'll have to give. It's as though you're continually priming your soul, priming your whole being. In the well, once you prime it and start to pump that handle, the water just gushes out effortlessly because you've taken the time and effort to prime it. Similarly, with the fire and the little shovel of coal starting the fire in another place, that's a form of priming. Again, all this leads to a form of self-sufficiency which means the stronger you are, the more self-sufficient you become, the less need you have for causeways.

The only need that will develop in you is the need to help, the need to give, the need to share and, as we've said, when you prime the well of your soul and your spirit, you will have bountiful water and grace; affection, optimism and light to share with the world around you. But always remember, if you do it with an air of pomp and ceremony and pride, and a sense of the benevolent, you will almost negate who you are and what you're doing. Give gracefully, give with love with no expectation of return and it will amaze you how much love will come back to you.

A few weeks ago I went to visit a friend who had just returned from a trip to Nepal where he had been trekking. We sat chatting in the living room and I noticed, on his coffee table, a little ornately carved metal bowl with a small club lying beside it. It looked like a mortar and pestle used for grinding up herbs and spices when you're cooking. The little bowl was sitting there and I said to him "what is that?" I can't remember the exact terminology he gave for it but I term it "the singing bowl."

He said, "In Nepal you take the bowl in your hand which you arc and then you strike the edge of the bowl with the little club rotating it round the bowl until it makes a singing sound, almost like a mantra." I picked up the bowl and struck it and this beautiful humming, singing mantra came from the bowl. I did it two or three times and each time this pristine, bell-like sound rang. My friend said "you have a real talent for doing that."

Several weeks later, back in the same home with some other friends, I noticed the bowl was still sitting on the table. This time I decided to show off.  I decided to show my great musical talents by playing this singing bowl.  I picked it up, struck it, rotated the little club round the edge and nothing happened!  I tried several times and each time – nothing happened.  The reason, I believe, is that I was doing it with an expectation of a return, an expectation of praise; "look how wonderful I am."

It was like gift giving.  I was going to give them the gift of this musical sound and they, in turn, were expected to give me approbation, praise as to how wonderful I was – and it didn't work; I had done it with intensity.  We spoke before about how when you hold the muzzle of your rifle too long on the target, you miss your target because you're too intense. So, there were several lessons learned there.  I was looking for praise "I will give you music, you will tell me how wonderful I am;" I did it with intensity and it didn't work.  I know the old Zen masters say similar things; that the harder you try, the less you can achieve. Less is better.

Think back to when you were a child or even as an adult; you taste something special, some delicious food that's been prepared, or some delicious dessert, and you that the taste is incredible, it's beautiful; my taste buds have never experienced a flavour like that.  So you take a little bit more and a little bit more, thinking to yourself that if a little bit is good, more is better.  But, ultimately you saturate your system with the taste until you feel uncomfortable; until you don't want to eat another bite and you no longer enjoy it.  You've taken too much. You've bitten off more than you can chew, or your eyes are bigger than your stomach.

So, because something is good, don't become so intense that you devote every second of your existence to it otherwise you may create a fire which is going to engulf you.  Do not become a slave to your senses. Less is actually better than more.

Again, as kids in Scotland, we would play games of improvisation before the days of T.V. , so we were always outside playing, and our favourite game was playing with bows and arrows.  This was in the days of Davie Crocket, Cowboys and Indians and all that; so we played with bows and arrows.  We would venture into the countryside and

260 | Bill Kimmett

cut branches and twigs for bows and arrows. I remember one day I came home with the requisite branch for the bow and the twigs for the arrows, and we arranged to meet later so we could do target practice and try to hunt some birds – which we never actually hit.

I remember I spent that day making my bow. I took all the bark off the wood and sanded it and even painted what I thought was a nice primitive motif on it with water colour paints. I even found a bit of string and a feather and hung the feather on it. But, when the time came to play and I ran outside, all the other boys had their bows and arrows and they were firing the arrows and were having a whale of a time. I realized I'd spent all my time making the bow and there had been no time to make the arrows. So, again, balance in everything. If you devote yourself exclusively to one thing, you're going to miss out on another.

It was the same when I made my flintlock pistol when I was a teenager. The pistol was only as good as the black powder and lead ball that you put into it. So, again if you spend all your time making the pistol with no time to find the black powder – it would also be useless.

## forty eight

# Yachts Without Wind: Dreams Without Action

**Journey without movement.**

You often hear people saying things like "I like to see the big picture." Think about that. Let us revisit our house which overlooks the ocean. The ocean is far enough away that I cannot hear the waves; I don't hear the lapping of the tides. I can see the general hazy spindrift of the wind blowing over the water and the waves, but I don't get an intimate closeness. But what I lose on that side, I get from the viewpoint of a bigger picture, I can see the horizon, I can see over the islands and I can see boats miles away. I can see an expansive view.

I drove down to the beach and took a walk along the sand and, yes, there was the ocean. My feet were crunching through the sand and I could hear the waves lapping and the symphony of the tide. I could see and hear the seagulls drifting close beside little boats which were rolling back and forth. And I could smell the spray in the air, the salt. I looked at the houses on that waterfront and they were almost eye-level with the water with a limited view of the horizon because they looked straight into the islands. They didn't look over them and they couldn't see the horizon; although there were certainly compensations. I guess life is like that in some ways; it's a compromise. In other words, you can't have everything.

I can't live in the house that I do, high on the mountainside overlooking the whole world below; the ocean, the boat, the islands and also sense the tactile, sensory feeling of the water lapping on my toes. I can get it if I live on the waterfront, but then I lose the big picture.

In life, there are probably two kinds of people: those who enjoy the big picture and those who are quite happy, on the micro level looking at small segments of their lives.

When you talk in terms of the big picture and the little picture, again, there are increments to it. Think in terms of the feather syndrome or the straw that broke the camel's back. I remember when I was a child there was a question that people used to always throw around thinking they were extremely smart: "what would you rather have, a ton of coal dropped on you or a ton of feathers?" Of course we would always say a ton of feathers. So, analytically, I mean a ton of feathers weighs the same as a ton of coal, so the smart answer would be "it doesn't matter, they both weigh the same." But the reality is a ton of feathers falling on you is going to be less abrasive than a ton of coal falling on you. Obviously, the combined weight is going to suffocate you, but for a moment it's going to be more pleasurable if the feathers fall on you.

The point of this seemingly mindless story is that in life we accept pressures, we accept demands and oftentimes we find it hard to say "no," until we accept more than we should. It's like that extra feather that suffocates.

I received a telephone call yesterday from the coordinator of a volunteer agency. It's a good organization and each year I'm asked to volunteer to go door-to-door and collect donations for this charitable cause. I've done it for quite a few years and that's fine. Usually I do one route but in this phone call I was asked if I would do an extra route because someone was sick. I said "yes, I can do that," and there was a silence, and then the voice said "would it be possible for you to co-ordinate your whole area?" I asked what it would entail and the answer was that there were 23 canvassers and I would be responsible for all the packages and ensuring they each got one, and to make sure they were complete in time. At that stage I knew it would be too heavy for me to bear.

It's hard to say no sometimes because we all like to be liked, we all like to be loved, and to say yes is often easier than saying no. But, how many of us have said yes to something that we really don't want to do? And when we leave that situation we say "I really wish I had not done that, my heart isn't in it. Back to knowing your limits.

Earlier we spoke of the Plimsoll Line of security. The Plimsoll Line on ships is painted on the hull and, when a cargo is loaded, the ship should not sink below that mark because below that is an unsafe level. That's what we do when we learn to say no. When I said I couldn't become a coordinator I knew that would be the feather that would push me below the Plimsoll Line of safety and security.

Supports come in many forms, like the causeways that we've talked about. I was in South Carolina on the east coast of the U.S.A. last year staying at a beach front resort. The island that we stayed on was essentially a sandbar with houses on it. When you sat on the beach, from one end of the island you would see a flock of pelicans; they would fly just above the roof line, cruise to one end of the island, turn and cruise back again. It took me a few minutes to realize that the birds were relying on thermals that were rising from the island. The sun was heating the sand, and, I guess, the roofs of the houses. The thermals would rise and then the pelicans would just cruise back and forth relying on them.

It's the same on my island, Savary Island in British Columbia, which is similarly a sand island. In the summertime, obviously, the sand heats up and the thermals rise - and here we have bald headed eagles which cruise and spiral overhead supported by the thermals. They don't really have to work; they just extend their wings and pretty well lie on top of these warm thermals of air and allow themselves to be supported. Now, when the thermals vanish, like the causeways, the birds again have to rely on their own momentum, their own self-sufficiency, to fly through the air.

So, again, if we rely on our causeways, lifelines, support systems and thermals; if we totally rely on thermals then we're going to be inept when these things end. Certainly we can enjoy and use all of these systems, but using and relying are two different things. When you rely on something and it's no longer there, it leads to despair. When you use something, not as a crutch, not as a support, when it ends you can retrench, reach inside and become the self-sufficient person you've always wanted to be.

We are always surrounded by opposing viewpoints. An example is, "I believe that more is better," or someone else will say I "think the

Spartan aspect of less is better." How does that relate to what we're trying to do here?

Years ago when I was hiking in the Scottish Highlands, I found myself on a very precipitous mountain trail heading towards a youth hostel. The night was classically black and dismal; the wind was howling and, of course, my flash light had died but I knew that if I kept on this one little, rugged path, on the other side was a lake, or as we call them in Scotland, a Loch, and the hostel was on the other side.

So through the blackness I climbed the mountain over the trail and got to the top. I looked to where the Loch was and, of course, all I could see was a darker semblance of pitch! Then, suddenly, way in the distance I could see a pinprick of light as the trees in the forest moved in the wind and opened this little avenue, and I could see this flicker. Knowing that it had to be the hostel I got there; I got to my sanctuary.

Now, the light that I was heading for was a candle in a window. So, in the blackness of that night, all it took was the flickering of one candle in a window to let me know where my destination was. In that circumstance that was all I needed – the minuscule flicker of a candle.

On the same trip I was walking along the coastline and, again, it was a very dark, dismal day. I saw on this rocky bluff, a lighthouse. The lighthouse was illuminating the world around it with its light because that's what it needed to do. If the lighthouse relied on the minuscule glimmer of a candle, ships would never see it and it would not serve its purpose. So there's a duality of purpose – a flickering candle miles away really was enough for me to find my destination; but the lighthouse needs a multitude of light. How they do it is through a complex system of prisms and mirrors and basically they magnify the lights in the lighthouse. They're magnifying. Again, if they relied on one little spark, the ships would be foundering on rocks all the time.

Magnifying! I was sitting on my deck one night in the pitch black just looking at the sky. It was at that twilight time when the stars would be appearing and when I looked through the naked eye, I couldn't see any stars. However, when I picked up my binoculars and looked at the sky, suddenly I could see little pinpricks appearing in the heavens. Like little buds of flame appearing that you couldn't see with the naked eye. But when you magnified, you could see them. Like a prayer that

I learned as a kid, "my soul doth magnify the Lord." Magnify, expand, enlarge, make better?

Just as I was looking at the sky with the binoculars and seeing stars that I hadn't known were there a minute before, just imagine if we could fine tune our senses and look internally and see the inner star within us. But we never really learn to do that. We never go a step beyond; we rely on our eyes to see inside. Try that. With your eyes open you're surrounded by a multitude of distractions. Just as I'm sitting here, I can see the ocean, the trees, the mountains, the islands, I hear the wind. I see my room and my photographs. There is a multitude of stimuli that discourage me from focusing and finding my inner star. You really have to fire yourself with passion. You must make a commitment: "I'm going to be the best person I can possibly be."

Resolutions are only as good as the follow-through. I have a set of scales in my bathroom and if all I do is perpetually weigh myself, I'll never lose weight. Just the act of standing on the scales doesn't strip off the pounds. I have to have commitment, a passion to lose weight. I have to look after my nutrition and I have to exercise. I have to have that strong commitment that I will lose weight, so standing on the scales after I've done all these other aspects of weight loss, then I will see a change. But if all I do is stand on the scales, nothing will happen because I must follow through on these resolutions.

When we make resolutions and say "I will move forward, reject negativity, find my inner star and seek my passion." A lot of people say "what's the point, what difference can I make, I'm just me. I'm just one minuscule microbe in this whole universe." But think again, back to the story of the light. If you're in the blackest, darkest room, with all the blinds closed, no light at all – only utter stupefying blackness – and you open your eyes, all you see is blackness. You can't pierce that gloom. But if you just light a little match, that tiny flicker will illuminate the whole room and it makes a difference. So, similarly, if you feel that you can't make a difference, you're just you, just inconsequential; think in terms of that little spark that illuminates.

I mean, every bonfire starts with a little spark. In other words, if you want to make a bonfire for the world, a bonfire that's going to illuminate the heavens and the whole universe, you don't need to light that bonfire with another bonfire. All you need to do is take that little spark that is you and ignite the bonfire. But you need commitment.

All my life I've believed in having projects. It could be an artistic project – doing a water colour painting, or a building project - building rock walls in my half acre on the mountainside is a project; thinking is a project. My children always said "Dad has a project."

Now, a project is something you do, it has a beginning, middle and an end to it. Although by saying that, sometimes projects are never-ending because they're so meaningful and filled with so much joy you don't want them to come to an end. It's almost like some of the books I've read; you're reading the book and totally engrossed in the story and you can feel the idealism of the writer, you can feel his passion, you can sense the drama. You're totally enthralled; wrapped in the passion of that book and you turn the page and, suddenly it's finished. Now that's a project you don't want to end, you want it to go on forever.

To do a project properly, you must project yourself into it. The two words side-by-side look the same, they're spelled the same but the meaning is different. The project is a task. To project yourself into it, it means you're throwing yourself into it; you're hurtling yourself into it; you're lighting the beacon of the lighthouse that's within you. You're lighting the bonfire with a spark; you've found your inner star and you are throwing yourself into that with a great commitment.

Problem! We spoke a minute ago about distractions. Again, a play on words! I remember a long time ago when I was driving through Scotland, coming upon a tiny village. I drove into the village along the main street and the road suddenly had a tight ninety degree bend with a little hump back bridge over to the other side of a river. Now, if I had gone hurtling down that street at high speed into that ninety degree bend which, obviously, you wouldn't do, I would have missed it, or if I'd turned obliquely, too quickly, I'd have smashed into that wall.

So, we need to assess the cadence of that little road, the little bridge and we need to slow down and then gently drive over that ninety degree bend and make another

Ninety degree bend to go down the other side of the street to get back onto the main road. Another play on words. If we jam on our brakes at the last minute at high speed we lose traction and again we'd go off the road and smash into the bridge.

So I guess if we're doing a project and throw ourselves headlong into it, distractions are going to occur and, as we've said, distractions lead to losing traction and we go off the road and, again, the analogy of that little ninety degree bridge in Scotland. If we lose our focus at that moment we end up hitting the bridge.

You have to stay focused when you're doing your projects, leaving your mind open. Some people say "how can you do two things at the same time?" Well, I guess in the terminology of the present time, we talk about multi-tasking. It's pretty well doing many things and I believe it's one of the things you have to learn to do in life. Like a beehive with the bees coming and going, they all go into the one hive and there's one goal at the end of it, although they're all coming at different times. You have to be able to open and close your mind; to focus on more than one thing at a time.

Once again, remember if all you ever do is make resolutions, you won't achieve. If you sit with your eyes open and all the distractions are just coursing around you, you will never learn to be a focused person and achieve what you want.

I have always talked in terms of being able to "tack" in life. Compare it to being in a ship; you are moving back and forth going towards a destination, and you are veering off but always coming back to it. Almost like the cartoon "Family Circus" where the child, in order to go from A to Z is all over the place, but eventually gets there.

Now, if you think of what "tack" means – let's say in a relationship, and trying to understand other people as well as ourselves! The T stands for trust, so again when you're dealing with improving yourself you have to have a sense of trust that your intentions are good. Trust that you are going to get to your destination. Trust that distractions will drift and blow away like the summer breezes. Trust that the person with whom you are trying to build a relationship is committed to that as well. And trust that you will resolve your issues; trust that you will have a perfect relationship with both your partner and yourself.

The A is acceptance. No one of is perfect, so it's hard to live with yourself if you're going to think that it will be doubly hard to live with your partner. Once you accept your differences and your imperfections, you will accept the fact that there are different definitions of perfection. Learn to accept your own faults; be understanding of your faults. Then you can accept that you are both trying to achieve a loving, caring, solid relationship.

We talked about losing traction because of distractions. It's like the old analogy of the bicycle; when you fall off you have to be committed to getting back on again.

Don't give up and say "what's the point; I'm not achieving anything, so I'm going to Switch my light off and go away." Just think of the lighthouse. I mean it's there as a preventive mechanism to stop chaos on the oceans. To prevent ships being shipwrecked and people dying and cargoes being lost. So that lighthouse must sustain its life on an ongoing basis. It can never allow the light to flicker and die or chaos is going to develop.

Similarly, if we're doing a project, and in this case the project is to make yourself the best you possibly can be. Just visualize one day saying "you know we've been working on this for ever and nothing's happening and I'm going to call it quits and just forget it." Now, at that particular moment you could be 99.9999 per cent towards achieving that goal. You switch it off, you turn the light of in your lighthouse, the beacon's dead and there's a distraction; you lose traction and you lose your commitment – and you don't achieve.

Just like the lighthouse, you must keep your light illuminating you so that when issues arise you're always ready to tackle them. You can't just switch the light off and think you'll switch it on again tomorrow. At that particular moment, if you're walking through a forest and using your flash light and think to save the light you'll switch it off – then over the cliff you may go. So you have to keep it going all the time!

The C in Tack means a couple of things, conciliatory and also compromise. I don't mean be judgemental. Don't place yourself or your partner on a scale and perpetually weigh-in to see if you're at the ambient temperature you want to be. We said before if all you ever do is weigh yourself you'll never lose weight. If all you ever do is judge with recriminations, belittling, demeaning, by saying "you should be doing better, I don't like the way you did that, improve yourself." You're saying that to yourself as well. Accept your own frailties because no one is perfect.

There are different levels; perfections and some not so; and some of these people are huge coursing rivers; mega rivers like the Nile of the Mississippi. The rest of us should be content if we find that we can provide a trickle toward the overall good, toward the current. That's our vocation in life.  So, we compromise and we accept; and when all is said and done you make your own karma.

The K in Tack is your Karma.  You may have struggled; you've entered this relationship with yourself or your partner with a sense of trust. You've become accepting of the differences, accepting of both your imperfections. You are conciliatory towards it, you've compromised and you've made karma.

People say "hang on for a second here, I think we can do a lot better than this, let's raise the bar."  Now, here's an "au contraire" thought. If you say to a limbo dancer "let's raise the bar," he's going to be happy because it's going to make his task easier.  In other words, that's a different way of looking at it.  To a limbo dancer his degree of difficulty is in direct relationship to how low the bar is from the ground. So, to challenge him you would say lower the bar and then he or she has to dance under that bar.

To a high jumper you would say raise the bar and again the degree of difficulty is in direct relationship to how far the bar is from the ground. They're both trying to achieve perfection; they're both trying to achieve that athletic degree of difficulty – one by going high, the other by going low. The end result is they're pushing their own personal limits; they are trying to be, and they are being, the best they possibly can by going in different directions. In other words, things are not always the way they seem to be.  We have to be able to think in a different way.

Years ago I had a tent trailer and for me reversing that tent trailer was a nightmare because in order to turn it to the right I had to spin my wheel to the left – always thinking of the opposite tack.  It's the same when you're steering a small boat with a tiller.  If you want to go right you push the tiller to the left, and if you want to go left you push the tiller to the right.  If you are entrenched and you're pigheaded, you may say that in life in order to go right you will always turn right. In order to turn left you will always go left.  If you do that with your trailer or your boat, you'll always end up going in the wrong direction. So you must accept that there are differences.

I remember reading in a Western novel that in some Indian tribes, some of the people had become "contraries" in which they lived their lives backwards. When they were on their horses they would literally sit backwards; when they met someone instead of saying hello they would say goodbye. They'd walk into the water backwards and when they were bathing they would throw dust over themselves. Now, that's an extreme example, but it is how they perceived their lives; they would go against the flow. And the strange thing is, and it is a strange thing, they were respected because they were hearing a drum beat, a cadence, that was different from everyone else and they were doing it their way.

Think about it like a musical group. Years ago when I was a teenager, I spent a little time in a musical group. There was a lead guitar, a rhythm guitar, a base guitar and a set of drums. In some cases there was a singer and in some cases, basically everyone sang. Now, the lead guitar would define the individual notes of a tune, he would play an identifiable melody; the rhythm guitar would play a rhythmic, musical cadence that complimented and provided a background for the lead guitar. The base guitar and the drums were sort of the heartbeat and they provided that rhythmic background.

The interesting thing was, I think, that everyone in the group chose their particular instruments possibly to suit their individual personalities. The lead guitar would be defining the tune and playing individual musical notes; the rhythm guitar would play chords which would again give that musical cadence in the background; and the drums and the base guitar were the throbbing hypnotic heartbeat. All of these instruments added dimension to the music in discrete yet meaningful layers.

In life there are people like that. We're all like musical instruments really. Some of us are quite content to be the background people who provide the cadence in life, while other people enjoy being the upfront person delineating the musical notes of life. We're all like that! If you say to some people "if you had to become a musical instrument what would you be?" Some would say "I don't like to be in the public eye, I'd like to be in the background, I'd like to be the drums." So, you can visualize what we're saying, where we all fit in.

I did some work as an extra in the movie industry years ago. Now, extras in movies are, as I've said before, called "moveable furniture." I guess living moveable furniture. In most scenes there would be the stars and the lead actors up front in the limelight. In the background you would see the extras, literally background, just providing a living mosaic upon which the lead actors were superimposed. Again it's like the duality of a lot of us in life; most of us are background people. And there are a few people who are in the forefront, in the limelight sometimes whether they want it or not.

The limelight stars we've spoken of before in terms of the Mississippi, the Nile, the Deltas; these huge currents – and in the background are the rest of us who are integral to the whole thing.

If you watched a restaurant scene in a movie and the two stars were sitting at a table chatting and in the background was a scene of empty tables and chairs, there would be a lack of vitality; there would be nothing to superimpose the actors onto, so the background provides that cadence, that rhythmic vitality of life. We're all dispensable, so those background actors have that little spark that's helping to illuminate the stars, and the stars would be the first to admit that the scenes are so relevant when there are background people providing that backdrop for them.

As we go along in life and we turn and say "I think I'm doing well, I think I'm achieving, but this job I'm doing is draining my vitality." On the one hand you've fired yourself with passion, you've used that minuscule spark inside to light that bonfire that is filling you with fervour and the desire to be the best you can. Just as you fire yourself with passion you must learn to fire yourself from negativity and the things you don't like and the job you're doing.

I realize I've said before that you have to put bread and butter on your table and you have responsibilities, but at the very least when you're fired with passion you're going to melt the ice around you and you're going to fire yourself from the negativity of life.

We have already talked about "back to less is more; or poor little me I can't make any difference in the world, or let my flame flicker for a second here, it's been going for many years and putting it out for a second won't make any difference." However we have learned that a little can make one heck of a difference.

There is a television show I used to watch fairly frequently called the Crocodile Hunter, filmed in Australia. The hero, who was tragically killed while filming, was an Australian Tarzan with a great zeal to protect reptiles, crocodiles. Invariably in every show he would be rescuing a crocodile by throwing one little line over it. The crocodile totally entangles himself until he's immobilized and taken to a safer environment.

Think about it! One little line thrown to that crocodile can totally immobilize him. That's like us. You've been trying to get rid of all your negativity and there's one little fault that we have; again, we're not perfect and that little fault if it starts to lead to guilt is going to be like that little rope thrown to the crocodile, that large aggressive beast, you're going to become so entangled in that one little thread it's going to be as though you're trapped, entangled in a fishing net.

It's like telling a white lie. You tell one lie and think it won't make any real difference. It will resolve the issue right now you think, but it comes back to haunt you. That little lie emanates from you like that fine line that has been thrown to the crocodile. You turn quickly and you trip over the line and you crack your head or turn the other way and it gets wrapped around your ankles and you have trouble getting out, you're entangled and it comes back to haunt you.

Just as you say "one little me will make no difference in the world," on a positive note you could be like that line that's thrown out and it's going to entangle the negativity of the world, and that's a good thing. Or that one little spark in the forest that showed me the little hut, the hostel, I was looking for on the Scottish moors. One little light was all that was needed. So, in some instances less is better but in the case of that line, less is worse. The crocodile hunter is achieving his end by one line as opposed to throwing huge nets and traumatizing the beast.

In the show we're talking about, The Crocodile Hunter, the setting for this wildlife refuge is set in gorgeous tropical gardens. Now, I live on the West Coast of Canada, which really is not the tropics, but recently I was walking along the foreshore in West Vancouver and I passed a large garden. This was winter so the garden was dormant and the plants had been cut back and there was a sense of inactivity; there was no colour but there was a sense of anticipation. A sense that in the springtime life would return to this dormant garden and it would become a cornucopia of colours and fragrances, bees and butterflies. A feeling of fresh life to come. There was a sense of trust that although it was now dormant the awakening of this garden would happen

The garden was surrounded by a rickety wooden fence which provided the garden with a frame. Interestingly enough, beside the garden there was a little art gallery and in it was a display of hand woven carpets, most of which had flower motifs. So, here we had the dormant garden outside, the living garden awaiting rebirth and inside the gallery the beautiful woven carpets which were almost like a reincarnation of the living garden. Beside the carpets there were also paintings of gardens, some framed and some not, and it was quite interesting that while the paintings may have looked the same, those that were framed seemed to be trapped somehow.

The eye would look at the painting then somehow it would bump against the frame that contained it. Those without a frame seemed to leap off the walls and just move progressively until the whole wall became a garden. People often say "would you frame that question differently, would you re- frame that?" What they actually mean is "would you rephrase that?" A frame is a box.

We've talked in terms of trying to be open, free and committed. Open to all the influences around us, negating the negativity and affirming the positive. So we are thinking outside that box, outside that frame. We're not limiting our questions to the so-called accepted, the so-called tried and true. In some ways we are becoming contraries and we're thinking in a different way. Instead of saying "raise the bar," we're saying "lower that bar." Instead of saying turn right to go right, we say "no, to turn right you have to go left sometimes." We are thinking in a different way. We are thinking outside that frame. Interestingly enough, to some people sometimes the frame becomes more relevant than the picture.

The frames are like rules and regulations, the bureaucracies, the hypocrisy. The fences that hold people in and instead of focusing on the painting which is the spark of life, which is the vitality that we must have, too many people spend their time on the frame, the fringes, on the externals and they ignore the internals.

So, the painting itself is the internal, it is the soul, the heart and should be the focus. So what is the frame? It is a fence, it's a gate; like a picture that is holding in the spark.

When my eldest daughter was at university, one of the jobs she had was selling frames to art stores. It amazed me that there were hundreds of different types of frames. I'm sure sometimes these frames, particularly the really solid gilt frames, would cost as much as the painting in some ways. Again, the painting is the spark of life, the internal focus, the inner star we're struggling to see. The frame is the box that we've been forced to place it in; the fence.

Try an experiment sometime. Look at some of your paintings and visualize it without the fence, the frame. Visualize it as being more relevant than the frame.

Good intentions, often times when we're trying to communicate them, are only as good as the words you use and the tone you take; the cadence in our voice, perhaps the strident tone of our voice. We can say one thing, but it sounds as though we mean something else.

When we talk in terms of communicating, I often think we can put our words in gentle, shushing slippers and let the words move across to the person. Or we can take the words and put them in steel toed work boots and let them clank across the room until they reach the person. They can be the same words but we've couched them in different intonations, different cadences, or stridencies. Low pitch, high pitch, gentle, understanding, dogmatic – all these various ways of communicating. With the best of intentions, sometimes the words come out in the worst way because people hear things in different ways.

In the bad old days, when we spoke in terms of lighthouses, there were people who were ship-wreckers and they would light "pretend" lighthouses on really wild, rugged, rock- strewn bays. They would douse the proper lighthouse so that the ships would see this "lie" which was the wreckers' bonfire. Ultimately the ships would hit rocks when they went from the safe route to the false route.

So that's the lie. In other words if you illuminate yourself with this negative bonfire pretending to be what you're not, you'll cause yourself and all the relationships around you to founder. What you see often times really isn't what you get.

A while ago my wife and I were out and in a store we bought something and as a special gift we were given a fan. If you looked at this fan, and you didn't know what it was, you'd see a long flat object and stuck in the middle of it there was a dark, dull, sort of hieroglyphic shape that was totally indecipherable to the eye. Now, when you opened the fan slowly the hieroglyphic shape took a different configuration until when it was totally opened there was a beautiful painting of a garden with a mountain, trees and an ocean behind it. A complete vignette of life, of a beautiful maritime scene and only when it was open could you see that.

So, people with a classic closed mind are like that fan. The mind is closed and if you ask them what they see inside all they're going to see is this negative, unclear image because they never try to open their mind and explore beyond it. If only they would slowly and incrementally open the fan they would see something and they would get the big picture. The lights would shine and they'd get a clear, clean, opaque vision.

The fan is almost like a bird when it's sitting on a fence with its wings folded tightly against its body. If you had never before seen a bird and you suddenly saw this, you'd see an ungainly, asymmetrical creature there, but then you see the bird slowly openings its wings and fly. Just think about that. We all have wings.

A lot of people dream about angels, and angels have wings and can fly. Angels can fly above the turmoil and strife of the world, they don't have negative issues and they're close to the Godhead and they can fly, they have wings.

We have all heard people say "I just want to fly out of here." Or fly-by-night which is a negative expression. We all have wings discreetly folded tightly inside us. Ponder what happens when we don't unfold them and learn to fly. Like the Dodo bird, the Penguin, the Ostrich and the Emu. A lot of these birds have wings but in many ways they've never had to use them, so consequently, the wings atrophy and they can no longer fly.

Think of all the various components in your life that if you don't use them, if you don't utilize them, you are going to lose the ability. If you never think, your brain is going to be like that steel trap we spoke about, it will snap shut and will freeze with rust. If you don't use your body, if you don't exercise, each time you stand on that scale you won't have a decrease in weight but probably an increase in weight because you're not using your body. If you have creativity in your soul and you don't use it but think one day you will, when that one day comes there's so much silt and sediment and sand that's blown around it, it will take a lifetime to excavate it – but only if you have the desire to do that. If you don't use these things you lose them.

The same with your spirit deep inside! Why do we say "deep inside?" Spirits really are the essence of us, they're the light but a lot of us keep the drapes closed and when they're closed the sun cannot come in the window and the room stays dark. A lot of people don't like the light; they don't spark the bonfire, so the spirit stays inside. Like the birds we spoke about and the fish we catch; the glow they had initially fades. You know that beautiful iridescent colour you see in fish when they're pulled out of the water and then it fades. It's like our spirits. If we don't let our spirits see the sun, if we don't let them witness the horizons, our eyes become opaque and dull.

You know, our eyes are truly the windows to our soul, and think about that. Some people's eyes sparkle and it's almost like looking at the sparkle of the sun on water and they're blinding in their beauty. It could be mischief, or love and empathy, but their eyes speak and you can see their soul through their eyes. Other people's eyes are bland, almost opaque, dull and unfocused; they're not really seeing the world around them.

They're certainly not seeing the interior of their soul or their bodies. They've never bothered to search or bothered to take the negativity like weeds in the garden and throw them out. Yes, if they've done it occasionally and they've come back like boomerangs they say "oh, what's the point, what difference can I make; life is meaningless, there's no purpose to it, I can't see any light around here, it's black and blah."

Like the Children of the Mist we spoke about, these people live in a continually mist environment. They've never seen the sun, they don't even reach for the sun, they are crippled by their inactivity; there is no lustre. People like that, if they're exposed on a regular basis to positive thinkers, the opposite should happen. As we spoke about earlier, the glow, the illumination, the love, the compassion, the positive outlook and the willingness to share should gradually bathe that person and they should come out of their shell. Almost like a little bird in its shell!

We have all seen little birds being born, the beak pecks away at the shell and a little hole appears and gradually becomes bigger and bigger until the little bird emerges from that cocoon of the egg. We don't want to stay in a shell, we want to burst out and flap our wings, and we want to fly. We do want to light that light to illuminate the world. We don't want to be closed tight fans with beautiful imagery that the world never sees because it's always kept closed. Our fan is never opened.

So let us all fly! The very fact that we have now given ourselves wings and we can now fly, and the act of flying above something gives different perspectives and you have to learn and understand and appreciate the new visions you're seeing and experiencing.

We talked in terms of using binoculars, which in essence brings things closer; a form of magnification. We've all used a magnifying glass to make things larger, but when you get into the super scientific microscopes, small routine objects become impossible to decipher and they take on a new life because they look so different. A small mite, a small insect magnified a million times or so, becomes totally different and we've no idea what it was unless somebody tells us.

So if you're exploring into your soul and you magnify areas, you're going to be experiencing feelings and emotions that are different from anything you've ever experienced. The minuscule notes that you never heard before are going to become crescendos; the tiny spark that you hardly knew was there is going to be magnified a million times until there is a huge glow coming from you.

Now, sparks and fire are things we understand. You know fire generates heat and light, it burns and we know that and understand it. We know what music is and we understand it. But there are going to be some things, like the stars, that are there but we've never seen them before in our soul, in our being, and we'll have no idea what they are. Through trust and acceptance and positive thinking we will use these to regenerate.

Life is like that, it's a book. It's a series of thoughts and feelings, emotions and questions and resolutions; and some passion. But just visualize; if this book had no punctuation, if there were no moments of pause between sentences and paragraphs, no commas or periods, the whole thing would be an indecipherable rush of chaos. In order to decipher the meaning it would take a scientist and it would take a long, long time to do it. Life is like that, life is filled with our inner pilgrimage, emotions and feelings and thoughts that we have, and the questions and answers. But we have to pause, take time to stop and relax between events.

We don't want to be like that so called river of life, that flood that goes so quickly that it erodes the banks. We want to find nuggets of truth in our search to be the best we possibly can. But if you go to a river to find nuggets of gold, to find grains of gold, to find pay-dirt, you won't find it in the mainstream of the river. You won't find it in the deep dark depths of the river. You're going to find it in the quiet back eddies, the tranquil pools that form where the river takes turns and in those quiet tranquil places you will find the nuggets of gold.

In our search for perfection that is where you are going to find the nuggets of truth. Not in chaos, not in the mad rush, not in an anxiety ridden panic stricken push to resolve everything. No, it is going to be in the quiet back eddies. It's going to be in gentle, peaceful moments where you sit and reflect; where there are no disturbances or distractions to throw you off your traction.

Yes, you are going to be projecting yourself into those quiet, reflective moments and that is when you will find the nuggets of truth.

Talking about gold and the search for gold reminds me of the fable of the Goose that Laid the Golden Egg. The goose was captured and held hostage by a King. Instead of being thankful for the golden eggs the goose was laying, and there were certainly enough eggs to sustain the King and his household; ultimately enough to gold to buy anything of material value and improve the lives of the people in his kingdom

But instead of being thankful and grateful, the king decided that if he could find out how the goose managed to lay the golden eggs, he could breed additional geese and have even more gold. With greed and avarice and total thoughtlessness the King had the goose eviscerated, cut open, and of course all he was left with was a dead goose. So be thankful for the gold "nuggets" you receive when you sift through the debris, the silt and sediment in the quiet back eddies of your mind; be thankful to find the nuggets of truth.

We started this book talking about plodding Clydesdale horses wearing blinkers, like us! We spoke in terms of throwing off the blinkers to become less focused, less driven to have tunnel vision. And we spoke in terms of how deep inside the Clydesdale - that draft horse, there was a soul, a spirit, vitality and the spark of a warrior's horse.

We spoke in terms of reaching inside and becoming a lean Nomadic warrior, someone who doesn't need armour. We spoke in terms of the armour that encases us and how we must throw off the armour; we must be the true person that is lying deep inside.

We spoke in terms of the chameleon layers; that mask of duplicity, of untruth, of pretentiousness that really is not us. We talked about how, in order to find ourselves and to build relationships, we must get rid of the chameleon complex and remove those layers and become the true person.

We also spoke of dreams, of how it's all right to be a "Johnny Head in the Air;" to be someone who sees life in a different light. We spoke of how we can get that light and how there is a spark deep inside, but how most of us keep the drapes closed all of our lives. We spoke in terms of how we must never let that light die. Instead the brightest beacon in our soul is lighted by a small, infinitesimal spark that can be the spark of life. We have become beacons; we have become lighthouses.

On our journey, our pilgrimage through life, our goal in the pH of goodness is to be the best we possibly can. Again, we know that we cannot all be at the top of every profession. We know we cannot be those things, but what we can be is a small rivulet that feeds the flow of life.

We spoke in terms of the intellectual bully. When we're given a talent, when we're given a sense of who we are and an ability to help others, we must do it. We don't build our progress, our prowess, on the backs of others. We don't use them as foundations to help us climb higher.

Remember, we do not want negativity! So, people and places and circumstances that tend to negate your goals must be avoided. Discard them; don't discard your problems with the boomerang that we spoke of. Yes, throw your problems as far as you possibly can, but if you use the same methods time after time and they keep coming back like a boomerang, you have to innovate. You have to find new ways to problem solve with yourself and also with your partner. You have to do that!

We spoke of extremes. If you want to go from A to Z, you don't always have to go in a straight line. You can tack through life. And remember, T is for Trust. A is for Acceptance. C is for Conciliation and being able to compromise. And K is, ultimately, for the Karma that you are making.

We spoke of how you don't always have to tackle problems head on but obliquely, like the bullfight. If the bull headed straight for the matador, would he get him? – I don't know. The bull is diverted by the cape and sometimes he throws his head in desperation and impales the matador.

We talked in terms of problem solving by the skipping stone principle. With that principle, you decide to tackle an issue or a problem with yourself or your partner. And you go in like a ton of bricks with a loud splash, a huge road. But as a very light stepping stone, or skipping stone, you throw it in the water; throw it at the problem and it skips many times and touches the issue many times, but it doesn't make a huge splash, it doesn't make a huge ripple. It seems a bit innocuous but ultimately it will resolve the issue because you're tackling it more than once.

You know, we talked in terms of how on this pilgrimage, on this voyage, we're heading off into unexplored territory and, like the early pioneers, sometimes we need a pathfinder; a coach or a guide to lead us through a wilderness that we've never seen before.

We also spoke of the time that must come when you can discard your coach, when you stand on your own two feet; when you no longer need all the lifelines or all the causeways, when you must be self-reliant. We spoke in terms of the journeys across those wilderness plains. If you stayed inside your coach or waggon with all the drapes closed around you, when you get to your final destination you are really back to where you started from. You have seen nothing, you have learned nothing; you have let others carry you; you've let others pull you through a multitude of experiences and you've learned nothing. You must be willing to discard your lifelines, your causeways, your coaches and climb out of that waggon and stand on your own two feet and fly.

We also spoke in terms of how flying would give you a different perspective. You know, if you stand on a beach and look out you see one perspective at eye level. You really don't see the horizons but if you fly like an eagle you can see horizons and you can soar effortlessly. You can soar on thermals of enthusiasm, of achievement. In reaching that horizon the neat thing is it always moves further and further away and it gives you an incentive to keep on exploring. When you think you've reached the horizon and say "this is as good as I'm going to get, I've reached my perfection," then you develop that complacency and you give up the eternal search.

So you must keep looking beyond the last horizon because, ultimately, there is no such thing as the last horizon.

You must allow your mind to be open to every experience as long as it is positive. The only weeds you will dig out of your mind, your heart and your soul, are the negative weeds because, after all, in many ways weeds may be a misnomer. At one time all flowers and plants could have been classified as God's creations as flowers and plants, but man called them weeds. So, once the negativity is discarded, the little nuggets of positive information, trivia and whimsy that come into our minds can be stored in the background and then at the appropriate time used to season and flavour the "soup of your life."

Every part is important – and we spoke of the parts in my Grandfather's fob watch. All the little whirls, wheels and springs are equally important. Some are smaller than others but you cannot discard any of them because all the parts make the whole thing work. We talked in terms of how beings are like that; all the parts make you who you are. It's your mind, you heart and soul, it's your spirit and how we want to illuminate ourselves and make those around us enjoy a better life. If we feel better about ourselves, those close to us will also feel better. We won't be the creative, intellectual so called spiritual bully who retains knowledge and information within himself. We will allow our light to shine; we allow others to benefit from our experiences

We spoke in terms of our house in Scotland where we would take a shovel of lighted coal from one fire to prime another fire and that's what we do. When we see people in need we reach inside and take the warmth and heat and light, the sparkling coals from within our heart and give them to someone else to help their lives. They in turn will pass it on to someone else until the whole world is lit with a glow from everyone.

We spoke in terms of our lives being like a ship that is going through the oceans of life, but if you don't clean the debris from the hull the barnacles and weed growth will slow you down until you're hardly moving. But if you clean the hull, instead of ploughing through the water you will plane above the waves and it becomes effortless.

We talked in terms of the tug boats, and most of us are like that – towing behind us a barge full of problems, dilemmas, unresolved issues, wishes and, maybe, chains. We have to let that barge go, sever the line and let it drift off because that's negativity and we do not need that.

Most of all we talked in terms of resolutions and commitment. We've said you cannot lose weight by repeatedly standing on the scales. You must work towards losing weight. Resolutions are only as good as the follow-through. To say repeatedly "tomorrow I'm going to…," in other words, the manana syndrome; tomorrow's another day. You have to start now because the tomorrow after today is yesterday. Like the three in one situation.

We spoke in terms of the bonsai tree; how we are all individuals; how we are all snowflakes. No one is identical to us and because of that we're growing in a specific way and we're influenced by the breezes around us. But we sink deep roots and we are different from the clone-like Poplar tree or the tree in a forest.

We spoke in terms of problems arising, like topping the trees in my garden. If you just cut off the top of the tree, ultimately the side branches will grow up and become the same tall tree again, just like the problems.

And when all is said and done, everything we're doing is done without an expectation of a return. When we improve, we improve others and we are not giving a gift and expecting anything in return. Neither are we bartering our new found self, we're giving ourselves and in giving we shall receive.

Ultimately, we will become like the Nomads with the Nomadic spirit. We will have pared down the extraneous paraphernalia that encumbers us; all the armors and chameleon layers, the material wealth that we think is important; the frame around our spirit and our soul. We will learn to smash that frame and become a true Nomad. There is no such thing as an obese Nomad. A Nomad is lean, is pared down and he wanders with a destination.

And finally we talked in terms of visualization. How we can wander through the plains and deserts in our minds and spirit. The desert is, after all, a pared, lean version of the world. These thoughts are philosophical tidbits all leading towards us becoming Nomadic spirits with Bonsai wisdom.

Always remember to retain your vision.

Preserve and maintain your vision.

Sustain and nourish your vision.

Achieve the bounty of your ultimate vision.

www.ingramcontent.com/pod-product-compliance
Lightning Source LLC
Chambersburg PA
CBHW030914090426
42737CB00007B/186